fair employment
in Northern Ireland

a generation on

fair
employment
in Northern Ireland

a generation on

**edited by Bob Osborne
and Ian Shuttleworth**

THE
BLACKSTAFF
PRESS

BELFAST

This product includes mapping data licensed
from Ordnance Survey of Northern Ireland®
reproduced by permission of the Chief Executive,
acting on behalf of the Controller of Her Majesty's Stationery
Office. © Crown Copyright 2004, Permit No. 40019.

First published in 2004 by
Blackstaff Press Limited
4c Heron Wharf, Sydenham Business Park
Belfast BT3 9LE, Northern Ireland
and Equality Commission for Northern Ireland
Equality House, 7–9 Shaftesbury Square
Belfast BT2 7DP, Northern Ireland

© Foreword, Garret FitzGerald, 2004
© The contributors (except chapters 2 and 8), 2004
© Chapters 2 and 8, Equality Commission for Northern Ireland, 2004

The contributors have asserted their right under the Copyright,
Designs and Patents Act 1988 to be identified as the authors of this work.

Typeset by Techniset Typesetters, Newton-le-Willows, Merseyside

Printed in Ireland by ColourBooks Ltd, Dublin

A CIP catalogue record for this book is available from the British Library

ISBN 0-85640-752-6

www.blackstaffpress.com

Contents

Foreword

GARRET FITZGERALD

Fair employment in Northern Ireland: a generation on serves two very important functions. At the level of methodology it demonstrates the remarkable progress that has been made in social research in Northern Ireland during the last couple of decades – both in the range of issues being tackled and in the quality of the work being undertaken. Substantively, it provides valuable insights into the scale of social changes that have been taking place during a period of continued political deadlock.

This book establishes authoritatively that problems of ethnic/religious discrimination in Northern Ireland have been tackled with considerable success – including the achievement of a marked increase in integration in workplaces, despite the fact that within this same period segregation of living accommodation has become more intense. All this has, however, been accompanied by the emergence of new and as yet underrated social issues within the Protestant community of Northern Ireland.

The authors remark that up to and including the early 1970s 'discussions concerning inequality, discrimination and disadvantage in the labour market in Northern Ireland were bedevilled by the absence of systematic empirical data . . . it was not until the analysis of the 1971 census data by Aunger (1975) that the evidence of Catholic disadvantage in the labour market was revealed'. The authors add that as late as 1981 Compton was still suggesting that 'discrimination was a minor factor and that factors such as the higher birth rate of Catholics and geographical location were far more important'.

Given that the scale of the problem of discrimination in Northern Ireland had been a matter of public knowledge and of passionate political debate during the first half century of its existence as a separate political entity, and led in the second half of the 1960s to a virtual revolt by the nationalist minority culminating in the violence of 1969, it is difficult to understand the failure of the Northern Ireland academic community to recognise the need for, and undertake, necessary research into this issue prior to 1975. This demographic argument was, they say, later subjected to 'comprehensive refutation'.

There is a heartening contrast between that past academic neglect, and even denial of the existence of a fundamental problem, and the scale and quality of the research undertaken in more recent times, upon which this book has been able to draw with great success.

There can be no doubt about the impact of legislative changes, outlawing discrimination and providing for some forms of affirmative action. The Fair Employment Act 1989 was enacted following the Report of the Standing Advisory Commission on Human Rights but was, of course, one of the fruits of the Anglo-Irish Agreement of 1985, the terms of which reflected concern on the part of the Government of the Republic at the inadequacies of earlier anti-discrimination legislation in Northern Ireland.

As Barry Fitzpatrick points out, this legislation contains 'statutory novelties' such as monitoring and review, 'fair participation' and affirmative action, which are not found in British sex and race discrimination laws of the 1970s, and which mark the Northern Ireland legislation as having more of a focus on a 'redistributive approach'. The huge cash penalties on offending employers who behave badly had a profound effect, and through affirmative action agreements with the regulatory body, as shown by McCrudden and his colleagues, substantial changes in employment profile have been achieved.

As a consequence of the progress made, Catholics, as Hughes notes, no longer have the same perceptions of unfairness and inequality as in the past – and Protestants have become more supportive of equality measures, as they have begun to feel themselves relatively disadvantaged. For, while Catholics are still underrepresented in the higher grades of the civil service and in security-related employment, Protestants are underrepresented in the health and education sectors.

Raymond Russell's detailed comparison of data from the monitoring returns submitted by employers in the years 1990–2001 confirms that major changes have taken place in the monitored Northern Ireland workforce, which includes the public and private sectors. Catholics have made least gains in the manual and security sectors (generally one to three percentage points, with a small increase in the Catholic share of employment amongst skilled workers). However, in management and the professions, and in clerical and sales occupations, they have gained between seven and ten percentage points within the space of eleven years. Almost universally these gains have been greater for males than for females.

It is clear that education has had a considerable impact upon the social changes that have taken place during the past couple of decades. Robert Miller suggests that the fact that in the past Protestants enjoyed routes to skilled manual jobs in traditional industries that were not open to Catholics may have made the latter more likely to view education as an avenue of upward mobility. In other words, the frustration caused by discrimination against a particular group in one era may in the longer run have transformed itself into an actual social advantage for that group.

Professor Osborne's analysis of this educational factor is thus especially interesting. At the outset he points out that twenty years ago study of the education factor was rendered very difficult by the failure to distinguish statistically Catholic schools from others, which made it necessary laboriously to build up data from individual pupil records for each school.

At that time Protestant school-leavers were more likely to move to employment by using family and other contacts, whereas Catholic school-leavers were more likely to enter training or to remain unemployed. The collapse of traditional industries and a general restructuring of the labour market in the 1980s, together with improved access by Catholics to education, subsequently led most Catholic young people to remain in the education system beyond the school leaving age, either undergoing training or entering further or higher education. At the same time improvements in state aid for Catholic schools helped to reduce curriculum differences, which particularly affected access of Catholic school pupils to science teaching.

Noting that evidence in other countries suggests that Catholic schools produce a better performance, Professor Osborne observes that in Northern Ireland Catholic schools have exhibited 'a greater capacity to overcome the negative effects of social disadvantage relative to other schools'. In support of this view he cites a striking superiority in the performance of pupils in Catholic primary schools with a high level of disadvantaged pupils and in Catholic secondary (i.e. non-grammar) schools as against other schools – the differential in the latter case, in terms of entry to higher education, being in excess of two to one.

As a result of this progress, the one-third lower proportion of Catholics with higher education recorded in 1971 has given way to a situation in which, although the proportion of Catholics with no educational qualification is still slightly higher than for Protestants, the proportion of Catholics with a university degree is now above that of Protestants.

Professor Osborne remarks on 'parity of participation between Protestants and Catholics' in higher education. It is not clear, however, to what extent the equality in proportions of Catholic and Protestant residents of Northern Ireland up to age 44 who are graduates, and the higher proportion of Catholics with doctorates, reflects the achievement of something like parity in the proportions from the two sections of the community *entering* third level education in recent times. For this 'parity of participation' in higher education could be due to the differential (which seems to have been as high as two to one in the late 1990s) in the proportions of Protestants and Catholics going to universities in Britain rather than Northern Ireland – for, as Professor Osborne points out, most of these higher education migrants do not return to Northern Ireland.

The resultant brain drain is mainly from the Protestant community – which, *pace* Professor Osborne, means that it does not just reflect a shortage of higher education places in Northern Ireland but must also reflect social factors. This large, and in religious terms, unbalanced net outward movement of young people entering higher education is of fundamental importance to the future of Northern Ireland – both in relation to its capacity to achieve more dynamic growth, comparable with that of the neighbouring Republic, and in relation to its internal population balance.

If the differential migration for higher education between Protestants and Catholics were to continue at the rate of the late 1990s, it can be calculated that the long-term impact of this factor would be equivalent to an additional 7.5% birth-rate differential between the two sections of the community, on top of what, at least until recently, has been a somewhat higher Catholic fertility rate.

This higher-education migration phenomenon clearly merits further social research. Moreover, it raises a quite different question that also merits further study: the character of migration flows *into* as well as out of Northern Ireland. For if, as seems to be the case, the flow to higher education in Britain has been depleting each new age cohort by about 12% (a net outflow of about 3,000 higher-education students each year) the fact that since 1990 overall net emigration has averaged only about 500 a year implies an average net inflow of about 2,500 other people each year

Comparisons with social developments in the Republic could also be a fruitful field for further research. On both sides of the Border there has been a striking lack of comparative North–South studies. Both parts of the island tend to look almost exclusively elsewhere when making social and economic comparisons. My own experience in undertaking economic North–South economic comparisons between 1956 and 1973 (and to a very limited degree more recently) has been that these can be illuminating. And, with their first two jointly-produced Statistical Profiles of North and South, the statistical services of Northern Ireland and the Republic have begun to provide a useful framework for such North–South comparative research.

Acknowledgements

A number of people have assisted in the preparation of this book. We would like to thank the Equality Commission for supporting the idea of a book on fair employment. Eileen Lavery of the Commission assisted authors in accessing key source material and generally encouraged the development of the book. We would also like to thank Hilary Bell, who read the manuscript with a keen eye for missing information and inconsistencies as well as helping to identify infelicities of style. We would like to acknowledge the support and encouragement of Patsy Horton, Wendy Dunbar and Rachel McNicholl of Blackstaff Press. Our thanks also go to Yann Hoffman-Kelly for the preparation of the index. Of course, as editors we must take responsibility for any errors.

Any mention of fair employment in Northern Ireland in the last generation has been inextricably linked to Bob Cooper. Bob Cooper chaired the Fair Employment Agency from its inception and became Chair of the Fair Employment Commission when it replaced the Agency. He also assisted in the preparations for the creation of the Equality Commission and was a member of the Review Team on the Senior Civil Service. At a time when documenting religious inequality in the labour market and promoting fairness by employers in the public and private sectors was, for some, a controversial cause, Bob Cooper steadfastly worked for greater equality, knowing that its achievement would help provide a more stable and prosperous society. Bob Cooper's role in promoting fair employment for all has been key to the changes which the contributors to this book document.

Disclaimer

The views expressed by the editors and contributors do not necessarily represent the views of the Equality Commission, with the exceptions of Chapters 2 and 8, where the authors do represent the Commission.

List of contributors

BOB OSBORNE holds a Chair in Applied Policy Studies at the University of Ulster. He has been a member of the Standing Advisory Commission on Human Rights and the Equality Commission for Northern Ireland and has advised legislative committees in Westminster and Belfast. He is currently a member of the Economic and Social Research Council's Devolution and Constitutional Change Advisory Board. Research interests lie in equality policy, education and higher education policy. Recent publications include: *Higher Education in Ireland: North and South* (London, Jessica Kingsley, 1996); and *Devolution and Pluralism in Education in Northern Ireland* (Manchester, Manchester University Press, forthcoming).

IAN SHUTTLEWORTH is a Lecturer in the School of Geography at Queen's University Belfast. His main interests lie in census analysis, labour market change, and migration. Recent or ongoing projects include: an examination of young people's labour market perceptions in Belfast; an analysis of commuting patterns in Northern Ireland; and political interpretation of census results in Northern Ireland. He has undertaken many research projects for Northern Ireland government departments and has also contributed to debates about employment equality and social deprivation.

BARRY FITZPATRICK has been Head of Legal Policy and Advice at the Equality Commission for Northern Ireland since April 2002. Before joining the Commission, he was Jean Monnet Professor of European Law and inaugural Head of the School of Law, University of Ulster, where he remains a Visiting Professor. Before April 2002, he was a part-time Chairman of Industrial Tribunals for four years, specialising in equality law cases, and was also Chair of the Equality Sub-Group of the Committee on the Administration of Justice. He remains Deputy Chairman of the Industrial Court for Northern Ireland. Much of his research has been in the field of European equality and employment law, particularly on issues of enforcement.

ROBERT FORD is a Research Officer working with the Department of Sociology, Oxford University.

ANNE GREEN is a Principal Research Fellow at the Institute for Employment Research, University of Warwick. She has a background in geography, and her particular interests are in spatial aspects of economic, social and demographic change; regional and local labour market issues; information and indicators; migration and commuting; and urban, rural and regional development. She has undertaken research for a variety of government departments, research councils and foundations. Recent projects have focused on skills issues at regional and local levels, and the development of associated indicators. She is a member of the Regional Studies Association, the Royal Geographical Society with the Institute of British Geographers and the Regional Science Association.

ANTHONY HEATH FBA is Professor of Sociology at the University of Oxford and a Fellow of Nuffield College. He is co-director of the Centre for Research into Elections and Social Trends (CREST). His main research interests are currently in social stratification, social inequality and ethnic minority disadvantage. He is currently organising a cross-national project on ethnic minority disadvantage in the labour market. His recent books include: *Ireland North and South: Perspectives from the Social Sciences*, edited with Richard Breen and Chris Whelan (Oxford, Oxford University Press, 2000); *Educational Standards*, edited with H. Goldstein (Oxford, Oxford University Press, 1999); and *The Rise of New Labour*, edited with J. Curtice and R. Jowell (Oxford, Oxford University Press, 2001).

JOANNE HUGHES is a Senior Lecturer in the School of Policy Studies, University of Ulster. Her main research interests are community relations/community development and urban regeneration. Current research projects include: comparative analysis of integrated schools in Northern Ireland and bilingual/bi-national schools in Israel; and analysis of Northern Ireland Life and Times data relating to community relations in Northern Ireland. Her publications include: *Partnership Governance in Northern Ireland: The Path to Peace*, co-authored with C. Knox, M. Murray, and J. Greer (Dublin, Oaktree Press, 1998); and *Community Relations and Local Government*, co-authored with C. Knox, D. Birrell, and S. McCready (Coleraine, Centre for the Study of Conflict, University of Ulster, 1994).

CHRISTOPHER McCRUDDEN is Professor of Human Rights Law, Oxford University; Fellow, Lincoln College, Oxford; Overseas Affiliated Professor of Law, University of Michigan Law School. He has served on several governmental committees, including the Northern Ireland Standing Advisory Commission on Human Rights and the European Commission's group of legal experts on equality law. His publications include: *Regulation and Deregulation*, editor (Oxford, Oxford University Press, 1998); *Equality in Law between Men and Women in the European Community: United Kingdom* (London, Office of Official Publications, 1994); *Equality between Women and Men in Social Security*, editor (London, Butterworths, 1994); *Individual Rights and the Law in Britain*, editor (Oxford, Oxford University Press, 1994); *Racial Justice at Work: The*

Enforcement of the Race Relations Act 1976 in Employment, co-author (London, Policy Studies Institute, 1991).

ROBERT MILLER is Deputy Director of the ARK project – the Northern Ireland Social and Political Archive (www.ark.ac.uk). His research interests throughout his career always have had social mobility as a theme, with regard to academic theoretical issues as well as its practical application to Northern Ireland politics. His current research interests use biographies to investigate family strategies of mobility.

RAY RUSSELL is a Research Officer with the Equality Commission for Northern Ireland. He specialises in fair employment issues and is a major contributor to the annual fair employment Monitoring Report. Prior to joining the Commission, he worked as Investigations Officer with the Equal Opportunities Commission. Much of his research has been in the field of medical psychology, particularly in relation to complementary therapies for asthma.

Abbreviations

AA	affirmative action
BHPS	British Household Panel Survey
CA	Court of Appeal, English
CCRU	Central Community Relations Unit
CCT	compulsory competitive tendering
CRE	Commission for Racial Equality
DED	Department for Economic Development
DEL	Department for Employment and Learning
DENI	Department of Education for Northern Ireland
DETI	Department of Employment, Trade and Investment
DHFETE	Department of Higher and Further Education, Training and Employment
EAT	Employment Appeals Tribunal
ECHR	European Court of Human Rights
ECJ	European Court of Justice
ECNI	Equality Commission for Northern Ireland
EComm HR	European Commission on Human Rights
EOC	Equal Opportunities Commission
ESRC	Economic and Social Research Council
EU	European Union
FE	further education
FEA	Fair Employment Agency
FEC	Fair Employment Commission
FEED	Framework Employment Equality Directive
FET	Fair Employment Tribunal
FETO	Fair Employment and Treatment (Northern Ireland) Order 1998
FSM	free school meals
GDP	Gross Domestic Product
HE	higher education
HL	House of Lords
HMSO	Her Majesty's Stationery Office
IER	Institute for Employment Research
ILO	International Labour Organisation
IRA	Irish Republican Army
IRLR	*Industrial Relations Law Reports*
J	Justice
LCJ	Lord Chief Justice
LJ	Lord Justice
LFS	Labour Force Survey
MP	member of parliament
NICA	Northern Ireland Court of Appeal
NICS	Northern Ireland Civil Service

NICRA	Northern Ireland Civil Rights Association
NICVA	Northern Ireland Council for Voluntary Action
NIE	Northern Ireland Electricity
NIHE	Northern Ireland Housing Executive
NIHEC	Northern Ireland Higher Education Council
NILT	Northern Ireland Life and Times Survey
NISRA	Northern Ireland Statistics and Research Agency
OECD	Organisation for Economic Co-operation and Development
ONS	Office of National Statistics
PAFT	Policy Appraisal and Fair Treatment Guidelines
PANI	Police Authority of Northern Ireland
PSNI	Police Service of Northern Ireland
QBD	Queen's Bench Division
RUC	Royal Ulster Constabulary
SACHR	Standing Advisory Commission on Human Rights
SDO	Sex Discrimination Order 1976
SIC	Standard Industrial Classification
SOC	Standard Occupational Classification
SRHE	Society for Research on Higher Education
SSRC	Social Science Research Council
TSN	Targeting Social Need
TTWA	Travel-to-Work Area
UDR	Ulster Defence Regiment
UK	United Kingdom
US	United States
UUP	Ulster Unionist Party

Chronology

1973   van Straubenzee report recommends legislation

1976   Fair Employment Act; Fair Employment Agency created

1978   *Guide to Manpower Policy and Practice* published

1986   government consultation paper on equal opportunity; suggests bringing fair employment and sex equality together

1987   SACHR review of fair employment calls for reform of legislation

1988   Fair Employment White Paper and Fair Employment Bill

1989   Revised Fair Employment (Northern Ireland) Act; further SACHR report calls for equality mainstreaming

1990   Fair Employment Commission replaces Fair Employment Agency

1991   Employment-monitoring extended to small firms

1992   Targeting Social Need (TSN) and Policy Appraisal and Fair Treatment (PAFT) guidelines announced by government as policy imperatives

1994   Revised PAFT guidelines published

1996   SACHR research on fair employment, TSN and PAFT published

1997   SACHR policy recommendations published

1998   White Paper on Equality; Fair Employment and Treatment (Northern Ireland) Order; Belfast Agreement; Northern Ireland Act includes Section 75, statutory duty to promote equality of opportunity

1999   Equality Commission for Northern Ireland created, which replaces CRE, FEC, EOC and Disability Council

2000   Section 75 – statutory obligations put into effect

2001   Northern Ireland Executive commitment to Single Equality Act

I

Fair employment in Northern Ireland

R.D. OSBORNE AND IAN SHUTTLEWORTH

Introduction

This book is designed to provide an assessment of how matters stand in Northern Ireland in relation to fair employment, which has been one of the most important areas of public policy interventions in the region in the past generation. Fair employment policy and issues of equality have been at the heart of the conflict and its resolution. A peaceful and inclusive society can only be created if substantial inequalities can be eroded or eliminated. Moreover, attempting to resolve the inequalities in the labour market has produced highly innovative legal and policy interventions and, since they date from the mid-1970s, it is important to begin an evaluation of their effectiveness and to identify both those areas where there has been change and the nature of the tasks that are still outstanding. This first chapter, therefore, sketches out the origins and development of fair employment policy and discusses some of the key background issues, before introducing the themes of each of the subsequent chapters.[1]

Complaints of religious discrimination in employment, alongside other matters including housing, electoral arrangements and policing, were a recurrent theme during the period of devolved government at Stormont from 1921 to 1972. Whyte (1983) evaluated the record of this period, testing allegations against available evidence. He found sufficient evidence to suggest that unfairness existed in the labour market in both public and private sectors. Barritt and Carter (1962: 93), almost a generation before, noted that 'the existence of *some* discrimination on grounds of religion, on the part of Protestants and of Catholics, is beyond doubt' but that 'the extent of discrimination cannot always be proved'. These findings echo work undertaken on the first half of the twentieth century, which identified patterns of Catholic labour market disadvantage (Hepburn, 1983). The evidence of unfairness and discrimination in areas of public sector employment, published by the Northern Ireland Civil Rights Association (NICRA) during the 1960s, played an important part in pushing the issue to the fore (for example, NICRA, 1964). The data from the 1971 Census, which took place almost at the end of the devolved government (but which was not available for analysis until the middle of the decade), revealed incontrovertible evidence of considerable Catholic labour market disadvantage (Aunger, 1975). Of course, not all disadvantage can be attributed to discrimination but neither can it be denied that discrimination played a part in sustaining disadvantage. Moreover, attempts by opposition MPs at Stormont in the 1960s to introduce anti-discrimination legislation, at a time when the first race relations legislation was being introduced in Britain, were consistently rejected by the then Unionist government. It was only with the outbreak of civil disturbances, and subsequently the suspension of the local parliament and the introduction of Direct Rule from London in 1972, that moves to introduce comprehensive religious anti-discrimination legislation in employment took place.

It has been a characteristic of the public debate about fair employment over the past generation that the adoption of absolutist positions has become the norm. On the one hand, there has been the denial of the existence of any religious discrimination; on the other hand, there has been the attribution of all inequalities in the labour market to discrimination. These absolute positions have been adopted by political groupings and their apologists and have also underpinned some of the academic debates. Both these positions represent major oversimplifications of complex processes in the labour market. As Chapters 5 and 6 demonstrate, the labour market in Northern Ireland is being radically transformed by worldwide processes. Yet the political debate over fair employment is often conducted as though nothing has changed in thirty years. It is a major theme of the contributions to this book that not only has the structure of the labour market been radically altered, but the positions of the two ethno-religious communities has also changed since the early 1970s, and the issues and problems remaining are different from those that existed a generation ago.

The Chronology shows some of the key milestones in the evolution of fair employment policy. Many aspects of these developments have been analysed and discussed elsewhere and it is not proposed to reiterate this discussion. For a consideration of both the evidence and its interpretation from varying perspectives see Ruane and Todd (1996); O'Leary and McGarry (1993); Rowthorne and Wayne (1988); Smith and Chambers (1991); Cormack and Osborne (1983; 1991). However, it is worth highlighting some of the lessons and key changes that have taken place over the years.

- After the introduction of Direct Rule in 1972, a review committee was set up to consider whether there was a need for a policy intervention. Chaired by a Conservative Minister of State, William van Straubenzee, the committee's report in 1973 recommended statutory anti-discrimination legislation and a regulatory agency to police it. The report was also notable for reviewing the arguments for an intervention that would incorporate positive discrimination in the form of quotas. In the early 1970s federal anti-discrimination policy in the United States (US) had begun to incorporate strict numerical ratios or quotas, and the political backlash that subsequently occurred had yet to take place. In the van Straubenzee report the case for numerical quotas as the basis for a general anti-discrimination policy was rejected on three grounds. First, it was believed that that such a policy would involve discrimination, even if for positive reasons, at a time when the committee regarded the elimination of discrimination as essential. Second, the committee believed that a quota policy would be a difficult technical exercise to put into operation. Third, it did not believe that such a policy would improve relations between the two communities.

  By and large, policy interventions in the thirty years since this report have taken place with this rejection of a quotas-based policy as a basic assumption (for example, see White Paper, 1988). However, one major exception has come about as a result of the acceptance of the recommendations of the Patten Report (1999): a 50:50 Protestant/Catholic recruitment ratio into the new Police Service of Northern Ireland (PSNI), including civilian employees, has now been instituted. This policy represents a form of positive discrimination, and its introduction required amendment to the existing fair employment legislation for the ten years it is to operate. Many supporters of fair employment found the acceptance of this policy difficult, but the political prize of a fully accepted police force, representing the wider community in its ranks, has been seen as an essential part of the political settlement.

- The 1976 fair employment legislation, which was introduced following the van Straubenzee report, incorporated one important difference compared with the parallel race relations legislation in Britain of the same year. Unlike the Commission for Racial Equality (CRE) in Britain, the Fair Employment Agency (FEA) in Northern Ireland was not required 'to have a belief' that discrimination existed in an organisation before using its investigatory powers (Appleby and Ellis, 1991). During the 1980s, the FEA notably used this power to investigate large sections of the public sector, universities and a range of other employers. By far the most politically important investigation was that undertaken in the Northern Ireland Civil Service (NICS) (FEA, 1983). This report stopped short of accusing the NICS of discrimination but provided a devastating critique of the failure of the NICS to implement the basic provisions of the guidelines prepared under the 1976 Act. In response, the NICS rapidly moved to institute comprehensive equality provisions, including equality monitoring (Harbison and Hodges, 1991). The actions of the NICS subsequently became the template for the rest of the public sector.

- The major changes to the legislation in 1989 reflected a long campaign for strengthened policy which derived from the acknowledged limitations of the 1976 Act. The push for strengthened legislation originated from a number of sources. First in importance came from the MacBride Principles campaign. This was primarily a US-based group from mainly the Irish-American community, which urged US companies operating in Northern Ireland to adopt a series of employment principles which themselves had been based on the Sullivan Principles applied to US employers in South Africa. In order to apply political pressure, the campaign urged state and city legislatures in the US to endorse the principles. These local governmental bodies could then apply further pressure by threatening to shift their investments from those companies operating in Northern Ireland which did not endorse the campaign. Questions were also asked at annual shareholder meetings. The British government fought the campaign, in part on the basis that some of the principles were illegal and also fearing that US companies would close their Northern Ireland plants when faced with this agitation. Local Northern Ireland politicians were enlisted to testify on the British government's behalf in the US. Commentators in the US increasingly queried the bona fides of the British government's rejection of the principles, as they seemed relatively innocuous when compared with affirmative action measures in the US (Booth and Bertsch, 1989; Osborne and Cormack, 1989).

A second important source of pressure for reform came from the increasing evidence from FEA investigations of the employment profiles of public bodies, which revealed Catholic disadvantage, which in turn added to the sense that reform was needed. Additionally, after the Anglo-Irish Agreement in 1985, which gave the Irish government an input to some Northern Ireland policy issues, pressure for reform was exerted by the Irish government. Finally, the Standing Advisory Commission on Human Rights (SACHR) began a review of the effectiveness of the existing intervention, which concluded that extensive reform was required (SACHR, 1987).

- The 1989 reform of the fair employment legislation was strongly influenced by emerging Canadian federal employment equity policy. This policy was based on the recommendations of the Abella Report (1984). Employment equity policy incorporated rigorous employment monitoring and permitted affirmative action which did not incorporate quotas. Interchanges between civil servants, as well as academics, together with a visit by Abella to Belfast, helped condition key individuals' views and shape the new policy (Osborne, 1992).

- The key dimensions of the 1989 legislation, which took policy beyond anything else that existed in the rest of the United Kingdom (UK), were the introduction of compulsory religion monitoring by employers and the range of affirmative action that could be used. Permitted affirmative action involved the possibility of setting goals and targets for improving employment patterns of an employer based on a comparison between the existing patterns and the profile of the relevant geographical catchment. It also, for the first time, explicitly outlawed indirect discrimination. Remarkably, neither the Fair Employment Commission (FEC, successor of the FEA) nor its successor, the Equality Commission for Northern Ireland (ECNI), has had to make more than limited use of the considerable investigatory powers available under the legislation, because employers, by and large, have been willing to enter into voluntary affirmative action agreements (see Chapter 7). A voluntary approach to compliance, however, has been largely determined by the knowledge that the investigatory powers existed and had been used, and out of a desire to avoid public identification. So the investigatory individual redress 'sticks' have been a necessary part of the success of the legislation (see Chapter 8).[2]

• The final extension of the fair employment legislation came in the Fair Employment and Treatment (Northern Ireland) Order 1998 (FETO). This legislation extended anti-discrimination laws to the provision of goods, services and facilities. It also extended the monitoring requirements of employers to part-time workers in recognition of the restructuring of the labour market involving the major expansion of part-time employment (see Chapter 6). Together with the 1989 legislation, it provided for specific forms of affirmative action by employers, which include: the encouragement of applications for employment or training for people from underrepresented groups; targeting training in a particular area or at a particular class of person; the amendment of redundancy procedures to help achieve fair participation; and the provision of training for non-employees of a particular religious belief, following approval by the ECNI. The Order also includes a new provision permitting recruitment from the unemployed (a specific protection was needed, otherwise such action might have constituted indirect discrimination).

• Arising from the 1987 SACHR review of the fair employment legislation, a second report argued that, in order to pursue fair employment objectives, it was crucial that government policy as a whole should put equality concerns at the heart of policy-making (SACHR, 1990).

Government responded to this call with two major equality-related policy initiatives, both of which were announced in 1992 by the Conservative government under the leadership of John Major. The first of these was called Policy Appraisal and Fair Treatment (PAFT) guidelines. The initial version of these guidelines, which were based on UK civil service measures to 'gender proof' policymaking, was extensively criticised as only restating existing anti-discrimination legislation. The guidelines were withdrawn and subsequently relaunched in 1994. Under the revised guidelines, equality considerations were to be applied in the making of any new policy, the review of existing policies and the provision of services. The equality grounds went substantially beyond fair employment by extending from religion and political opinion to include gender, disability, race and ethnicity, marital status and those with or without dependants. The guidelines were to be applied by all government departments and related agencies and bodies.

Notwithstanding the NICS indicating its full commitment to implementing PAFT, research reported in 1996 demonstrated that the government departments and the public sector as a whole had made only a very patchy effort. There were major problems of co-ordination across departments, highly variable understandings of the purpose of the guidelines, failure to apply the guidelines where appropriate, and in several instances a failure of government departments to advise agencies of the existence of the guidelines (Osborne et al, 1996). As a result of these deficiencies, SACHR called for the guidelines to be put on a statutory basis (SACHR, 1997). Government accepted this recommendation and indicated the intention to legislate in a White Paper (1998). This proposed action then became a part of the Belfast Agreement in 1998 and was subsequently included as Section 75 of the Northern Ireland Act later that year. Section 75 of the Act is now the statutory framework for the mainstreaming of equality by all designated public bodies, including many of those UK departments and bodies which operate in Northern Ireland. While this particular version of mainstreaming equality in the policy process is distinctive to Northern Ireland, it is not unique. Rees (1998) and Mackay and Bilton (2000) have examined European and other international examples, while all public sector bodies in Britain must mainstream race equality under the terms of the Race Relations Act of 2000, and will do so in relation to disability with a revised Disability Discrimination Act scheduled for 2004.

Similar criticisms emerged of the second policy initiative, known as Targeting Social Need (TSN). As Osborne (1996b) has shown, the policy was launched with multiple objectives and goals, which led to substantial confusion amongst civil servants and commentators. At the heart of the ambiguity was the intention under TSN to skew public expenditure towards the less well-off groups and areas in Northern Ireland, but this skewing was designed to reduce the differential experience of socio-economic disadvantage by Catholics. A subsequent debate arose: if the intention was to reduce community differentials, was TSN to result in a skewing of resources *only* towards Catholic areas and communities? A counter-argument suggested that this would raise moral difficulties, as it would ignore disadvantaged Protestant communities. Moreover, at a time when Protestant political disenchantment was growing, such an approach was likely to prove counterproductive. Subsequent evaluations found that this debate, and the confusion it generated, paralysed implementation (McLaughlin and Quirk, 1996a; McGill, 1996; NIEC, 1998). The White Paper (1998) indicated that the policy would be relaunched as New TSN and aimed at areas and communities based on need and with a focus on enhancing employability. The policy was to be 'religion neutral' but with the indirect impact of reducing community differentials. However, it is known that a report commissioned by government, unpublished at the time of writing, evaluating the implementation of New TSN is highly critical, and its criticisms echo many of the administrative weaknesses and failures identified in the 1996 evaluation. A concern with process rather than outcome has characterised implementation. While many in the voluntary and community sector give conditional support to New TSN, others would prefer an anti-poverty strategy (NICVA, 2001). New TSN in Northern Ireland seems at one level similar to the Labour government's concern with social exclusion in Britain (Hills, Le Grand and Piachaud, 2002). However, its failure to clearly conceptualise the problems it is seeking to tackle fundamentally reduces its impact.

After a decade, the mixed record of the NICS in implementing these two major equality initiatives puts the focus on an organisation which emphasises its central role in holding Northern Ireland together during almost thirty years of civil disturbances (although this is a role to which the trade unions and voluntary and community sector might also lay some claim). While there is little questioning of the NICS commitment at the top level to these policy initiatives, critics express doubts about the NICS capacity to achieve effective implementation when faced with all-department initiatives such as these. It is not clear to those who are frustrated by a lack of substantial progress whether what is perceived as a modest performance to date arises from initiative fatigue and/or an inability to effectively co-ordinate actions. A continued lacklustre performance will inevitably prompt a further view that there is also the possibility that, as an essentially conservative organisation, the NICS may not be fully convinced of the equality agenda, either as a policy imperative or as a set of actions capable of being successfully operationalised. The stop–go experience of devolution has masked the extent to which the Northern Ireland Executive has the capacity to ensure that politically agreed priorities can be effectively implemented. In the event of a return to devolution, it will be a major question of whether the Executive can ensure that Section 75 of the Northern Ireland Act and New TSN will become embedded in the policy process and create the transformations which many groups and organisations expect and where the delivery of significant strides towards equality are part of the political settlement.

Continued failure to achieve greater equality may require Section 75 to be recast with a new emphasis on regulation (including sanctions) and outcome measures. The current approach uses the voluntary and community sector to drive implementation, utilising ideas about participatory policymaking known as 'community governance'. This may confuse two ideas in one policy. Is the objective to achieve greater equality or a more inclusive and participatory way of making policy decisions? Evaluations of the implementation of Section 75 should take this duality into account.

- The creation of a single Equality Commission was a groundbreaking development in the UK. Many disagreed with the policy outlined in the White Paper of March 1998, fearing that some areas of equality would lose out to fair employment. However, the proposal became part of the Belfast Agreement later that year and was subsequently legislated for in the Northern Ireland Act of 1998. The logic of bringing together the regulatory bodies responsible for anti-discrimination legislation and the promotion of equality of opportunity is to attempt to unify the anti-discrimination legislation.[3] The first *Programme for Government* announced by the Northern Ireland Executive stated that this would take place. The work on developing a Single Equality Bill raises many complex issues, including the scope (which includes age and sexual orientation in line with European Union [EU] directives), monitoring, definitions of discrimination, investigatory and enforcement powers, and the scope for affirmative action. The ECNI has sought to put forward a strategic and detailed approach to this forthcoming legislation in a series of papers (see www.equalityni.org).

Social science research, fair employment and policy

It is worth noting and commenting on the central role that social science research has played in the discussion of fair employment in Northern Ireland. During most of the 1960s and early 1970s, discussions concerning inequality, disadvantage and discrimination in the labour market in Northern Ireland were bedevilled by the absence of systematic empirical data. Although NICRA tried to provide hard evidence (NICRA, 1964), it was not until the analysis of the 1971 Census data by Aunger (1975) that the evidence of Catholic disadvantage in the labour market was revealed. The newly created FEA spelled out these differences in greater detail (FEA, 1978) and for the first time revealed the 'unemployment differential', which at that time was 2.5:1. With this evidence in mind, social researchers, often funded by the FEA and latterly by SACHR, began to explore factors other than discrimination that might account for the patterns revealed in the Census.

Conducting research in a divided society which was characterised by widespread violence posed particular problems to the social science community (Taylor, 1988). While social science itself was questioning whether research could ever be 'value free' or 'objective', attempting to spell out the realities of inequalities in Northern Ireland in a way that could provide policymakers with a solid basis for introducing reform seemed worthwhile. This presupposed that Northern Ireland was reformable, a position questioned by some academic commentators (O'Dowd, Rolston and Tomlinson, 1980). Early research dismissed the idea that there were any differences in attitudes to work between Catholics or Protestants (Miller, 1978b), while educational qualification differences were identified as a possible factor contributing to inequality (Osborne and Murray, 1978). The first study of social mobility in Northern Ireland suggested that religion was an independent determinant of mobility chances (Miller, 1979). Other research identified the operation of informal recruiting practices, widespread in the UK and Ireland, which in the Northern Ireland context operated as a means of perpetuating existing inequalities and disadvantages (Cormack, Osborne and Thompson, 1980; Darby and Murray, 1980). Cormack and Osborne (1983) brought most of this early research together and laid out what was then known empirically about labour market disadvantage and the processes sustaining it.

These early researches made it clear that, although they were identifying and exploring factors other than discrimination operating in the labour market, they accepted the existence and importance of both contemporary and past discrimination. However, as this debate developed, other researchers began to suggest that discrimination was a minor factor and that factors such as the higher birth rate of Catholics and geographical location were far more important (Compton, 1981). Eversley (1989) produced a comprehensive refutation of the demographic argument as developed by Compton, and pointed out that only in Northern Ireland had there been an attempt to give such prominence to demographic characteristics when analysing minority inequalities. In any case demographic factors will play a less important role in future analyses of communal labour market inequalities. Birth rates have tended to fall generally in the last thirty years, and fertility differentials between Catholics and Protestants have also lessened. Geographical factors, however, have figured in the analysis of black disadvantage in the US and Britain, and there is no doubt that residential segregation in Northern Ireland does impact on equality issues in terms of access to jobs and the 'chill factor' (see Chapters 6 and 7).

Research commissioned by SACHR in the analysis of the first decade of fair employment and leading up to its recommendations for reform reflected these divisions (see SACHR, 1987; Smith and Chambers, 1991; Cormack and Osborne, 1991). At this time, the polarised nature of the debate seemed to echo the acrimonious and zero–sum political tenor of the times. At the heart of the debate was the absence of any significant improvement in the employment profiles of Catholics relative to Protestants, notwithstanding the major collapse of manufacturing that had occurred in the 1980s. The unemployment rate differential seemed stuck at a rate about 2.5 times higher for Catholics and, crucially, there was little evidence of employment change elsewhere. Part of this absence of change subsequently was identified as a function of the growth of security-related occupations (Royal Ulster Constabulary [RUC], Ulster Defence Regiment [UDR], and civilian security staff), which recorded Protestant proportions of 90 per cent or over and occurred as the British government sought to substitute local security forces for the British army.

Additional research commissioned by SACHR identified the possible links between education and labour market inequalities. Specifically, SACHR wanted to know if there were any resource and policy issues concerning education which had implications for fair employment. The research programme undertaken represented the most comprehensive overview of the education system at the time. It was reported in a series of annual SACHR reports between 1989 and 1991. Gallagher, Osborne and Cormack (1994a) summarised the key dimensions of the research. Amongst other matters, this research demonstrated an underprovision of grammar schools in the Catholic system and that recurrent school funding, which had evolved incrementally, appeared to place Catholic schools at a disadvantage. The research also revealed that the operation of the 85 per cent state support for capital programmes in all Catholic (and other voluntary) schools placed a significant financial burden above the 15 per cent, was very bureaucratic and may have acted indirectly to inhibit more expensive science development in Catholic schools. Similar funding arrangements in the Canadian province of Ontario had also resulted in a similar lower uptake of science in Catholic schools, whereas Scottish Catholic schools that had received 100 per cent capital funding since 1918 did not exhibit these curriculum differences. Moreover, this research is one of the few examples of social science research which can demonstrate specific policy changes arising from its findings. Policy changes during the 1990s saw the opening of two new Catholic grammar schools (in Belfast and Londonderry/Derry), the introduction of formula–funding with a weighting for pupils from disadvantaged backgrounds, and the availability of 100 per cent capital funding for

Catholic schools in return for some adjustments to governance arrangements. In addition, some of the backlog of capital programmes, especially in the Catholic sector, began to be rectified. It is also likely that these changes have contributed to the educational changes reported in Chapter 4.

The most recent instalment of this debate took place after the SACHR report and its recommendation that the reduction of the unemployment differential should be a policy objective. The government's Central Community Relations Unit (CCRU) at that time sponsored a series of research investigations of the unemployment differential (Murphy and Armstrong, 1994; Gudgin and Breen, 1996). This brought to a head not only the academic proponents of the competing perspectives, but academic perspectives themselves became perceived as becoming closely aligned to political perspectives. On the one hand, factors such as migration and other demographic factors were argued to be substantial explanatory variables, leaving little role for discrimination, while, on the other hand, the role of discrimination was depicted as providing a crucial part of the explanation for the unemployment differential, and demographic and geographic variables were insignificant. An acceptance of the importance of demographic and other factors was depicted as amounting to 'blaming the Catholics' and thereby reducing the need for strong anti-discrimination intervention, while acknowledging the importance of discrimination seemed tantamount to 'blaming the Protestants' for Catholic disadvantage and implying that the only policy issue was to strengthen legislation in order to end discrimination. At this time, Bew, Patterson and Teague (1997) complained that much of the research was undertheorised and argued that fair-employment-related research ought to pay more attention to theoretical models of the labour market.

It is also a little noted fact that the 1971 Census revealed significant differences between various Protestant denominations in their experience of unemployment, with Church of Ireland members more likely to experience unemployment rates similar to Catholics than Presbyterians and Methodists, a factor at least partially attributable to class differences in the Anglican community (Cormack and Rooney, n.d.; Cormack and Osborne, 1991). This difference is still found in the 2001 Census. Such evidence poses further challenges to those who would depict the overall Protestant:Catholic unemployment differential as resulting from a single cause.

The second major SACHR review of fair employment, undertaken in the mid-1990s, produced more significant research, which was published in three edited collections. The first volume (McLaughlin and Quirk, 1996b) examined long-term unemployment, training and access of the unemployed to jobs, job creation and public sector job losses, and included the first evaluations of the two new equality policies of TSN and PAFT. A second volume included an assessment of fair employment case law, the definition of 'fair participation', examined 'merit', assessed the role of the tribunal system, and included a general discussion of equality issues (Magill and Rose, 1996). The third volume concentrated on public attitudes to fair employment, including public opinion and the views of employers and the political parties (McVey and Hutson, 1996). Since this substantial activity surrounding the SACHR research, most academic and related activity has concentrated on the new provisions of Section 75 of the Northern Ireland Act 1998 and New TSN (McCrudden, 2001; Dignan, 2003a; 2003b; Osborne, 2003b).

The value and quality of the fair employment and related research was attested by an external commentator in 1995:

> Where the Northern Ireland situation does differ [from elsewhere] is that because of the sorts of exercises we have surveyed in this chapter, our understanding of the nature and interplay of most of the factors (including discrimination), which create employment inequality, is considerably more sophisticated than it is in either Britain or America. And, though some of those involved might not think so, the level of debate in Northern Ireland in relation to religious inequalities is considerably more sophisticated than it is in Britain, in relation to race. (Edwards, 1995: 72)

Part of the reason for the more recent reduction in academic focus on the unemployment differential, notwithstanding its policy significance, has come from the substantial lowering of all unemployment rates during the 1990s to historically low levels, as revealed by the Labour Force Survey (LFS). True, Catholic rates remain at a higher level, but even here, depending on the measure used, there does seem to have been some reduction in the differential (see Table 1.1). Moreover, it is also worth noting that rising numbers of those aged 50+ who are not economically active, especially males, are starting to mask the true nature of labour market participation and status (Anyadike-Danes, 2003). In addition, clear evidence of rising numbers of Catholics in employment, and their securing of professional and managerial occupations especially in the public sector, began to emerge from monitoring returns during the 1990s (see Chapter 2). In these circumstances, attention has focused on the particular problems of the economically marginalised (McVicar, 2000) and the evaluation of the success of the New Deal programme in channelling people into employment and specific activities designed to combat long-term unemployment (DEL, 2001; 2003). These actions, although religion-neutral, will impact more significantly on the Catholic population because of the continued unemployment differential, but this will change as the differential is eroded.

There can be little doubt that the fair employment and related research conducted over the past generation by the social science research community, mostly, but not exclusively, based in Northern Ireland, has not only illuminated the nature and content of the problem but has been influential in shaping the case for intervention and, in some cases, specifically influencing the nature of reform (Osborne, 1993).

Table 1.1

Unemployment rates by religion in Northern Ireland
(economically active aged 16+)

	Prot. Males %	Cath. Males %	Prot. Females %	Cath. Females %	Prot. %	Cath. %
1971 Census	6.6	17.2	3.5	6.9	5.5	13.8
1981 Census	12.4	30.2	9.6	17.1	11.4	25.5
1991 Census	12.7	28.4	8.0	14.5	10.7	22.8
2001 Census	5.9	10.8	3.9	6.2	5.1	8.7
1990 LFS	10.4	20.5	6.3	9.2	8.6	16.0
1991 LFS	9.3	22.9	5.6	11.9	7.8	18.4
1992 LFS	10.1	24.2	7.6	10.3	9.1	18.4
1993 LFS	11.1	23.1	7.2	10.6	9.4	18.1
1994 LFS	10.9	22.1	5.6	7.8	8.6	16.1
1995 LFS	10.1	20.0	5.5	10.4	8.1	15.9
1996 LFS	9.8	15.4	5.3	9.4	7.8	12.8
1997 LFS	5.5	16.0	4.9	6.9	5.3	12.2
1998 LFS	5.4	12.6	5.5	7.6	5.4	10.4
1999 LFS	5.6	10.4	4.3	6.9	5.0	8.8
2000 LFS	6.0	9.3	4.2	8.2	5.2	8.8
2001 LFS	4.7	9.9	3.9	6.1	4.3	8.3

Source: NISRA (2001) and 2001 Census

The political debate

While some of the academic contributions have arguably been col-
oured by a political perspective, the public debate of fair employment
by the political parties has shown little genuine awareness of the evidence that has become available over the last decade. Unionist parties
seem to have great difficulty in acknowledging that disadvantage and
inequality in employment existed for Catholics in Northern Ireland.
Politicians from the unionist tradition, and those working with them,
try to continue the debate over the differential in unemployment with
a view to explaining it away. These politicians fail to acknowledge the
reality of the processes for change or the actual changes that are under
way. Little public comment by these leaders, for example, is made
about the long-term consequences for Protestants of the continuing
haemorrhage of young Protestants to universities and colleges in
Britain, with little evidence of their return to live in Northern Ireland.
These movements, which have been ongoing for two decades, are
having an impact on the representation of Protestants in the highly
qualified workforce (see Chapter 4). Already sections of the public
services, for example health, record an underrepresentation of Protestants in professional and managerial positions. Taken together with the
older age structure of Protestant employees in most of the public sector
compared with Catholic employees, there is likely to be ever further
growth of the share of Catholics in this sector. Rising proportions of
Catholics are most unlikely to result from 'discrimination', but could
have a great deal, ironically, to do with the effects of this long-standing
migration. How many Protestant/unionist political leaders are discussing these issues and their implications within their community? While
unionist politicians have attacked and continue to attack equality
measures and institutions, how many acknowledge that the significant
numbers of affirmative action agreements between employers and the
FEC/ECNI under the fair employment legislation are concerned with
the underrepresentation of Protestants? By the same token, how many
leaders in the main unionist groupings openly recognise the huge problems of educational underachievement of working-class Protestants,
especially boys?

Few Catholic or nationalist leaders acknowledge the nature and scale
of the positive changes that have taken place and continue to take place.
The past couple of decades have transformed the employment profiles
of the Catholic community. Participation in higher education has

advanced substantially and many of these graduates have come from the poorest Catholics areas. The growth of the Catholic middle class, identified in the early 1990s, has continued apace (Cormack and Osborne, 1994; Gallagher, Osborne and Cormack, 1994a). How many nationalist political leaders openly say that the circumstances for their community are much better than twenty-five years ago? The Catholic community still shares a disproportionate burden of disadvantage, although the most recent evidence suggests the *scale* of this difference is declining because of the reduction in overall unemployment levels (Dignan, 2003a; 2003b). It is correct that public policy should continue to focus, both directly, where appropriate, and indirectly, through New TSN, on this disparity, but there is still a strong tendency of politicians to focus only on this and not to discuss the major positive changes that have taken place and continue to do so.

Perhaps the most striking example of the lack of leadership commentary regarding these issues was the predictable and ultimately sterile exchanges between opposing sides over the publication of the results of the 2001 LFS and its measure of the unemployment differential (see *Irish News* and *News Letter*, 24 February 2003; *Belfast Telegraph*, 25 February 2003). There seems to be a significant time-lag between actual changes in fair employment and how politicians discuss these matters. Moreover, as Hughes in Chapter 9 demonstrates, attitudes held by members of the public are generally more positive than positions expressed by politicians representing the two communities.

To a significant extent this volume seeks to assist in the stimulation of a mature discussion of this policy area. All the contributors seek to carefully present their evidence and how it can be interpreted. It represents an up-to-date snapshot of the current situation and how matters have changed in the last generation, and covers key dimensions of fair employment policy.

Finally, it is appropriate to spell out the importance of the regulatory framework for achieving greater equality, of which fair employment is a fundamental part. Periodically, those committed to the principles of the free market argue that anti-discrimination measures, especially when they involve affirmative action, impose unfair burdens on employers and that the natural forces of competition will ensure that employers, in order to maximise their competitive edge, will inevitably appoint the best person for the job, as to do otherwise will result in a lack of competitiveness and, eventually, failure. Glazer (1988), for example, noted that the major advances for the black community in the US came after the initial Civil Rights Act in the mid–1960s and before affirmative action measures developed. He argued that the market should have been left to operate and the black community would have found its place across US society. In Canada, similar free-market views were published at the time the employment equity legislation was being developed there (Block and Walker, 1985). The debate in Northern Ireland has been more muted but occasionally those associated with the private sector, in particular, will refer to the 'burden of equality' and its capacity to harm competitiveness.

These views have had little impact in Northern Ireland, as the consequences of failing to provide fairness in access to jobs and other parts of society have been all too clear over the past thirty years. Nor can employers isolate themselves from the society in which they are located. It is also worth noting that employers themselves, in evidence to a parliamentary committee reviewing fair employment, testified to the importance of the legislation in changing recruitment procedures and thereby helping to produce change (Northern Ireland Affairs Select Committee, 1999). Chapter 7, moreover, produces important new evidence of the success of the application of affirmative action agreements with employers in improving the employment of under-represented Protestants and Catholics. The economic success of the last decade, when the new fair employment measures were introduced, suggests that the 'burden', to the extent it exists, has been modest.

Chapter themes

The chapters in this book are loosely organised on the basis of examining the current situation – a snapshot of present-day circumstances and how employment opportunities are changing. These form the subject of Chapters 2 and 3. Chapter 2, written on behalf of the ECNI by Ray Russell, presents an analysis of the monitored returns of employers on their patterns of employment and recruitment over the decade or so since compulsory religious monitoring of employees was introduced. It should be recalled that, since monitoring covers approximately 70 per cent of the workforce, by definition the unemployed are omitted, as are those concerns with fewer than 11 employees (that is, small businesses and the self-employed). Russell's chapter, as he makes clear, does not include those employed part time, which have only been the subject of one year's returns. It should be noted that the monitoring of part-time employment covers many of the lowest paid workers, most of whom are female, and these patterns will need careful scrutiny in the next few years, as the monitoring information enables trends over time to be examined. But Russell's careful presentation of the data reveals that substantial progress has been attained in the 'equitable distribution of employment and employment opportunities between Protestants and Catholics'. He introduces the idea of the patchwork quilt to suggest that within this positive message there are variations that do not fit a simple description. Catholics are still underrepresented in security-related jobs, in district councils and, more generally, in the private sector. On the other hand, there are now significant areas of the public sector where Protestants are underrepresented, including education and health. Moreover, the dynamics are for increasing Catholic proportions, arising from recruitment levels that are in line with their representation in the younger and qualified groups. He also notes that there is evidence of increasing integration of workforces (as is also found in Chapter 7) – at a time when increasing segregation has been noted in so many other facets of society. The basic message of Russell's chapter is of substantial change which is likely to continue.

In Chapter 3 Robert Miller has one simple but crucially important message. His research finds that the recent study of social mobility in Northern Ireland, compared with that conducted a generation ago, indicates no independent influence of religion. That means that religious background does not independently influence the chances of any individual achieving a higher social status than their parents:

> Once the effect of occupational structure is taken into account, Catholic and non-Catholic males show the same pattern of occupational mobility between generations. The same result had been obtained in 1973/74, but the difference for 1996/97 is that the *current* occupational structures of the Catholic and non-Catholic men do not differ significantly. These results hold when the analysis is extended to include men and women. The main reason for this convergence in the occupational structures of the two religious groups can be attributed in large part to the educational reforms of the postwar era. At the same time, however, the present-day absence of religion from the coefficients of mobility from first job to present occupation, observed in the path models, suggests (in contrast to Breen's [2000] conclusion) that fair employment legislation *has* had a demonstrable effect, equalising Catholic and non-Catholic mobility chances. Unlike the previous generation in the 1973/74 data, if Catholics and non-Catholics begin their working lives with the same levels of

education and first job, their mobility through their careers will not be directly advantaged or disadvantaged by religion.

This is perhaps one of the most significant conclusions for this book as a whole and conclusively demonstrates that the circumstances of Catholics have been transformed in the past generation. Sceptical readers might query the results of one piece of research but it is also significant that it closely ties in with the evidence in Chapter 2 of improving employment profiles, and also that in Chapter 4 of a substantial evening up of educational outcomes.

In Chapter 4, R.D. Osborne sets out the latest evidence on the output of the education system and the current stock of those with qualifications. He starts by noting the changing relationships between education and the labour market. While many commentators have depicted a tightening relationship between the possession of qualifications and labour market access and success and that, in broad terms, the higher the qualification held the better the job obtained, two caveats to this general position are suggested. The first is the possible evidence that possession of intermediate qualifications may not deliver the success they did for earlier generations, leading to the possibility of overqualification for some. The second relates to the possible use of criteria other than educational qualifications as part of 'merit', thereby allowing employers to seek out those who 'fit' within an organisation – a process which can include discrimination on the grounds of class, gender, religion, race, disability, etc.

This chapter demonstrates that there has been a substantial shift over the past generation so that the qualifications of school-leavers across both communities are now very similar and that this equivalence is broadly evident amongst the general population. Within this general parity there are several variations. The first is that Catholics are still overrepresented amongst those with no qualifications, both in the general population and in terms of those leaving school. Second, Catholics now show a higher representation than Protestants amongst those with the highest level of qualifications in the population (degree and equivalent and above) – a major change in the past generation. The continuing overrepresentation amongst those with no qualifications is likely to be a result of higher Catholic disadvantage, which, in turn, will help in perpetuating that overrepresentation.

In Chapters 5 and 6, Ian Shuttleworth and Anne Green lay out just how extensively global processes are reshaping both the context for the economy in Northern Ireland and the structure of the labour market. It is salutary to look at the 1971 Census and note the occupations that belong to a distant and pre-computing past, such as rope-makers, smiths and forge-men and weavers, while the dramatic drop in those employed in agriculture is a reminder of the scale of change. Chapter 5 takes a broad perspective looking at general patterns of economic and social change experienced in the advanced economies of North America and Europe, and introducing some interpretations of these changes. The authors' objectives are to show that Northern Ireland cannot be understood in isolation from these wider trends and to illustrate the changed background for employment equality policy.

In contrast to the abstractions of Chapter 5, Chapter 6 presents information on the outcomes of these general developments in Northern Ireland. It discusses changing levels and patterns of employment, patterns of economic activity, alterations in unemployment, and local geographical variations. In dealing with this empirical material, the chapter seeks to examine the specific environment in which employment equality policy has had to operate and to discuss the challenges and opportunities it currently faces.

In Chapter 7, Christopher McCrudden, Robert Ford and Anthony Heath focus on the operation of one of the key innovations of the 1989 Act. Under the legislation, alongside compulsory religious monitoring of employees, the FEC/ECNI can develop affirmative action agreements designed to increase the representation of the minority. In this highly innovative chapter, the authors reveal that such agreements have covered both the underrepresentation of Catholics *and* of Protestants. They highlight the reduction of segregated workforces (subject to the qualification that multi-site employers cannot be assessed) and the growth of more integrated workforces. At a time when so many different indicators suggest that the two main communities in Northern Ireland are becoming more segregated and polarised, this represents a major contrary and positive finding. Although there are many methodological caveats to their analysis, they conclude that there is evidence that the affirmative action agreements have played a role in improving the employment profiles of participating employers. This is a crucial finding, as it not only demonstrates that the affirmative action powers of the 1989 Act have been a vital tool in securing change but that it also, indirectly, goes some way to historically validating the strategy of the FEC in utilising its powers during the 1990s. Researchers and policymakers elsewhere in the UK, who have tended to require convincing that policy innovations in Northern Ireland could have a wider utility, should reflect on this evidence for achieving greater racial equality. In the light of the proposed single equality legislation for Northern Ireland, this chapter suggests that the affirmative action powers currently available under fair employment have a much wider relevance.

In Chapter 8, Barry Fitzpatrick examines fair employment case law. Building on earlier analyses, he notes the crucial role the redress of individual grievances has played in cases of unfairly treated individuals and suggests that the Fair Employment Tribunals (FETs) have had a hitherto unrecognised role. Their work has created an environment that makes it clear to employers that discrimination, including harassment, would attract severe penalties. In this way, the redress of individual grievances has complemented the strategic enforcement mechanisms analysed in Chapter 7. He argues that the expertise of the FET should be utilised by creating a specialist equality tribunal as part of the single equality legislation.

In Chapter 9, Joanne Hughes examines how the two ethno–religious communities' attitudes to equality and fair employment have changed over time. She notes some key positive indicators. For example, fair employment is less of a concern to Catholics and Protestants than in the past. Catholic attitudes are now markedly more positive towards their position than in the early 1990s. More Protestants and Catholics believe that equality should permeate social and political life. She also notes, however, that Catholics increasingly believe themselves to be better treated than Protestants; that the equality framework protects their interests. Protestant responses, however, although more nuanced, suggest that they believe they may be starting to lose out in jobs. Hughes suggests that just as positive attitudes from Catholics are evidence of policy success, so the concerns of Protestants must not go unheeded.

These varied contributions show that the context for debates about equality between Catholics and Protestants have substantially changed since the 1970s. This is hardly surprising given the economic, political and institutional changes that have been experienced in Northern Ireland. It is true that some differentials remain and that further work is needed to secure greater equality between the two communities. Data from the 2001 Census show, for example, that the Catholic employment rate lags behind that of Protestants, and residential segregation remains a significant problem for some communities. But despite these problems, the overall picture presented by the essays in this book is one of major labour market, social and legal changes. In many arenas Catholics as a group have caught up with or surpassed Protestants, and there is no longer consistent Catholic relative disadvantage to the same degree as in the 1970s and 1980s. Consequently, discussions about equality are now inevitably more complex. The new situation poses novel political challenges for equality policy in the future, with the requirement to engage more with the Protestant/unionist community. At the same time, new types of jobs, new ways of life and new institutions give pressing reasons for policymakers to think about equality in fresh ways. Facing these challenges is the main test for equality policy as it enters the twenty-first century.

2

Employment profiles of Protestants and Catholics
A decade of monitoring[1]

RAYMOND RUSSELL

Introduction

In 1991, in the first policy statement of the newly formed Fair
Employment Commission, the chairman, Robert Cooper (now Sir
Robert Cooper), wrote:

> The Commission has set itself the target of bringing about an equi-
> table distribution of employment and employment opportunities be-
> tween Catholics and Protestants in Northern Ireland. It will measure
> achievement in terms of changes within those areas of employment
> in which the Commission has been actively involved and also in
> terms of the overall changes in the employment profile. (FEC, 1991)

The main purpose of this chapter is to ascertain how much progress has
been made in achieving this goal.

One method of measuring progress towards the goal of 'fair participation' in employment is by evaluating change over time in the annual
monitoring returns submitted by employers to the FEC and its successor, the ECNI.[2] As the requirement to monitor the part-time workforce was not introduced until 2001, the analyses which follow focus
entirely on the full-time workforce (those working sixteen or more
hours per week). Percentages in [square brackets] refer to Protestants

and Catholics only, with the non-determined excluded. For purposes of clarity and simplicity, the tables generally contain data on one community only, usually the Catholic community. The corresponding percentages for the Protestant community can be deduced by subtracting the Catholic percentage from 100.

A note about underrepresentation

Throughout the chapter, attention will be drawn to underrepresentation in the monitored workforce. At the aggregate level, as used in the annual monitoring reports, the FEC operationally defined underrepresentation as meaning any numerical disparity between the availability of a relevant group and the utilisation of that group. *Availability* refers to that community's representation within the economically active population, while *utilisation* concerns the community's share of the monitored workforce.[3]

When evaluating data on underrepresentation, it is important to note that the community composition of the economically active is changing over time, with a clear upward trend in the Catholic share. The 1991 Census revealed that the Catholic share of the economically active of working age was 40 per cent (both genders), [40.4] per cent for males, and [39.4] per cent for females. By 2001, the corresponding figures were [42.7] per cent for both genders, [42.3] per cent for males, and [43.2] for females (NISRA, 2001; 2003a).

The factors which contribute to underrepresentation are as myriad and complex as the fair employment debate itself. They may include geographical location, chill factors, job type, rates of pay, requisite training, access to a car or public transport, historical educational and career preferences, and past discrimination.

The monitored Northern Ireland workforce

The monitored Northern Ireland workforce is comprised of the combined workforces of public authorities and private sector concerns. In 2001, the monitored Northern Ireland workforce stood at 405,109 employees, with a community composition of [60.5] per cent Protestant and [39.5] per cent Catholic. In 1990 only those private concerns with 26 or more employees were required to submit monitoring returns to the FEC. In 1992 this requirement was extended to smaller employers – those employing between 11 and 25 workers. Therefore, in order to compare trends over time, we must examine the same sections of the workforce in 2001 as in 1990. Thus, it is necessary to exclude the smaller private companies (11–25 employees) from the analysis.

In 1990, the monitored Northern Ireland workforce stood at 349,400. Analysis of these first returns revealed that the Catholic share of all monitored employment was [34.9] per cent – which was [5.1] percentage points lower than the figure for Catholic representation (both genders) in the economically active of working age, [40.0] per cent (see Table 2.1). For males, the gap was significantly higher, at [8.4] percentage points. For females the Catholic share was [38.5] per cent, indicating substantial representation at the aggregate level, compared with a labour availability figure of [39.4] per cent. However, it was acknowledged that monitoring data covered full-time employment alone, and that only an enumeration of part-time and full-time employment would adequately profile the employment position of women.

Looking at the same sections of employment, by 2001 the monitored Northern Ireland full-time workforce had grown to 380,791, an increase of 9 per cent. By 2001, Catholic representation had increased by [4.6] percentage points; [5.0] percentage points for males and [3.9] percentage points for females. The number of Catholic employees rose from 115,266 to 143,339. Over the same period, the number of Protestant employees also increased, although by a smaller margin, from 214,691 in 1990 to 219,366. As a result of the comparatively larger rise in Catholic employment during the decade, by 2001 the Protestant share of the monitored full-time workforce had declined from [65.1] per cent in 1990 to [60.5] per cent in 2001.

Table 2.1

Change in the Catholic percentage of the Northern Ireland workforce (public sector concerns and private sector concerns with 26 or more employees) by gender, 1990–2001

	1990 %	1992 %	1994 %	1996 %	1998 %	2000 %	2001 %	Overall Change %
Males	32.0	32.8	34.2	35.3	36.4	37.0	37.0	+ 5.0
Females	38.5	39.4	40.6	41.2	42.1	42.4	42.4	+ 3.9
Total	34.9	35.8	37.2	38.1	39.1	39.6	39.5	+ 4.6

Source: FEC and ECNI (1991–2002), Monitoring Reports Nos. 1–12

Monitoring data also permitted an examination of the occupational profiles of the two major communities. It was found that Protestants were overrepresented in the higher Standard Occupational Classification (SOC) groups, namely professional and managerial, while Catholics, particularly males, had a larger presence in the lower SOC groups – generally those with lower status and remuneration, such as unskilled and ancillary workers.

Table 2.2 illustrates the changes which have occurred in Catholic representation in the monitored Northern Ireland workforce by SOC group and gender. In 1990 only one of the nine major groups had a Catholic representation of 40 per cent or over, namely SOC 3 (which includes nursing and the professions allied to medicine). In SOC 6, which contains police officers as well as private security staff, it was as low as [28.5] per cent. In SOC 4 (clerical and secretarial) the Catholic share was [34.1] per cent – an underrepresentation of [5.9] percentage points.

Decomposition by gender revealed very substantial underrepresentation within certain sectors of employment. For men, only in one occupational group did the Catholic proportion equal or exceed [40.4] per cent, and this was in SOC 9 (other occupations). In three groups the proportion was below 30 per cent. The Catholic male share was lowest at 20 per cent in SOC 6 (personal and protective services), a group containing almost 27,000 employees in 1990. The low Catholic share in this group was largely due to the inclusion of security-related employment (police, army, and prison service), which was (and still is) largely male and Protestant.

Examination of the 1990 figures for females revealed a Catholic share of [39.4] per cent or more in five of the nine SOC groups. In SOC 3, the Catholic share was as high as [45.3] per cent. However, in SOC 4, the largest group (with nearly 43,000 employees), Catholic representation was [33.9] per cent. At the aggregate level (both genders), leaving aside the small female SOC 5 group, which contained less than 6 per cent of employees, the only category where Protestant representation was less than might be expected was the female SOC 3 group, which contains nurses and midwives.

Table 2.2 shows that, between 1990 and 2001, Catholic representation (both genders) rose in every SOC group. The largest increases were recorded in SOC 1 (managers and administrators), [8.6] percentage points; and SOC 2 (professional occupations), [10.5] percentage points. During this period a significant increase of [7]

Table 2.2

Change in the Catholic percentage of the Northern Ireland workforce
(public sector concerns and private sector concerns with 26 or more employees)
by SOC, 1990–2001

	Males			Females			Both Genders		
	1990 %	2001 %	Change %	1990 %	2001 %	Change %	1990 %	2001 %	Change %
SOC 1 Managers and administrators	28.5	36.8	+ 8.3	36.0	42.5	+ 6.5	30.5	39.1	+ 8.6
SOC 2 Professional occupations	29.7	39.6	+ 9.9	41.4	49.8	+ 8.4	33.4	43.9	+ 10.5
SOC 3 Associate professional and technical occupations	32.8	40.0	+ 7.2	45.3	48.0	+ 2.7	40.1	44.7	+ 4.6
SOC 4 Clerical and secretarial occupations	34.9	43.6	+ 8.7	33.9	40.4	+ 6.5	34.1	41.1	+ 7.0
SOC 5 Craft and skilled manual occupations	32.3	34.9	+ 2.6	42.6	39.5	− 3.1	34.3	35.4	+ 1.1
SOC 6 Personal and protective service occupations	20.0	22.4	+ 2.4	40.5	41.7	+ 1.2	28.5	32.1	+ 3.6
SOC 7 Sales occupations	31.1	39.5	+ 8.4	34.8	41.0	+ 6.2	33.3	40.4	+ 7.1
SOC 8 Plant and machine operatives	36.5	39.7	+ 3.2	42.4	41.8	− 0.6	38.6	40.2	+ 1.6
SOC 9 Other occupations	40.6	42.0	+ 1.4	36.8	40.1	+ 3.3	38.8	41.2	+ 2.4
Total	32.0	37.0	+ 5.0	38.5	42.4	+ 3.9	34.9	39.5	+ 4.6

Source: FEC and ECNI (1991–2002), Monitoring Reports Nos. 1–12

percentage points was also observed in SOC 4 (clerical and secretarial occupations).

Between 1990 and 2001, the Catholic male share of the Northern Ireland workforce increased in every group, with the largest increases occurring in SOC 2 [9.9] percentage points and SOC 4 [8.7] percentage points. For females, the Catholic share rose in eight groups. The largest increases were reported in SOC 1, [6.5] percentage points; SOC 2, [8.4] percentage points; and SOC 4, [6.5] percentage points. SOC 5 (craft and skilled manual occupations) was the sole group in which Catholic female representation declined, from [42.6] per cent to [39.5] per cent. By 2001, SOC 5 was also the smallest group for females, containing only 2.3 per cent of female employees.

This composite picture of the monitored Northern Ireland workforce for 1990 illustrates the aggregate level of participation for Protestants and Catholics. The data for 2001 shows that significant changes occurred in community composition during the intervening period. However, more detailed decomposition of the data by sector reveals the complex nature of the fair employment debate.

Public sector

The public sector is a major component of all employment within Northern Ireland. In 2001, more than one-third of the monitored full-time workforce was employed in the public sector (Equality Commission for Northern Ireland, 2002). As a ratio of total employment, public sector employment has always been high in Northern Ireland, and whilst such employment declined during the 1990s, Northern Ireland still has a much higher proportion of public sector employees than the rest of the UK.[4]

Employment within the public sector is dependent upon a number of factors, the most salient of which are trends in public expenditure and government policy on the provision of public services. A slowdown in total spending, plus increased emphasis by government upon value for money in the provision and delivery of public services, occurred within the 1990s, with the implementation of policy initiatives such as privatisation, compulsory competitive tendering (CCT) and the market testing of ancillary services, including cleaning and catering. The absolute change in employment, which occurred in the public sector during the period 1990 to 2001, is shown in Table 2.3. The effects of government policy are seen in the figures. Privatisation, internal restructuring and downsizing are evident in a workforce which is 6.2 per cent (9,626) smaller than at the beginning of the period.

Table 2.3 demonstrates that monitored public sector employment gradually declined from a peak of 154,845 in 1990 to a trough of 140,460 in 1998, before recovering to a figure of 145,219 in 2001. Examining the period as a whole, the fall in public sector employment notably affected the Protestant community. While the overall number of Catholics employed in the public sector increased by 8.8 per cent,

Table 2.3

Absolute change in monitored public sector employment, 1990–2001

Year	Protestant	Catholic	Non-determined	Total	Change
1990	92,149	50,300	12,396	154,845	
1991	91,589	50,647	11,178	153,414	− 1,431
1992	90,649	50,589	10,940	152,178	− 1,236
1993	85,993	50,145	9,788	145,926	− 6,252
1994	84,493	49,944	9,237	143,674	− 2,252
1995	84,177	50,011	9,007	143,195	− 479
1996	82,935	50,315	9,187	142,437	− 758
1997	81,711	50,593	9,195	141,499	− 938
1998	81,151	51,247	8,062	140,460	− 1,039
1999	81,326	52,036	8,199	141,561	+ 1,101
2000	81,686	53,873	8,465	144,024	+ 2,463
2001	82,260	54,717	8,242	145,219	+ 1,195

Source: FEC and ECNI (1991–2002), Monitoring Reports Nos. 1–12

Table 2.4

Absolute change in employee numbers within major divisions of the public sector, 1990–2001

	Health Count	Education Count	District Councils Count	Civil Service Count	Security-related Count	Total Public Sector Count
1990	49,725	16,591	8,678	35,853	20,713	154,845
2001	48,065	18,698	8,289	37,035	19,563	145,219
% change	− 3.3	+ 12.7	− 4.5	+ 3.3	− 5.6	− 6.2

Note: The public sector count includes a number of public bodies that are not covered by any of the five categories.
Source: FEC and ECNI (1991–2002), Monitoring Reports Nos. 1–12

from 50,300 in 1990 to 54,717 by 2001, the number of Protestants declined by 10.7 per cent during this period, from 92,149 to 82,260. The largest recorded fall in Protestant public sector employment occurred in 1992–3. Among the factors implicated in the decline was the privatisation of Northern Ireland Electricity (NIE), which resulted in the transfer of around 4,300 Protestant employees to the private sector.

Although the public sector experienced an overall reduction in size during the first twelve years of monitoring, disaggregation by the major divisions within the sector reveals a more complex picture of gains and losses. Table 2.4 shows the distribution of employment over the period within the major groups. While two sectors, namely education and the Civil Service, experienced employment growth, the remaining three major divisions (health, district councils, and the security-related sector) witnessed a contraction in employment.

Employment in the health sector, which is the largest segment with around one-third of public sector employees, fell by 3.3 per cent during the period 1990–2001. The reduction was mainly a result of the contracting out of hospital cleaning and catering services to the private sector, especially during the early years of the 1990s. The education sector experienced gradual growth during this period, primarily as a consequence of the expansion of further education in Northern Ireland during the 1990s, and was 12.7 per cent larger in 2001, compared with 1990. The Civil Service, which accounts for almost a quarter of public sector employees, expanded by 3.3 per cent over the twelve-year monitoring period, while the security-related sector, which employs over one-in-seven public sector employees, contracted out by 5.6 per cent during this period.

Feminisation of the public sector

One of the most salient features of public sector employment trends during the 1990–2001 period has been the gradual feminisation of the workforce.

Figure 2.1 reveals that the male and female sections of the public sector workforce, though similar in size in 1990, experienced a reversal of fortunes during the reference period. While the female workforce underwent a decline over the first few years of the decade, after 1994 the number of employees grew steadily and by 2001 was 5.9 per cent larger, an overall increase of 4,437 employees. In contrast, male employment underwent continuous decline during this period, and

Figure 2.1

Public sector employees by gender, 1990–2001

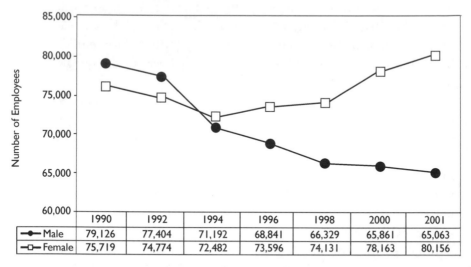

	1990	1992	1994	1996	1998	2000	2001
● Male	79,126	77,404	71,192	68,841	66,329	65,861	65,063
□ Female	75,719	74,774	72,482	73,596	74,131	78,163	80,156

Source: FEC and ECNI

by 2001 the workforce was 17.8 per cent smaller than it had been in 1990, a loss of 14,063 employees. As a consequence, the female share moved from slightly under half (48.9 per cent) in 1990 to over half of the workforce (55.2 per cent) by 2001. The decline in male employment was spread over all of the major divisions of the public sector.

Trends in community composition of the public sector

The increase in the overall number of Catholics employed in the public sector since 1990 (see Table 2.3) is also reflected in their share of the workforce. Table 2.5 reveals that in 1990 [35.3] per cent of all monitored public sector full-time employees were Catholic. By 2001,

Table 2.5

Trends in the Catholic percentage of monitored public sector employees by gender, 1990–2001

	1990 %	1992 %	1994 %	1996 %	1998 %	2000 %	2001 %	Overall Change
Males	30.4	30.8	32.1	32.8	33.5	34.7	34.9	+ 4.5
Females	40.4	41.1	42.1	42.3	43.3	43.9	44.0	+ 3.6
Total	35.3	35.8	37.2	37.8	38.7	39.7	39.9	+ 4.6

Source: FEC and ECNI (1991–2002), Monitoring Reports Nos. 1–12

Table 2.6

Change in the Catholic percentage of public sector full-time employees by gender and SOC, 1990–2001

	Males			Females			Both Genders		
	1990 %	2001 %	Change %	1990 %	2001 %	Change %	1990 %	2001 %	Change %
SOC 1 Managers and administrators	28.6	36.3	+ 7.7	33.9	42.3	+ 8.4	30.3	39.0	+ 8.7
SOC 2 Professional occupations	28.9	40.6	+ 11.7	40.5	50.1	+ 9.6	33.1	45.4	+ 12.3
SOC 3 Associate professional and technical occupations	38.7	42.1	+ 3.4	46.5	48.1	+ 1.6	43.9	46.3	+ 2.4
SOC 4 Clerical and secretarial occupations	44.5	50.9	+ 6.4	38.5	43.1	+ 4.6	39.8	44.8	+ 5.0
SOC 5 Craft and skilled manual occupations	29.4	29.3	− 0.1	31.7	29.9	− 1.8	29.5	29.3	− 0.2
SOC 6 Personal and protective service occupations	16.5	17.6	+ 1.1	39.9	40.7	+ 0.8	25.4	28.1	+ 2.7
SOC 7* Sales occupations	24.1	40.0	+ 15.9	26.5	33.6	+ 7.1	25.8	34.9	+ 9.1
SOC 8 Plant and machine operatives	36.5	43.7	+ 7.2	23.6	47.1	+ 23.5	36.2	43.8	+ 7.6
SOC 9 Other occupations	41.5	44.7	+ 3.2	38.3	41.2	+ 2.9	39.9	43.1	+ 3.2
Total	30.4	34.9	+ 4.5	40.4	44.0	+ 3.6	35.3	39.9	+ 4.6

*SOC 7 contains a negligible number of public sector employees.
Source: FEC and ECNI (1991–2002), Monitoring Reports Nos. 1–12

this figure had increased to [39.9] per cent. Disaggregation by gender, however, reveals that Catholic females fared better than their male counterparts. Although the percentage point increase over the twelve-year period was similar for both, by 2001 the Catholic female share of the female public sector workforce had reached [44.0] per cent, almost one per cent higher than their representation among the economically active of working age, [43.2] per cent. In contrast, Catholic male representation was [34.9] per cent, over [7] percentage points less than their share of the economically active, [42.3] per cent.

Community composition by SOC group

Table 2.6 presents data on the changes which have occurred in Catholic representation in the public sector during the reference period by gender and SOC group. Monitoring data reveals that substantial change has occurred at the aggregate level (both genders). Comparing the data with Catholic labour availability figures, in 1990 only one of the nine occupational groups had a Catholic share of [40.0] per cent or greater; by 2001 Catholic representation was [42.7] per cent or greater in five groups. The most significant changes were recorded in the higher occupational groups. In SOC 1 (managers and administrators), the Catholic proportion rose by [8.7] percentage points, while in SOC 2 (professional occupations), Catholic representation increased by [12.3] percentage points since 1990. Similar changes were observed for both males and females. In only one occupational group, the small SOC 5, which contains only 2.5 per cent of employees, did the Catholic share decrease during the reference period.

Community composition by sector

The observed flow of Catholics into the higher SOC groups at an aggregate level in the public sector is even more pronounced when the data is decomposed by sector. Table 2.7 illustrates the changes which have occurred in the community composition of the health, education and district council sectors by SOC.

Between 1990 and 2001, Catholic representation in SOC 1 increased by [17.6] percentage points in the health sector; by [16.2] percentage points in the education sector; and by [11.0] percentage points in the twenty-six district councils in Northern Ireland. The Catholic share of SOC 2 rose by [10.9] percentage points in the health sector; by [10.2] percentage points in the education sector; and fell by [3.4] percentage points in the district councils.

Table 2.7

Change in the Catholic percentage of the health, education and district council sectors of the public sector workforce by SOC, 1990–2001

	Health Sector			Education Sector			District Councils		
	1990 %	2001 %	Change %	1990 %	2001 %	Change %	1990 %	2001 %	Change %
SOC 1 Managers and administrators	27.8	45.4	+ 17.6	26.2	42.4	+ 16.2	24.9	35.9	+ 11.0
SOC 2 Professional occupations	37.8	48.7	+ 10.9	39.8	50.0	+ 10.2	41.8	38.4	− 3.4
SOC 3 Associate professional and technical occupations	48.3	49.1	+ 0.8	41.0	48.2	+ 7.2	32.5	43.4	+ 10.9
SOC 4 Clerical and secretarial occupations	36.3	42.8	+ 6.5	39.3	43.4	+ 4.1	32.5	38.1	+ 5.6
SOC 5 Craft and skilled manual occupations	28.0	29.4	+ 1.4	26.4	31.2	+ 4.8	31.0	34.0	+ 3.0
SOC 6 Personal and protective service occupations	45.3	47.6	+ 2.3	43.8	45.9	+ 2.1	40.7	39.3	− 1.4
SOC 7 Sales occupations	33.3	20.0	− 13.3	40.0	32.3	− 7.7	43.8	34.2	− 9.6
SOC 8 Plant and machine operatives	37.1	35.3	− 1.8	43.4	49.6	+ 6.2	30.5	31.5	+ 1.0
SOC 9 Other occupations	43.1	48.1	+ 5.0	41.9	46.8	+ 4.9	36.6	39.4	+ 2.8
Total	43.5	47.1	+ 3.6	41.0	46.1	+ 5.1	33.8	38.0	+ 4.2
N (includes Non-determined)	49,725	48,065		16,591	18,698		8,678	8,289	

Source: FEC and ECNI (1991–2002), Monitoring Reports Nos. 1–12

At an aggregate level, Table 2.7 shows that, while Catholics were still underrepresented in the district councils, the picture is one of Protestant underrepresentation in the health and education sectors. In this regard, it is worth noting that the fair employment legislation provides for the implementation of specific affirmative action measures by employers to address community underrepresentation in individual companies. This topic is covered more fully in Chapter 7.

The Civil Service

Monitoring information relating to civil servants employed in Northern Ireland includes both the NICS and the Home Civil Service. In 2001, the Civil Service employed 37,035 people in a full-time capacity (more than sixteen hours per week), a quarter of the monitored public sector workforce. Catholic representation increased by [3.1] percentage points during the first twelve years of monitoring, from [36.8] per cent in 1990 to [39.9] per cent in 2001.

Security-related employment

Since 1990, monitoring returns have included the following security-related occupations: the RUC (now the PSNI), the Royal Irish Regiment, the Territorial Army, the Royal Naval Reserve, the Northern Ireland Prison Service, and civilian staff employed by the Police Authority of Northern Ireland (PANI).

The composition of the entire public sector is influenced by the large number of Protestants working in security-related occupations. In 1990, a total of 20,713 persons were employed in such occupations, of whom 17,426 [92.6 per cent] were Protestant. By 2001, there were a total of 19,563 security-related personnel, of whom [91.3] per cent

Table 2.8

Change in the Catholic share of security-related employment by gender, 1990–2001

	1990 %	1992 %	1994 %	1996 %	1998 %	2000 %	2001 %	Overall Change
Males	7.0	7.0	7.2	7.6	7.8	8.0	7.9	+ 0.9
Females	9.6	9.4	10.1	10.4	11.1	11.5	11.5	+ 1.9
Total	7.4	7.4	7.7	8.1	8.4	8.7	8.7	+ 1.3

Source: FEC and ECNI (1991–2002), Monitoring Reports Nos. 1–12

were Protestant. In 1990, one in four (26.8 per cent) of all Protestant male public sector workers were employed in the security sector, compared with one in twenty (5.3 per cent) of their Catholic counterparts. By 2001, the Protestant male ratio had increased to one in three (34.1 per cent), mainly as a result of an overall 21 per cent decline in Protestant male public sector employment during the intervening years, while the Catholic male ratio had remained unchanged.

Table 2.8 shows the trend in the Catholic share of security-related employment by gender, in the period 1990–2001. Little change can be detected in community composition, with the Catholic share in 2001 only [1.3] percentage points higher than the corresponding figure for 1990.

In order to increase the number of Catholic police officers, the Patten Report recommended a mandatory recruitment profile of 50 per cent Catholic and 50 per cent other over a period of ten years (Patten Report, 1999). The 50:50 rule, as it later became known, was enshrined in Article 46(1) of the Police (Northern Ireland) Act 2000. It is anticipated that Catholic representation in the new PSNI will gradually increase over the coming decade.

Summary of the public sector

The picture that emerges from an analysis of public sector data over the reference period is one of a growing feminisation of the workforce and a gradual change in community composition. By 2001, more than half the monitored workforce (55.2 per cent) was female. From a low of [35.3] per cent in 1990, aggregate Catholic representation rose to [39.9] per cent by 2001. When compared with the figure for Catholic labour availability of working age in 2001 [42.7] per cent, there is still an underrepresentation, but the gap is closing. Looking at the various segments which comprise the public sector, Catholic underrepresentation is still evident in a number of district councils, the higher grades of the Civil Service, and security-related employment in general, while Protestant underrepresentation is apparent in the health and education sectors and a number of district councils.

Private sector

In 2001, the private sector full-time workforce was comprised of 259,890 employees. The composition of those for whom a community could be determined was [60.7] per cent Protestant and [39.3] per cent

Catholic. However, as noted earlier, in order to make comparisons over the full twelve-year period of statutory monitoring, it is necessary to exclude the smaller companies (11–25 employees) from the analysis.

In 1990, Catholic representation in the private sector was [33.0] per cent for males, [36.8] per cent for females and [34.6] per cent overall. These figures represented a shortfall from the Catholic share of the economically active of working age [40.4 per cent for males, 39.4 per cent for females, and 40 per cent overall]. Analysis by SOC showed that, amongst most occupational groups, Catholic representation was below what might be expected, particularly for males.

For companies with more than 25 employees, employment rose by 41,017 (21.1 per cent) over the twelve-year period, from 194,555 in 1990 to 235,572 in 2001. The increase was 21.5 per cent for males and 20.4 per cent for females. Employment rose steadily during the 1990s, peaked in 1999 and fell back by 2001. Reduction in employment levels is largely accounted for by a drop in female jobs, which fell from 107,533 in 1999 to 97,563 in 2001. In contrast to the public sector, decomposition by gender reveals that by 2001 male/female proportions were virtually identical to what they had been at the start of statutory monitoring in 1990. In 2001, the female share of the private sector workforce (26+ employees) was 41.4 per cent , compared with 41.6 per cent in 1990, while the male share was 58.6 per cent in 2001, compared with 58.4 per cent in 1990.

Employment counts over the twelve-year period increased for both communities. The number of Protestants employed rose by 14,564 or 12 per cent, while Catholic numbers increased by 23,656 or 36 per cent. Fig 2.2 reveals that, overall, Catholic representation rose by [4.7] percentage points, from [34.6] per cent in 1990 to [39.3] per cent in 2001. For Catholic males, the increase was [4.9] percentage points, while the position of Catholic females improved by [4.1] percentage points.

Looking at the same sections of the workforce as were monitored in 1990, Table 2.9 shows the profile of the workforce by SOC in 1990 and 2001. In 1990 there were low proportions of Catholic males in managerial (SOC 1), professional (SOC 2), technical (SOC 3) and skilled manual occupations (SOC 5). At that time, although skilled manual occupations accounted for well over one in four private sector jobs amongst males, the Catholic share at [33] per cent was less than might be expected. By 2001, significant change had taken place, particularly in the higher SOC groups. The Catholic male share of SOCs 1, 2 and 3 rose by [8.7], [8.3] and [13.2] percentage points respectively. Although Catholic male underrepresentation is still evident in many of the occupational groups, the size of the gap has been considerably reduced.

Catholic female representation rose from [36.8] per cent in 1990 to [41.1] per cent in 2001. Using the figure for Catholic female labour availability in 2001, [43.2] per cent, as a benchmark, Table 2.9 reveals that considerable progress has been made, particularly in the higher status occupations. Catholic underrepresentation, however, is still apparent in a number of the nine occupational groups.

Analysis by industry sector

The major Standard Industrial Classifications (SICs) can be combined into three broad industry sectors, namely: *manufacturing*, which encompasses SICs 2, 3 and 4; *construction*, which is SIC 5; and *services*, which comprises SICs 6,7,8 and 9. In 1990, the two communities had differing employment profiles. Compared with Catholic employment, a higher proportion of Protestant employees (49.5 per cent) were concentrated within manufacturing, and a lower proportion within construction (5.3 per cent). Similar proportions of both communities worked in the services sector.

Figure 2.2

Change in the Catholic percentage of the private sector full-time workforce in concerns with 26 or more employees, 1990–2001

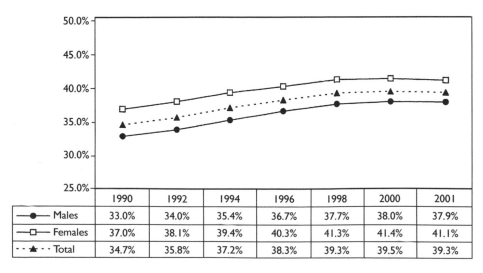

	1990	1992	1994	1996	1998	2000	2001
—●— Males	33.0%	34.0%	35.4%	36.7%	37.7%	38.0%	37.9%
—□— Females	37.0%	38.1%	39.4%	40.3%	41.3%	41.4%	41.1%
· · ▲ · · Total	34.7%	35.8%	37.2%	38.3%	39.3%	39.5%	39.3%

Source: FEC and ECNI

Table 2.9

Change in the Catholic percentage of private sector concerns with 26 or more employees by SOC, 1990–2001

	Males			Females			Both Genders		
	1990 %	2001 %	Change %	1990 %	2001 %	Change %	1990 %	2001 %	Change %
SOC 1 Managers and administrators	28.4	37.1	+ 8.7	38.0	42.6	+ 4.6	30.6	39.1	+ 8.5
SOC 2 Professional occupations	30.7	39.0	+ 8.3	43.5	49.3	+ 5.8	34.0	42.5	+ 8.5
SOC 3 Associate professional and technical occupations	25.0	38.2	+ 13.2	39.1	47.7	+ 8.6	29.9	42.0	+ 12.1
SOC 4 Clerical and secretarial occupations	26.9	36.9	+ 10.0	28.9	37.3	+ 8.4	28.3	37.2	+ 8.9
SOC 5 Craft and skilled manual occupations	33.0	35.5	+ 2.5	43.0	39.9	− 3.1	35.2	36.0	+ 0.8
SOC 6 Personal and protective service occupations	36.9	36.3	− 0.6	41.9	43.1	+ 1.2	39.6	40.5	+ 0.9
SOC 7 Sales occupations	31.3	39.5	+ 8.2	35.0	41.0	+ 6.0	33.5	40.5	+ 7.0
SOC 8 Plant and machine operatives	36.5	39.2	+ 2.7	42.5	41.8	− 0.7	38.9	39.9	+ 1.0
SOC 9 Other occupations	39.6	40.0	+ 0.4	34.8	39.4	+ 4.6	37.7	39.7	+ 2.0
Total	33.0	37.9	+ 4.9	36.8	41.1	+ 4.3	34.6	39.3	+ 4.7

Source: FEC and ECNI (1991–2002), Monitoring Reports Nos. 1–12

Table 2.10 illustrates the sectoral changes that have occurred since 1990. Looking at the same sections of the private sector workforce as in 1990 (26+ employees), while nearly half of employees (47.6 per cent) were working in manufacturing industry, by 2001 this figure had fallen to just over one-third (38.1 per cent). Conversely, over half (56.1 per cent) were engaged in service industries by 2001, compared with 45.9 per cent in 1990. Moreover, while the number of employees in manufacturing remained largely static, the number employed in services increased by 47.7 per cent, from 88,878 in 1990 to 131,300 by 2001. Similar numbers and proportions were employed in construction.

During the twelve-year period of statutory monitoring, the Catholic share of manufacturing and services increased by [4.8] and [4.7] percentage points to [37.6] per cent and [40.0] per cent respectively. In construction, the Catholic proportion rose by a more modest [0.5] of a percentage point.

The decline in traditional manufacturing industries, such as shipbuilding and heavy engineering, which employed a substantial number of Protestants, noticeably affected that community. Looking at the same sections of the workforce, the number of Protestants employed in manufacturing fell by 11 per cent, from 60,348 in 1990 to 53,742 in 2001. In contrast, the number of Catholics employed in manufacturing rose by 10.2 per cent during the same period, from 29,427 to 32,420.

Table 2.10

Change in Catholic percentage (private sector workforce of 26 or more employees) by industry sector, 1990–2001

	1990			2001			Change		
	%	Total Count	Total Workforce	%	Total Count	Total Workforce		%	Total Count
Manufacturing	32.8	92,172	47.6	37.6	89,048	38.1		+ 4.8	− 3,124
Construction	44.6	12,572	6.5	45.1	13,528	5.8		+ 0.5	+ 956
Services	35.3	88,878	45.9	40.0	131,300	56.1		+ 4.7	+ 42,422
TOTAL	34.7	193,622	100.0	39.4	233,876	100.0		+ 4.7	40,254

Note: The small SIC 0 and SIC 1 groups are excluded from the table.
Source: FEC and ECNI (1991–2002), Monitoring Reports Nos. 1–12

Company size and segregation

Historically, segregation in employment was a notable feature of the Northern Ireland labour market. Monitoring data, however, does not permit a detailed examination of this topic, as individual concerns collate data for the company as a whole, rather than by individual locations. Nonetheless, although it is a rather crude proxy for segregation, for illustrative purposes it is worth examining trends in those companies which employed a small proportion of one or other community in 1990. Before examining the data, however, it is important to note that low levels of representation of one or other community may reflect community composition in a very localised catchment area.

A feature of the early monitoring returns was the number of private concerns which employed either less than 10 per cent Protestants or less than 10 per cent Catholics. Table 2.11 illustrates the downward trend in segregation by company size which has occurred during the reference period.

In 1990, one in five of the smaller and medium-sized companies (26–50 and 51–100 employees) employed less than 10 per cent Catholics, while one in ten employed less than 10 per cent Protestants. Around one in ten of the larger-sized companies (100+ employees) employed less than 10 per cent Catholics. With the exception of the smaller companies (where progress has been slower), by 2001 the relevant proportions of concerns employing less than 10 per cent of one or other community had almost halved. By 2001, only one in twenty of the medium and largest-sized employers (100+) employed less than 10

Table 2.11

Prevalence of private sector companies employing either less than 10 per cent Protestants or less than 10 per cent Catholics by size-band, 1990 and 2001

Company Size	1990			2001		
	Number of Companies	Companies with <10% Prot. %	Companies with <10% Cath. %	Number of Companies	Companies with <10% Prot. %	Companies with <10% Cath. %
26–50	866	9.6	19.9	1,123	8.1	15.3
51–100	474	9.9	21.3	666	5.1	10.8
101–250	283	6.7	10.2	359	4.7	6.4
251+	170	2.4	11.2	180	1.1	5.0

Source: FEC and ECNI (1991–2002), Monitoring Reports Nos. 1–12

per cent Catholics, while one in a hundred had a workforce employing less than 10 per cent Protestants. Although a degree of segregation is still evident, particularly in the small companies, significant progress has been made in the intervening years towards the establishment of more representative workforces.

Summary of private sector

Considerable change took place in the community composition of private sector concerns during the reference period. Looking at the same sections of the workforce, in 1990 the aggregate Catholic share of the private sector workforce was [34.6] per cent. By 2001, this had risen to [39.3] per cent, with significant increases in representation re-corded in the higher SOC groups. However, with Catholic labour availability reaching [42.7] per cent in 2001, there is still some way to go before that community is fully represented in the private sector workforce.

The significant structural changes which occurred in the Northern Ireland economy during the 1990s are reflected in the monitoring data. Analysis by sector clearly reveals a decline in manufacturing and a large increase in service-type occupations. When the data is examined by company size, the medium and largest-sized employers (100+) had made the greatest advance in addressing underrepresentation. By 2001, the number of large concerns still employing either less than 10 per cent Protestants or less than 10 per cent Catholics had been more than halved.

Applicants and appointees

Previous sections have analysed trends in the community composition of the monitored workforce since statutory monitoring began in 1990. Compositional data on employees is often referred to as *stocks*. It is now appropriate to examine applicant and appointee data, usually referred to as *flows*. Tables 2.12 and 2.13 present data on the Catholic share of applicants and appointees, in both the private and public sectors,[5] during the period 1991–2001. Examining the eleven-year period of monitoring as a whole, Tables 2.12 and 2.13 demonstrate that in large private sector concerns (251+), the representation of Catholics among applicants and appointees has been broadly similar over the period 1991–2001. Decomposition by gender reveals a similar picture. Up until 1997, as NISRA (2001) pointed out, the same could be said about

the public sector. During the 1997–9 period, however, the representation of Catholics among appointees was approximately 3 percentage
points higher than their representation among applicants.

Table 2.13 also serves to highlight two other salient features of the
data. First, the Catholic share of female appointees was consistently
higher than that community's corresponding share of male appointees,
particularly in the public sector. This finding provides further evidence
of the growing feminisation of the public sector workforce. Second, an
upward trend is evident in the Catholic (both genders) share of
appointments since 1990.

Trends in appointments

Flows into employment are influenced by a cluster of factors, including
demography, educational attainment, and labour availability. Far from
being static, the 2001 Census of Population revealed that these factors
are quite dynamic, and have changed considerably since 1991. The
Census revealed that the Catholic community has a younger age profile than the Protestant community. Twenty-five per cent of people
with a Catholic community background are aged under 15, compared
to 18 per cent of those with a Protestant community background.
Conversely, 10 per cent of Catholics are aged 65 or over, compared

Table 2.12

Catholic share of private sector (251+ employees)
and public sector applicants, 1991–2001

	PRIVATE SECTOR			PUBLIC SECTOR		
	Males	Females	Both Genders	Males	Females	Both Genders
Year	%	%	%	%	%	%
1991	39.0	44.1	41.3	40.2	40.8	40.5
1992	41.0	44.9	42.8	39.7	41.9	40.8
1993	41.1	46.2	43.3	42.7	43.0	42.8
1994	41.3	44.8	42.9	39.6	43.5	41.5
1995	42.2	46.1	43.9	40.1	42.2	41.2
1996	46.0	50.1	47.9	42.9	44.3	43.7
1997	43.8	47.2	45.3	41.0	43.0	42.0
1998	43.6	48.7	45.8	42.7	45.3	44.1
1999	44.4	49.1	46.5	43.7	45.5	44.7
2000	44.0	48.8	46.1	45.1	46.2	45.8
2001	42.6	48.0	45.0	46.5	48.5	47.8

Source: FEC and ECNI (1991–2002), Monitoring Reports Nos. 1–12

with 17 per cent of Protestants (NISRA, 2003b). This is a continuation of the trend observed ten years earlier in the 1991 Census. As the under-15 cohort enters the labour market, both the number and proportion of Catholic applicants for employment are likely to increase.

In a knowledge-based economy, such as Northern Ireland, a graduate qualification is increasingly a prerequisite for employment. In 1991, [46.6] per cent of those in the under-35 age band with a degree, equivalent or higher were Catholic. Ten years later, the 2001 Census (NISRA, 2003b) revealed that in the under-35 age band, where many appointments are made, [56.0] per cent of those with a higher degree, and [48.1 per cent] of those with a first degree or equivalent were Catholic.

As Gallagher, Osborne and Cormack (1994a) observed, it is important to remember that most recruitment takes place amongst younger age groups. Thus, 'the relevant age-specific benchmark to judge recruitment patterns is not the representation of the two groups in the economically active population as a whole, but their representation in younger age groups' (p. 81). The 1991 Census revealed that Catholic representation in the under-35 age cohort of the economically active was [43.9] per cent (Gallagher, Osborne and Cormack, 1994a). By 2001, Census data demonstrated that while overall Catholic

Table 2.13

Catholic share of private sector (251+ employees) and public sector appointees, 1991–2001

| Year | PRIVATE SECTOR | | | PUBLIC SECTOR | | |
	Males %	Females %	Both Genders %	Males %	Females %	Both Genders %
1991	40.2	40.8	40.5	39.4	40.9	40.3
1992	39.7	41.9	40.8	39.7	40.4	40.1
1993	42.7	43.0	42.8	40.8	41.9	41.5
1994	39.6	43.5	41.5	40.6	41.4	41.1
1995	40.1	42.2	41.2	40.0	42.3	41.5
1996	42.9	44.3	43.7	43.7	44.4	44.1
1997	41.0	43.0	42.0	43.1	46.3	45.1
1998	42.7	45.3	44.1	45.5	47.8	47.0
1999	43.7	45.5	44.7	46.8	47.9	47.6
2000	45.1	46.2	45.8	45.1	45.5	45.4
2001	46.5	48.5	47.8	47.5	48.0	47.9

Source: FEC and ECNI (1992–2002), Monitoring Reports Nos. 2–12

Table 2.14

Community background (religion or religion brought up in) of economically active persons of working age in Northern Ireland by age-band and gender, 2001 Census.

	Protestant %	Catholic %
Both genders of working age	57.3	42.7
16 to 24	50.4	49.6
25 to 34	54.9	45.1
35 to 44	57.4	42.6
45 to 59/64	63.9	36.1
Males of working age	57.7	42.3
16 to 24	50.2	49.8
25 to 34	55.7	44.3
35 to 44	57.4	42.6
45 to 64	64.0	36.0
Females of working age	56.8	43.2
16 to 24	50.6	49.4
25 to 34	53.9	46.1
35 to 44	57.3	42.7
45 to 59	63.7	36.3

Note: The term 'Catholic' includes those respondents who gave their religion as Catholic or Roman Catholic. The data refers to Catholic and Protestants only, with 'other religions and philosophies' and 'none' excluded. Working age is 16–64 for males, 16–59 for females.

Source: NISRA (2003a)

representation in the economically active of working age had increased to [42.7] per cent, in the 16–24 and 25–34 age cohorts the Catholic share had grown to [49.6] per cent and [45.1] per cent respectively (see Table 2.14). In brief, it is clear that trends in demography and educational attainment are set to generate further change in the community composition of the labour market in Northern Ireland.

Conclusion

This chapter began by referring to the first policy statement of the FEC in 1991 when the Commission 'set itself the target of bringing about an equitable distribution of employment and employment opportunities, between Catholics and Protestants in Northern Ireland'. To what extent has this goal been achieved?

Fair employment is best understood as a patchwork quilt, rather than a seamless garment. For example, the data shows there are still areas where Catholics, particularly males, are underrepresented, notably in the security-related sector, district councils, and the private sector in general. At the same time, there is evidence of Protestant underrepresentation in the health and education segments of the public sector.

In broad terms, however, the data reveals that substantial progress *has* been made towards a more equitable distribution of employment and employment opportunities in Northern Ireland. In 1990, the community composition of the monitored Northern Ireland full-time workforce was [65.1] per cent Protestant and [34.9] per cent Catholic. Based on the figure for Catholic labour availability at that time, this represented a shortfall of around [5] percentage points in the Catholic share of monitored employment. Looking at the same sections of the workforce as were monitored in 1990, by 2001 Catholic representation had increased to [39.5] per cent, a shortfall of around [3] percentage points, again based on Catholic labour availability data [42.7 per cent]. In reviewing these figures, it is important to note that employment counts rose for both communities during the twelve-year period. The number of Catholics in monitored full-time employment rose from 115,266 to 143,339, while the Protestant count increased from 214,691 to 219,366 during the same period.

Looking at flows into employment, the Catholic share of appointments has been consistently higher than their share of employment over the reference period. In 2001, Catholic representation in appointments ranged from [45.3] per cent in the public sector to [47.9] per cent in the private sector. Given the younger age profile of the Catholic community, and their substantial representation amongst those with higher level qualifications in Northern Ireland, it seems likely that current trends in appointments will be maintained.

The story of fair employment monitoring, as outlined in this chapter, is, in a sense, a proxy for the story of the success or failure of the 1989 Act itself. The degree to which new recruitment and selection procedures, affirmative action programmes, employer advice and the workings of the FET led to changes in the community composition of employment is reflected in the data.

The answer to the question posed in the first paragraph of this conclusion must be a qualified 'yes'. The data presented here shows that the Northern Ireland labour market has moved, and is continuing to move, in the direction of a more equitable distribution of employment. More, however, still needs to be achieved before the target set by the FEC in 1991 can finally be realised.

3

Social mobility in Northern Ireland
Patterns by religion and gender

ROBERT MILLER

Introduction

The study of social mobility (usually considered as inter- or intra-generational movement between occupations) is a highly developed area in the sociology of social stratification and in the social sciences generally. Part of the 'mobility tradition' has been to apply advanced statistical techniques to the investigation of equality of opportunity. This chapter, a secondary analysis of data from the survey funded by the Economic and Social Research Council (ESRC), *Social Mobility, Political Preferences, Attitudes and Behaviour in Northern Ireland*,[1] draws upon that tradition. The survey was designed as a part replication of the original 1973/74 Irish mobility survey, *Determinants of Occupational Status and Mobility in Northern Ireland and the Irish Republic*,[2] and was undertaken in late 1996 and early 1997. Because of this, it can throw light on the patterns and determinants of social mobility in the 1990s in comparison with the earlier 1970s survey, which, of course, is a key period.

While not including all the 1990s, or bringing the story up to the early years of the twenty-first century, the data are the best currently available, and the dates of the two surveys bracket the first employment equality legislation of 1976 and the institutional, political, economic and social changes identified in other chapters. These have seen, for example, the improvement of the position of the Catholic community as revealed by ECNI monitoring returns (see Chapter 2) and wider labour market restructuring (see Chapter 6). One focus of this chapter, therefore, is to examine social mobility by religion to see if the 1990s pattern is different from that of the 1970s. Since the data have been underused, especially with regard to gender, a second theme considered is the social mobility of women. Consequently, the chapter will also concentrate on this aspect, with particular regard to the inter- action of religion with gender. Another rationale for this combined examination of religion and gender is that these two aspects are now under 'one roof' in the ECNI and gender can influence patterns by religion and vice versa.

As mentioned earlier, a number of advanced statistical techniques will be used and the outcomes of two types of analysis will be reported. First, a *path diagram* uses regression analysis to depict the factors that help or hinder the chances of an individual being upwardly mobile. This allows the independent effects of religion and gender after other variables, such as level of education or occupational background, are taken into account. Second, *loglinear analysis* is used to assess whether actual patterns of social mobility have changed between the 1970s and the 1990s by religion or gender. The technical details and detailed results of these analyses are available in a more comprehensive paper, which can be obtained from the author.

Social mobility
The 1973/74 study

The 1996 survey partly replicates the original 'Irish Mobility Study' that was carried out twenty-three years before. The original mobility study owes its origins in part to the political situation of its time. At the beginning of the 1970s, almost no reliable data existed about the amount of inequality experienced by Catholics. Much of the claims of discrimination being voiced by NICRA could be seen as claims of adverse social mobility chances. The original principal investigators on the first Irish mobility study submitted a research proposal to the British Social Science Research Council (SSRC, now the ESRC) for a small survey of occupational mobility that would be confined to the Belfast area. This proposal was turned down, but with the suggestion that a larger proposal encompassing the whole of the region might be more successful. John Jackson, professor and head of the Department of Social Studies at Queen's University Belfast, and Professor Sugiyama Iutaka, a visiting professor from the University of Florida, submitted the proposal for a massive study covering both parts of Ireland. This larger proposal was funded.[3]

Hence, the original Irish mobility study had questions of religious inequality at its core. These questions were answered by two analyses. A path diagram regression analysis (Miller, 1981) was carried out to establish the factors, or variables, that could be identified as independently affecting the current occupational status held by respondents to the survey. In effect, this analysis asked whether a person's religion had a role to play in their chances for upward social mobility that was independent of other features, such as a person's education or the high or low status of their family background. Second, a log-linear analysis (Miller, 1983) was carried out to establish whether patterns of intergenerational mobility were different for Catholics compared to non-Catholics. That is, whether people from the same social background exhibit the same patterns of mobility across a generation or whether Catholics or non-Catholics will be more effective at exploiting the advantages (and overcoming the disadvantages) of their origins.

The path analysis
Comparing males in 1973/74 and 1996/97

Blau and Duncan (1967) pioneered the use of standardised regression coefficients for the production of *path models* for the study of patterns of social mobility, and Miller followed their procedure to construct a path model of social mobility using the data from the 1973/74 study in Northern Ireland. The original path model looked at the factors, or variables, affecting the chances of social mobility between two generations. (For a complete report of the findings, see Miller, 1981.) The path model for the 1973/74 data demonstrated that the most important determinant of a person's present occupational status was their level of educational qualification, followed by the level at which they entered the labour market (the status of their first job). Social background, as indexed by the status of their father's job, also had a significant, though smaller, direct effect (as well as having an indirect effect through education – people from higher status backgrounds were more likely to secure higher educational qualifications). Other potential factors, such as geographic location and family size, did not have statistically significant effects that were independent of education, origin and first job status.

Once account had been taken in the model of all of these other variables, religion continued to have a statistically significant, though weak, direct effect upon occupational status, with Protestants being somewhat more likely to have a higher status occupation. The significance of the relatively small coefficient for religion was that it remained even when the effects of education, level of origin and first job were included in the model. The interpretation of the meaning of the persistence of the religion coefficient was that it could be taken as indirect evidence of religious discrimination operating against Catholics. In the political context of the time, the finding was seen as controversial. However, other subsequent multi-variate regression analyses using data from the same time period, which assessed the relative effects of a variety of variables upon income and unemployment rates (Smith, 1987; Smith and Chambers, 1991; Eversley, 1989; 1991), also found that religion remained significant and reached similar conclusions about the relative disadvantage of Catholics. Later analyses also reached the same conclusions (Murphy and Armstrong, 1994), although there were attempts to discredit these conclusions largely by reference to demographic factors (Compton, 1991; Gudgin and Breen, 1996).

A path model designed to be a replication of the 1973/74 results was developed from the 1996 data. Before turning to the model results themselves, several caveats that need to be kept in mind during their interpretation should be mentioned. The 1973/74 survey sampled men only. Hence, the 1996 replication path model presented below is limited to only the male portion of the sample. Both samples were designed as representative samples of the non-institutionalised population in Northern Ireland, but the age range of the 1973/74 data covers those aged 18 to 65, while the range for 1996 is 21 to 65. The response rate in 1972 was higher, 72 per cent as opposed to 64 per cent in 1996/97. Therefore, the 1996/97 respondents will be slightly older and the potential for biasing error due to non-response is greater. Three variables that appeared in the 1973/74 path model – father's education in years, experience of post-full-time education, and population size of respondent's birthplace – are not present in the 1996 data and therefore could not be included in the replication.

Given those caveats, however, the 1996/97 replication does provide a reasonable approximation of the 1973/74 analysis. Both samples are representative samples of the same target populations and the effect of the slight difference in age range should be minimal. The main variables of respondents' education and occupational status have been coded using very similar procedures, so the analysis should be equivalent in its most significant features. Additionally, the effect of the omission of those variables that were present in the 1973/74 data but not in the 1996/97 data can be assessed to some degree in the full analysis, extended to include both males and females, that is presented shortly.

The standardised regression (also called *path*) coefficients are displayed visually for the 1996/97 data in Figure 3.1. This diagram replicates the 1973/74 data as far as possible, dealing only with males and using comparable variables to the earlier analysis. The main benefit of using a diagram is that it is possible to picture the chains of causality with the earliest variables and coefficients appearing on the left. The coefficients are a measure of the amount of effect that an 'independent' variable A (assumed to be causal) has upon a 'dependent' (assumed to be caused) variable B. These coefficients range between –1 (a perfect negative relationship) to +1 (a perfect positive relationship). Values close to zero imply a weak association. Since the coefficients are standardised, direct comparisons can be made between the relative strength of each variable. Only statistically significant relationships are indicated by an arrow. An example of how to read the diagram is given by an

Figure 3.1

Replication of 1973/74 path model, males only

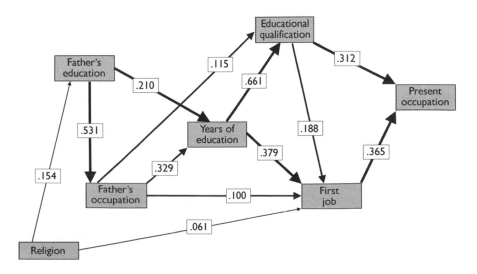

examination of the variables influencing present occupation. The largest direct effect (0.365) is from the status of first job with respondents' qualifications (0.312) coming a close second. Religion did not have a direct statistically significant effect on present occupation in the 1996/97 data once the effects of first job had been taken into account, although it had *indirect* effects via father's occupation and first job status.

Whilst the overall patterns of the 1973/74 and 1996/97 path models are broadly similar, there are some differences in the ordering and strength of the variables between the two datasets, although roughly the same amount of variance on occupational status (about 42 per cent) was explained each time. In 1973/74 the status of father's occupation was a significant influence on present occupation, as was religion. These two variables were not directly significant in the 1996/97 analysis. In both datasets the status of first job and educational qualification were the leading determinants of present occupation.[4] Unlike in 1973/74, father's occupation exerted a significant effect on the status of first job and there was also a small religion effect on this variable. However, there were also continuities, since first job status for both datasets was mainly determined by level of educational qualification and number of years in full-time education. The results for the influences of years of education were virtually identical for both the 1970s and the 1990s datasets.

Path analysis
The full 1996/97 dataset

It was crucial to extend the analysis to include women on several counts. First, it allows gender to be considered alongside religion and other variables. This is sensible given the probable interactions between religion and gender. Second, by incorporating women, the number of cases in the analysis is doubled over those in the replication of the 1973/74 research. Finally, variables were collected in 1996/97 that were not gathered in 1973/74 and the full analysis permits their inclusion. The results are presented in Figure 3.2.

The results do not differ radically from those in the male-only analysis reported in Figure 3.1. The main determinants of level of present occupation remain first job (0.346) and educational qualification (0.317). The number of periods of unemployment experienced by a respondent exerts a predictable, though weak, negative effect upon present job status. Significantly, being male implies having an advantaged chance of a higher job status, and this direct effect is independent of level of labour market entry, educational qualification or experience of unemployment. Once people enter the labour market and embark upon their careers, women who came in at the same level and with the same amount of education do not do as well as equivalent men.[5] Albeit circumstantial, the persistence of this coefficient can be taken as indirect evidence of gender discrimination.

The variables of qualification and years of education remain the most important explanatory factors for first job status (0.219 and 0.390 respectively). Father's occupation and religion are statistically insignificant. However, age is now important. Older respondents seem to have had a somewhat *higher* entry-level job once the effects of education have been taken into account (but note that younger respondents in general have greater amounts of education). Number of years of education remains by far the most important factor affecting level of educational qualification (0.609), but attendance at a grammar rather

Figure 3.2

Path model, 1996/97 survey, males and females

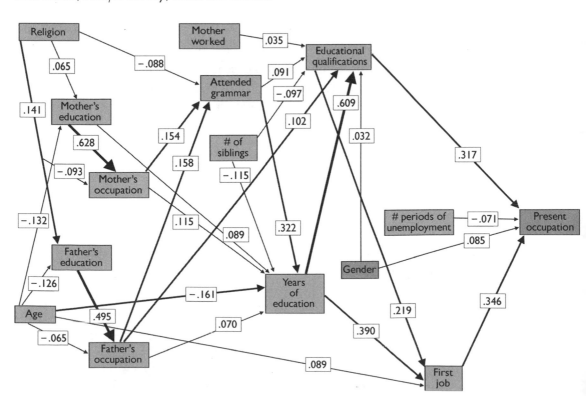

than a secondary school independently raises the expected level of qualification, as does having a father with a higher status occupation (and presumably more resources available to devote to the education of his children). The presence (or lack) of resources available in the family also is the likely cause underlying a negative association between family size (number of siblings) and educational attainment. Respondents from larger families are less likely to have higher educational qualifications, have fewer years of full-time education, and are less likely to have attended a grammar school: a large number of siblings lowers the likely years of education of the respondent, and higher occupational status of both the father *and* the mother raises the likely number of years of education and the probability of attending a grammar school. These findings are similar to those from the 1973/74 dataset (see Hayes, 1987; 1990; Miller and Hayes, 1990). The negative effect of age upon total years of education reflects both the rising amount of education experienced by the population over the years and, more directly, the effect of historical rises in the statutory school-leaving age.

The discussion of results should not centre solely upon the importance of variables that appear as significant effects in the path model – those paths that are *not* found to be statistically significant and those variables that do *not* appear in the path model are just as important. In effect, possible relationships that are found not to exist represent hypotheses that have been eliminated by the data. The 'lost' relationships that are of most significance are those that involve religion or gender. Once the influences of other variables are taken into account in the regression estimations, religion does not appear as a significant variable for any of the main variables that relate to the respondents: present occupation; first job; educational qualification; and years of education. Hence, compared to a generation earlier, religion in analyses based on the 1996/97 dataset appears to have lost its unique significance for people's mobility chances.

That is not to say that the broad religious community to which a person is attributed now has no significance in Northern Ireland. The less advantaged position of Catholics in Northern Ireland cannot be explained away simply by attributing it to other associated demographic or social factors. The correlations in Table 3.1 demonstrate that this is not the case. What the lack of significance for religion does demonstrate is that the effect of religion upon people's mobility chances is played out through the association of religion with other factors that affect mobility. For instance, the simple correlations in Table 3.1

demonstrate that being 'non-Catholic' is associated with having a higher job status, both at present and at the time of entry into the labour market, with a higher job status for the father, and with higher levels of educational attainment, particularly in the parents' generation. In turn, being Catholic is associated with larger family sizes and is somewhat associated with being younger.

The picture is different for gender. Being male does impart a statistically significant advantage to the standing of one's present occupation, and this effect holds even after the effects of level of labour market entry, educational qualification and experience of unemployment are taken into account. There is also a similar, though even weaker, positive effect upon level of educational qualification for males that remains after the stronger effects of number of years of education, whether the respondent attended a grammar school, the number of siblings they had, and level of father's occupation are taken into account. This continued persistence of gender in the path model is congruent with the presence of indirect sex discrimination working to the disadvantage of women. (As with religion, however, one should note that the real

Table 3.1

Correlations of religion and gender with other variables

	Religion†	Gender‡
Present occupation	0.047**	0.110***
No. periods of unemployment	−0.039*	0.177***
First job	0.057***	0.023^{ns}
Educational qualification	0.036*	0.059***
Years of education	−0.006^{ns}	0.027^{ns}
Attended grammar	−0.044**	0.008^{ns}
Number of siblings	−0.309***	−0.041*
Age	0.042*	0.010^{ns}
Father's occupation	0.093***	0.050*
Father's education	0.136***	0.021^{ns}
Mother's occupation	−0.055^{ns}	0.087**
Mother worked	0.073***	0.028^{ns}
Mother's education	0.059***	0.042*

*** = $p < 0.001$
** = $p < 0.01$
* = $p < 0.05$
^{ns} = not significant

† Catholic = 0; non-Catholic = 1
‡ Female = 0; Male = 1

Source: Social Mobility Survey, 1996/7

significance of gender is in its correlation with other, more significant, causal variables rather than in its unique direct effect. For instance, being male is positively associated with a higher present occupational status, a higher level of educational qualification and, in contrast, with more periods of unemployment.)

Finally, it is important to note those variables whose significance was tested but which did not exert any significant effects upon any of the main variables in the path model. Neither being 'ever married' as opposed to being 'single'[6] nor the occupational status of the spouse[7] had any effect upon present occupational status. The available measures of geographic location or mobility – location in the east or west of the region and whether respondents had migrated to Northern Ireland as children or adults – had no significant effects in the model. The total number of times that a respondent had been a 'homemaker' (working solely within the home) had no effect. Unlike 'total number of siblings', the number of older siblings had no separate effects.[8] Measures of the interaction of the job statuses of the parents or of the interaction of the educational attainment of both parents had no effects additional to those found for the direct effects of the occupational and educational levels of each parent considered singly.[9] Finally, measures of the number of organisational memberships of the respondent, and of the number of self-reported interests in 'cultural and sports' activities, had no effect upon current occupational level. This is interesting in terms of debates about 'social capital', in which arguments are made that membership of organisations, by providing social linkages, can provide advantage in the labour market over individuals who have no such ties.

Loglinear analysis
Comparing males in 1973/74 and 1996/97

A second perspective is provided by the use of loglinear analysis. If the same results, although using a different method, are derived as in the regression path analysis, then it is highly likely that they are robust. Loglinear analysis provides a means to discriminate between structural (or forced) mobility and exchange (or true) mobility. Structural mobility occurs when there are deep-seated changes in the availability of jobs or labour market opportunities (as outlined in Chapters 5 and 6). The chances of making the transition to white collar or service jobs in Northern Ireland, for example, have probably increased in the recent past simply because there are more of these jobs available and less manual and agricultural employment. True mobility occurs when individuals exchange places between types of job over and above what would be expected given structural changes in the labour market. The problem is to separate these two types of mobility from each other – large amounts of social mobility could either result from major structural changes in the available opportunities or from people moving freely between occupations in an egalitarian society. Loglinear analysis offers a way to make this separation. This is important in the Northern Ireland context because it permits an assessment of how mobility patterns of Catholics compare with non-Catholics and whether any differences are a result of structural differences in the opportunities open to each group or to differences in true mobility.

Miller (1983) carried out a loglinear analysis of Protestant/Catholic intergenerational mobility of the 1973/74 survey data by comparing the occupational statuses of the male respondents with those of their fathers. The result of this analysis was that differences in occupational mobility between the groups could be attributed solely to religious differences in the occupational distributions of the origin (fathers') and destination (sons') occupational structures. It was not necessary to posit any differences in ability to exploit mobility chances between the two religious groupings. That is, if the Catholics could be placed hypothetically into the opportunity structure enjoyed by the Protestants, their pattern of mobility would not differ significantly from that shown by Protestants and vice versa. These results were confirmed in Hout's (1989) analysis of the same data.

Using the 1996/97 data, Breen (2000) carried out a replication of the same analysis and directly compared his findings with those for 1973/74. He confirmed the original 1973/74 findings and found basically a similar pattern in the 1996/97 data. As in 1973/74, it is not necessary to posit any significant difference in exchange mobility between the two religious groupings. Differences between the intergenerational mobility of Catholic and non-Catholic males can be attributed solely to variance in the mobility opportunity structures of the two religious groupings. Whereas in 1973/74, the differences between Catholics and Protestants were both in the occupational structure of origin and in the occupational structure of destination, by 1996 occupational differences between Catholic and non-Catholic males had narrowed to the extent that it is only necessary to take into account differences in occupational structure in the previous (fathers') generation. Hence, both surveys agree that Catholics and non-Catholics will perform equally well given the same opportunity structures. Where the difference in mobility patterns between the two surveys lies, whose fieldwork took place almost a generation apart, is in the change in opportunity structures. In 1973/74 Catholics were doubly disadvantaged in that the opportunity structures of both origin and of destination were less favourable than those enjoyed by Protestants. By 1996, present occupational distributions have equalised to the extent that the Catholic disadvantage only persists for the origin distribution.

Loglinear analysis
The full 1996/97 dataset

The replication done by Breen (2000) was confined only to the male part of the 1996/97 sample as a direct comparator with the 1973/74 dataset using father's occupation as the sole measure of origin status. It also gave little information about actual substantive patterns of mobility. To address these issues, a loglinear analysis was therefore carried out on the whole 1996/97 sample. The association of gender with religion, as it influenced intergenerational social mobility, was the central focus of the analysis.[10]

It is useful to consider overall mobility patterns. 'Inheritance' (currently being in the same stratum as one's origin) is particularly pronounced for both the highest and lowest strata. There is little mobility into the 'upper service' strata from the lowest groups, and the highest proportion of individuals currently in this category is drawn from individuals who had this background to begin with, although the 'proprietors and farmers' are also a significant contributor to the 'upper service' strata. Similarly, if an individual starts in the 'semi and unskilled' strata, there is a good chance that they will remain there. Most people are located in strata different from their origins and there is some long–distance mobility from the very bottom to the top (although the odds of being socially mobile from bottom to top and top to bottom are much less than would be expected in a completely open society, where social background made no difference).

The analysis informs us that the main source of difference between Catholics and non–Catholics in their current patterns of mobility lies in their differing origins, since the origin of Catholics is skewed towards the lower strata. More came from the lowest 'semi- and unskilled' strata and fewer from the 'upper service' and 'skilled manual' strata. This weaker starting position has had adverse impacts on their mobility.

Despite this, while there are some differences between the current status of Catholics and non-Catholics, overall there has been a considerable evening out. This represents a significant change from the previous survey, which took place a generation ago, where Catholic mobility chances were adversely affected by downward skews in *both* the origin distribution *and* the (in 1973/74) present distribution. The present-day occupational structure has altered significantly towards more equality for Catholics.

Breen (2000) attributes this trend towards more equality in mobility chances to the effect of the postwar educational reforms, which removed the barriers to upward mobility routes through education for the working class and created a 'new Catholic middle class'. Catholics were disproportionately more disadvantaged than Protestants and hence can be expected to have benefited more from the enhanced opportunities (Osborne et al, 1983). One can note also that in the past Protestant males enjoyed routes to secure skilled manual jobs in the traditional industries of shipbuilding and heavy engineering that were not open to Catholics. Consequently, Catholics may always have been more likely to view education as an avenue of upward mobility. As the traditional industries in Northern Ireland declined and occupational opportunities switched to non-manual jobs that required educational qualification, Catholics may have been culturally better placed to benefit. Certainly, education, both in terms of quality, as indexed by educational qualification, and in terms of quantity, as indexed by years of education, are central to the path models in Figures 3.1 and 3.2.

Education may also have interacted with geographic mobility in a manner that has had the net result of enhancing chances of Catholic mobility into the upper non-manual strata in Northern Ireland. The proportions of young people attending university have burgeoned in recent decades (Cormack and Osborne, 1993). While Catholic students tend to attend Northern Irish universities and stay in the region upon graduation, a significant portion of the Protestant university cohort now go 'across the water' to Britain (Osborne et al, 1987). Most of these predominantly Protestant students remain in Britain after graduation and effectively remove themselves from competition for university degree level entry jobs in Northern Ireland (Miller et al, 1991). This would impact directly upon the relative mobility chances of Protestants and Catholics, to the advantage of educationally qualified Catholics who remain in Northern Ireland. Employers in the region seeking to fill new posts that require highly qualified applicants, and

having to troll from a disproportionately Catholic pool of local applicants, may find themselves facing a 'Protestant' labour market shortage, with the stark choice being appointing a Catholic or no one at all.

The impact of fair employment legislation implemented under
Direct Rule cannot be ruled out either, though its direct effect, to the
degree that could be picked up in a social mobility survey, is likely to
have been relatively minor in comparison to the more sweeping effects
of educational reform and changes in industrial structure. Fair employment legislation's main impact may have been as much on preventing
the evolution of new discriminatory mechanisms in developing areas
of the economy as on redressing traditional wrongs. Whatever the
reasons, these results demonstrate that, in comparison to a generation
ago, the direct effect of religion upon mobility is now largely due to a
'legacy' from the past.

This is not the case with regard to gender. For both religions, the
main difference in intergenerational mobility between women and
men can be attributed to differences in their distribution across the
categories of present occupational status that favour men. Proportionately three times more men are located in the highest 'upper service'
bracket, over four times more men are in the 'proprietor' category
and almost three times more are in the 'skilled manual' stratum. In
the non-manual categories, women cluster in the lower 'routine non-
manual' stratum and, in the manual categories, in the bottom 'semi-
and unskilled' stratum. For those from 'proprietors and farmers'
origin, men are quite likely to be in the same stratum at present
(presumably due in large part to the inheritance of a family farm or
business). In contrast, women originating from the 'proprietors and
farmers' stratum have moved disproportionately into the 'lower
service' stratum. The poorer 'structure of opportunity' to which
women are subject explains the lower mobility performance of
Catholic women and goes a long way towards explaining the same
pattern for non-Catholic women. In contrast to Catholics, there are
some differences in the mobility patterns of non-Catholic women and
men that cannot be attributed only to the adverse effects of the present
occupational distribution. Long-distance upward mobility is particularly pronounced among non-Catholic women compared to
non-Catholic men.

Summary

Comparison between the 1973/74 and the 1996/97 surveys shows a movement towards meritocracy. Point-of-career entry, as indexed by the status of first job, and educational qualification, were the most important influence on current occupational status. In contrast to the path analysis carried out on the 1973/74 social mobility survey, neither the social origin as indicated by the job status of the father nor religion had a direct effect on the occupational status of men in the 1990s. Social origin does still affect present standing to the advantage of those from relatively privileged backgrounds, but only indirectly through educational attainment. Religion was shown to have no direct effect on the current status of men in 1996/97, unlike in 1973/74, although it continued to have indirect effects.

Loglinear analysis confirms these findings of the path analysis. Once the effect of occupational structure is taken into account, Catholic and non-Catholic males show the same pattern of occupational mobility between generations. The same result was obtained in 1973/74, but the difference for 1996/97 is that the *current* occupational structures of the Catholic and non-Catholic men do not differ significantly. These results hold when the analysis is extended to include men and women. The main reason for this convergence in the occupational structures of the two religious groups can be attributed in large part to the educational reforms of the postwar era. At the same time, however, the present-day absence of religion from the coefficients of mobility from first job to present occupation, observed in the path models, suggests (in contrast to Breen's [2000] conclusion) that fair employment legislation *has* had a demonstrable effect, equalising Catholic and non-Catholic mobility chances. Unlike the previous generation in the 1973/74 data, if Catholics and non-Catholics begin their working lives with the same levels of education and first job, their mobility through their careers will not be directly advantaged or disadvantaged by religion.

A brief analysis of how Catholics and non-Catholics found jobs was also undertaken. 'Social capital' – access to networks of friends and contacts – has been hypothesised to be an important way in which jobs are found (Granovetter, 1995). These social ties were found to be important, especially at the start of careers, with 38 per cent of respondents saying that 'friends' or 'family/relatives' were the main way they found their first job. This finding is intriguing since it has been replicated in a number of studies (for example, Green, Shuttleworth and Lavery, 2003) but officially it should not occur, because jobs, particularly given the terms of fair employment legislation, are not supposed to be found by these means. However, the net effect of this job-search method could be small – Catholics and non-Catholics use it equally, and the more privileged labour market position of non-Catholics has been eroded, lessening the value of social networks by which 'lads follow dads'.

The picture is less optimistic when looked at by gender. The path analysis of the 1996/97 data showed that men still have a better chance than women of upward social mobility, even when the effects of labour market entry and educational attainment are taken into account, indirectly confirming the presence of job discrimination that advantages men. These findings are also confirmed by the loglinear analysis. The main reason that women have a smaller chance of upward inter-generational mobility is that the distribution of female jobs is less favourable than that of males.

These results together suggest that there is less clear evidence of Catholic disadvantage in the labour market than in the past but that gender remains a major issue. The declining importance of community background is part and parcel of the greater complexity of the labour market revealed in other chapters. These show that there has been a Catholic advance in some sectors of the monitored labour force (see Chapter 2), that there is Protestant underrepresentation in some activities, and that the labour market context of the 1990s differs markedly from that of the 1970s (see Chapters 5 and 6). As remarked earlier, it is probable that fair employment legislation has had some demonstrable effect, but it is difficult to attribute how much of this change is due to legislation and how much to the occupational and industrial shifts noted in the last decades of the twentieth century. This precision is probably impossible – it is highly problematic, to say the least, to pose 'what if' counterfactuals of what the situation would have been if there had been no or different legislation or no economic restructuring in a meaningful way. However, given the evidence presented in this chapter and elsewhere, it is likely that the legislation speeded changes that were already taking place, and that the legislation operated in the 1990s at least in a favourable economic environment of expansion. Forecasting future economic trends is a dangerous game, but the expectation of continued growth in female and white collar employment means that existing social mobility trends will continue or accelerate, with the possibility that women may close the gap with men.

4

Education and the labour market

R.D. OSBORNE

Introduction

This chapter seeks to examine the nature of the differences between Protestants and Catholics in the outputs of the education system. Educational issues in relation to fair employment are the focus of the chapter because of the postulated increasingly close relationships between the possession of educational qualifications and labour market access and success. Simply, the conventional wisdom suggests that in the past fifty years or so success in the labour market, whether measured in terms of unemployment, occupational level or earnings, is strongly influenced by the level of educational qualifications held. This relationship is not deterministic – not all those with qualifications succeed in the labour market and some do well notwithstanding that they have no formal qualifications; we can all think of the self-made entrepreneur. Nevertheless, eligibility to enter white collar and professional occupations has, it is argued, been increasingly determined by the possession of educational credentials. It follows, therefore, that a key issue for the securing of greater equality in the labour market between different social groups is their relative performance in the education and training systems. If, for example, one group achieves consistently less well than another group, then that group's capacity to achieve in the labour market, irrespective of other factors, will be reduced. Examining the educational achievements of each group opens up the further question of the background experiences and resources of each group, which may influence these outcomes. A cycle of disadvantage can exist when underattainment in the education system results in underachievement in the labour market, which, in turn, can perpetuate educational underachievement.

Even if groups may be similar in terms of educational characteristics, there is still the question of labour market fairness. One measure of fairness would be the extent to which each group can turn its educational credentials into labour market access and success. For example, if unemployment rates or earnings levels are lower for one group even if the qualification levels are the same, then this pushes the focus of analysis onto the operation of the labour market, where systematic factors such as discrimination may be present. This chapter will tackle some of these issues and try to answer the question of whether there are any educational issues between the two main communities in Northern Ireland that can have a significant influence on labour market outcomes.

Data context

This assessment of education is undertaken in a context where relevant statistical information for compulsory education is now plentiful, in contrast to when the issue was first examined over twenty years ago (Osborne and Murray, 1978; Murray and Osborne, 1983). At that time, no official data on the education system recognised the segregated nature of the schools in Northern Ireland. Indeed, the first study was only undertaken by laboriously transferring individual pupil records for each school into a suitable format – a process that took several months – so that the O level and A level patterns for 1967, 1971 and 1975 could be assembled and analysed. Now, however, most relevant educational data for schools are available as part of the main statistical series from the Department of Education. However, there are still substantial gaps in the statistical series in the further and higher education sectors of the system. In the past quarter of a century other significant sources of data have become available – notably the LFS – which incorporate a religion question. Finally, the Population Census provides additional relevant data.

Qualifications and the labour market

During the 1970s, considerable research demonstrated that for school-leavers the most common destination was to take up full-time jobs. Research at this time demonstrated that even the lowest level of qualification resulted in greater labour market success compared with those who had no educational credentials (Gray, McPherson and Raffe, 1983). The Northern Ireland studies, however, also highlighted the major differential in experiences of young male Protestants and Catholics, with Protestants more likely to enter work, often as a result of using family and other contacts, while Catholics were more likely to enter training or to be unemployed (Cormack, Osborne and Thompson, 1980). However, with increasing unemployment during the early 1980s, school-leaver unemployment began to rise as traditional industries collapsed and extensive labour market restructuring took place. Youth jobs in the labour market disappeared and lower educational credentials lost their effectiveness in securing employment, as the transition from school to jobs was replaced by state-funded youth training schemes (Youth Opportunities Programme in Britain and Youth Training Programme in Northern Ireland; McWhirter et al, 1987). For those seeking to leave school in the 1980s and 1990s, accessing jobs became increasingly difficult especially in areas dominated by more traditional industries. Youth training programmes were extended in duration and purpose. As jobs became more and more difficult to obtain, the pattern of leaving school to take up full-time work subsequently became an experience of only a small minority. Instead, the experience for many became an extended period of training and short-term jobs before finding a niche in the labour market. Labour market difficulties, except for those who proceeded directly to the labour market, also had an impact on the transition from the home into independent adult living. Many young men postponed leaving home, remaining dependent on their families, while some young women accelerated the transition into parenthood and only subsequently entered casual and part-time work. In contrast, opportunities for those with better qualifications improved as higher and further education expanded.

The election of the Labour government in 1997 resulted in a new policy concerning those 'excluded' and marginalised with the introduction of the New Deal programme and other social inclusion initiatives. However, the majority of young people now stay in education beyond the school leaving age to enter training, and further and higher education. As a result of direct government policy, participation in higher education, for example, has increased dramatically for 18–21-year-olds and is now approximately 45 per cent in Northern Ireland, a doubling over the past twenty-five years. The qualifications of school leavers have risen substantially in the same period.

Contemporary research on the relationship between education and the job market has benefited from new data sources that enable different parts of the relationships between education and jobs to be examined. One of the most researched areas relates to the transition from the education system to work. An impressive comparative study examined the nature of the relationships between education and jobs in the transition from school to work in fourteen countries and noted that in all countries education is strongly associated with labour market outcomes. It also noted that in most countries the returns on higher level qualifications are greater than for intermediate or lower qualifications (Shavit and Muller, 1998).

New data sources in the UK, for example the British Household Panel Survey (BHPS), have enabled the relationship between education and job outcomes to be closely examined, while another key source of data comes from two major continuing surveys of those born in one week in 1958 and those born in one week in 1970 – the birth cohorts. Comparing the experiences of these two cohorts demonstrates how educational experiences and qualifications have related to labour market access and experience over time.

Brynin (2002a), using the BHPS, examines some of the current relationships that exist between qualifications and jobs in Britain. While having no qualifications undoubtedly leads to higher rates of unemployment, low skill and lower earnings in employment, he suggests that the relationship for those with qualifications is changing over time. Trying to measure these relationships is complicated, as not only are more people gaining qualifications but the nature and skill levels of jobs are also altering. For older age groups it would appear that having O levels/GCSEs confers more of an advantage in the type of work obtained compared with younger age groups (as measured for first and second jobs obtained). This implies that, compared with the older age groups, younger people are more likely to be overqualified for the work they have obtained. In other words, having a qualification at this level brings less of an advantage to those born from the 1950s onwards. However, Brynin cautions that this does not mean that educational expansion should halt, since the skills demanded for jobs are increasing and educational expansion itself gives people more choice in the labour market.

In the study of the two birth cohorts, Bynner et al (2002) make essentially the same point. In summary, the pathways to adult life for those with qualifications are changing. The gap between those with good qualifications and those who have not is growing and the opportunities for 16-year-old school-leavers are reducing. While family background continues to exert a significant strong influence on prospects as young people enter adulthood, especially through its influence on educational attainment, the influence of high qualifications independent of family background is increasing for the younger age cohort as employers tighten the requirements for access to jobs. Nevertheless, the premium (extra earnings achieved as a result of having these higher qualifications) is declining.

Other studies have utilised these data to examine the class mobility of the two birth cohorts (Breen and Goldthorpe, 2001) and the role of qualifications in determining labour market experiences of women (Elliott, Dale and Egerton, 2001). The former study is interesting in that it suggests that there is little evidence in the British experience of a tightening influence of qualifications in the experiences of those born in 1970 compared with those in 1958. The authors argue that employers may well regard 'ascriptive' characteristics as constituting part of 'merit' as much or even instead of educational background. Hence, an employer may give preference to someone who will 'fit in'. There is, therefore, considerable scope for discriminatory behaviour in the process in terms of class, disability, gender, race, religion, etc. However, the authors also note that the scope for this is more likely to be in the parts of the private sector, rather than the public sector, where educational qualifications are mandatory to secure entry to many occupations. It is perhaps no coincidence that the greatest successes in fair employment have been achieved in the public sector (see Chapter 2). The influence of educational qualifications on the labour market experiences of women seem to be closely related to the possession of occupationally specific qualifications and those which are non-specific. Thus, 'occupationally specific qualifications appear to enable women to retain a closer attachment to the labour market during [. . .] family formation, and in addition would seem to protect women from the drop in earnings typically associated with taking time out of the labour market or working part-time' (Elliott, Dale and Egerton, 2001:163).

These studies seem to find that while there is a clear relationship between securing educational qualifications and job success, the nature of
the relationship varies with the level of qualification held – the higher
the qualification held the better the job success. However, there may be
evidence that overqualification is becoming a factor in the relationship.
Younger people are less able to convert similar qualifications into job
success than older people. There may also be some evidence that the
tightening relationship between educational credentials and jobs postulated by many commentators may not be taking place to the same
extent in the private as compared to the public sector. Lastly, the role
of vocationally specific higher level qualifications partially offset the
disadvantages of taking time out of the labour market by women.

Resources in the education system

Before we examine the relative performance of the two communities
in educational terms it is important to consider the extent to which the
two communities are similarly resourced. The most significant research in the recent past into these matters was undertaken for the
SACHR at the end of the 1980s and early 1990s (SACHR, 1990;
Gallagher, Osborne and Cormack, 1994a). This research, amongst
other matters, demonstrated that there was an underprovision of
grammar schools in the Catholic system and that recurrent school
funding, which had evolved incrementally, appeared to place Catholic
schools at a disadvantage. The research also revealed that the operation
of the 85 per cent state support for capital programmes in all Catholic
(and other voluntary) schools placed a significant financial burden
above the 15 per cent, was very bureaucratic, and may have acted indirectly to inhibit more expensive science development in Catholic
schools. Similar funding arrangements in the Canadian province of
Ontario had also resulted in a similar lower uptake of science in
Catholic schools, whereas Scottish Catholic schools that had received
100 per cent capital funding since 1918 did not exhibit these curriculum
differences. Policy changes during the 1990s in response to these findings saw the opening of two new Catholic grammar schools (in Belfast
and Londonderry/Derry), the introduction of formula funding with a
weighting for pupils from disadvantaged backgrounds, and the availability of 100 per cent capital funding for Catholic schools in return for
some adjustments to governance arrangements. In addition, some of
the backlog of capital programmes, especially in the Catholic sector,

began to be rectified. Some of the substantial anomalies generated by the existence of seven funding formulae for schools identified by the Northern Ireland Affairs Select Committee (1997) are being tackled through the development of a common funding formula.

In the contemporary situation, therefore, many of the resource/structural differences in the two main systems are being reduced, if not eliminated. The comparison between the two communities' educational attainments, however, needs to acknowledge a significant difference in the social profiles of the two communities. Simply, Catholics experience higher rates of unemployment (although the scale of that differential has reduced recently) and higher rates of dependency on state benefits. In all research on the determinants of educational attainment, these factors have been shown to depress or reduce educational performance. This factor alone would lead to a prediction of Catholic underachievement relative to Protestants. However, research in other countries where separate school systems exist has suggested that Catholic schools often produce a 'school effect', based in part on 'ethos' (see Donnelly, 2000; Morris, 1997), which enables these schools

Table 4.1

Religion of pupils in Northern Ireland schools, 2002–3 (row percentages)

	Protestant and other Christian	%	Catholic	%	Others	%	Not Stated	%
Primary								
Controlled	66,363	82.4	3,221	4.0	393	0.5	10,603	13.2
Catholic-maintained	808	1.0	77,775	98.4	72	0.1	387	0.5
Integrated	2,446	48.8	1,776	35.2	35	0.7	789	15.6
Preparatory	1,888	69.0	269	9.9	30	0.6	545	19.9
Secondary								
Controlled	33,947	90.0	808	2.1	67	0.2	2,888	7.7
Catholic-maintained	227	0.5	44,751	99.1	35	0.0	162	0.4
Integrated	5,132	52.2	3,971	40.4	140	1.4	581	5.9
Grammar								
Controlled	12,685	85.1	885	5.9	53	0.3	1,291	8.7
Voluntary Catholic	204	0.7	27,862	99.1	14	0.0*	34	0.1
Voluntary other	14,840	73.9	1,775	8.8	134	0.7	3,325	16.6

Note: 'controlled' are state schools, which are *de facto* Protestant schools; integrated schools include grant-maintained and controlled integrated schools; 'preparatory' refers to fee-paying but state-subsidised departments attached to Protestant grammar schools; 'voluntary other' grammar schools refers to *de facto* Protestant grammar schools; 0.0* denotes <0.1%

Source: adapted from DENI (2003)

to produce a better performance when compared with non-Catholic schools. To some extent Catholic schools have exhibited a greater capacity to overcome the negative effects of social disadvantage relative to other schools (Paterson, 2000). Finally, we should acknowledge that, although the education system is largely segregated, some mixing does occur and that religiously integrated schools now account for approximately 5 per cent of pupils. The relevant data are set out in Table 4.1.

Two measures will be used in the examination of the possession of qualifications by the two ethno-religious communities in Northern Ireland. The first will relate to the performance of schools, which is the main way in which the educational authorities release data. As a result of the cross-attendance of one denomination in the 'others'' schools, we cannot talk of Catholic or Protestant school performance but we can refer to Catholic-managed schools and those under 'other management'. The 'other management' sector includes all *de facto* Protestant schools, but also integrated schools, which by definition include a mix of Protestants and Catholics. The pupils in this category will also contain a higher proportion of the statistically very small ethnic minority populations in Northern Ireland. However, when the Census or other survey-based data are examined, it will be possible to refer to Catholics and Protestants, as the data substantially originate with individuals.

Performance in the education system

Data can be examined from a number of key points in the education system to assess whether there are any differences that are likely to have consequences for fairness in the labour market. Specifically, performance in the transfer test (eleven plus) and the qualifications and destinations of school-leavers will be reviewed. Thereafter, data relating to higher education entry and graduates will be examined. The 2001 Population Census will be used to examine the 'stock' of those in the population with qualifications. The final data examined will be from the LFS, which will enable a measure of the extent to which educational credentials give the same labour market access. A brief conclusion will refer to training and social inclusion.

The transfer test, or eleven plus

Although the current arrangements for transferring pupils from

primary to post-primary schools have been the subject of highly critical and thorough research (Gallagher and Smith, 2000) and are currently being reviewed in the aftermath of the Burns proposals (2001),
they provide the first assessment of performance in the education system. However, this statement has to be qualified by the fact that different arrangements exist for the transfer from primary to post-primary
schools in Craigavon, County Armagh,[1] and more significantly, the
growth in the numbers of pupils who are not entered for the transfer.
Nevertheless, the eleven plus is still the major determining gateway to
educational success and subsequent occupational success, by providing
the route into grammar schools, which, in turn, is a major predictor of
educational success (Gallagher and Smith, 2000).

In terms of the concerns raised in this chapter, the issue is: how do
Catholics and Protestants compare in the eleven plus process itself?
Taking those who do not sit the transfer (and hence cannot enter grammar schools), the proportions of those attending Catholic-managed
primary schools has risen from 30 per cent in 1995–6 to just below 34
per cent in 2001–2, while the comparable figures for other schools has
risen in the same period, from about 33 per cent to just over 35 per
cent. Altogether almost 9,000 pupils did not sit the transfer in 2001–2.
Of these pupils, a significantly higher proportion of boys (37.7 per
cent) compared with girls (31.4 per cent) were non-participants. It is
also evident that the higher the proportion of pupils entitled to free
school meals (FSM), the higher the proportion not participating in
the transfer process (24.9 per cent of pupils where the FSM proportion
is less than 11 per cent, compared with 49.8 per cent where it is more
than 51 per cent). (Shuttleworth (1995) sets out the case for using FSM
as a proxy for socio-economic disadvantage.)

The eleven plus process is, therefore, highly selective in social class
terms. Thereafter, performance can be examined in two ways: the first
is to examine the grade distribution. Overall, there is very little difference in the profiles of grades attained. For example, 37.8 per cent of
those in Catholic-managed schools attained an A grade, whilst the proportions of those in other schools is 39.9 per cent. Those attaining the
lowest grade, D, represented 28.8 per cent of candidates in Catholic-
managed schools and the comparative figure for other schools is 28
per cent. However, there is a substantial difference in the proportions
attaining grade A between the two school systems when FSM is taken
into account. The data are shown in Table 4.2. Bearing in mind that
these figures only relate to those entered for the transfer process, what

is revealed is that, generally, Catholic-managed schools are more likely to see pupils achieving a grade A but the differences are most striking the higher the proportion of pupils entitled to FSM. Taking schools where the FSM percentage is 31 per cent and over, the proportion of pupils in Catholic schools attaining an A grade is 26.4 per cent, whereas the figure for other schools is 16.3 per cent. In numerical terms, 725 attain grade A in Catholic schools with FSM levels at 31 per cent plus, compared with 144 in other schools. The scales of these differences suggest a substantially lower performance in the transfer test in non-Catholic schools which have high proportions of poorer pupils. There is clearly a major issue for public policy here.

Qualifications of leavers

Monitoring the qualifications and destinations of school-leavers provides an indication of the comparative flows of young people into higher and further education, training and employment. The basic figures are shown in Table 4.3, where the highest qualifications of leavers is shown, and Tables 4.4 and 4.5, where the same data are shown for males and females separately.

As it can be seen, there are very few differences between the qualifications in terms of the possession of A level passes or equivalent but there is a marginal advantage to leavers from Catholic schools. Thereafter, there is a marginal advantage to leavers from other schools for those with GCSEs, but leavers from other schools are slightly less likely to leave with no GCSEs or with no formal qualifications. These

Table 4.2

Religion and A grades in eleven plus transfer test by free school meal (FSM) band, 2001–2

FSM band %	Transfer Candidates (%)		No. of Candidates	
	Catholic-managed Schools	Other Managed Schools	Catholic-managed Schools	Other Managed Schools
<11%	52.7	47.4	858	2,336
11–20	40.6	35.6	699	715
21–30	38.6	32.2	791	315
31–40	31.2	21.1	365	77
41–50	28.8	17.8	142	36
51+	20.2	9.8	218	31

Source: DENI (2002)

data, as they are presented, reflect the concerns of those examining the outputs of the education system. From a labour market perspective, however, it is possible to say that lower grade GCSEs (that is, those grades below C) have only marginal credibility with many employers. On this basis, if we take those leaving with A levels (even if most of these young people continue full-time further and higher education) and those with GCSE grades A*–C, then the respective figures are 73.3 per cent of those leaving Catholic schools and 74.7 per cent of those leaving from other schools. On this measure there are still no significant differences in the contemporary qualifications of leavers from the two systems.

Within these basic patterns, it is possible to examine the differences by school type (grammar/secondary) and gender. The school type figures show a slightly higher proportion of those from Catholic grammar schools with A levels (79.5 per cent) compared to those from other schools (77.9 per cent). The real differences, however, emerge from comparing secondary schools. Here pupils from Catholic secondary schools are notably more likely to leave school with A levels (18.4 per cent) compared to other schools (11.0 per cent). But leavers from Catholic schools are more likely to leave with either no GCSEs (6.7 per cent compared to 5.0 per cent) or no formal qualifications (5.5 per cent compared to 4.3 per cent).

In relation to gender, the position for girls is shown in Table 4.4 and

Table 4.3

Highest qualification of school-leavers by management type, 2000–1

Highest Qualification Held	Catholic-managed Schools		Other Managed Schools	
	No.	%	No.	%
3 + A levels	3,521	27.6	3,766	27.1
2 A levels	1,099	8.6	1,019	7.3
1 A level	201	1.6	223	1.6
5 + GCSE (A*–C)	2,111	16.5	2,651	19.1
1-4 GCSE (A*–C)	2,423	19.0	2,728	19.6
Other grades (1+ D–G)	1,818	14.2	2,086	15.0
No GCSEs	802	6.3	660	4.8
Other qualifications	145	1.1	97	0.7
No formal qualifications	657	5.1	663	4.8
Total leavers	12,777	100	13,893	100

Source: adapted from DENI, special tabulations

for boys in Table 4.5. The differences for girls are small, although those from Catholic schools are more likely to leave with A levels (48.8 per cent) compared with non–Catholic schools (44.1 per cent); however, girls leaving from non–Catholic schools are more likely to leave with 5+ GCSEs grades A★–C. Taking school type into account shows few differences between grammar schools, but girls leaving secondary

Table 4.4

Highest qualification of female school-leavers by management type, 2000–2

Highest Qualification Held	Catholic-managed Schools		Other Managed Schools	
	No.	%	No.	%
3+ A levels	1,998	34.5	2,190	33.4
2 A levels	715	12.4	586	8.9
1 A level	112	1.9	115	1.8
5+ GCSE (A★–C)	1,068	18.4	1,337	20.4
1–4 GCSE (A★–C)	1,035	17.9	1,266	19.3
Other grades (1+ D–G)	643	11.1	817	12.5
No GCSEs	218	3.8	241	3.7
Total leavers	5,789	100	6,552	100

Source: adapted from DENI, special tabulations

Table 4.5

Highest qualification of male school-leavers by management type, 2000–2

Highest Qualification Held	Catholic-managed Schools		Other Managed Schools	
	No.	%	No.	%
3+ A levels	1,523	24.6	1,576	23.9
2 A levels	384	6.2	433	6.6
1 A level	89	1.4	108	1.6
5+ GCSE (A★–C)	1,043	16.9	1,314	20.0
1–4 GCSE (A★–C)	1,388	22.4	1,462	22.2
Other grades (1+ D–G)	1,175	19.0	1,269	19.3
No GCSEs	584	9.4	419	6.4
Total leavers	6,186	100	6,581	100

Source: adapted from DENI, special tabulations

Catholic schools are significantly more likely to leave with A levels (27.5 per cent) than those leaving non-Catholic schools (15.5 per cent).

For boys, the differences are smaller than for girls, with the main differences being the slightly higher proportion of those from non-Catholic schools with 5+ GCSEs grades A★–C (20.0 per cent compared to 16.9 per cent), and the higher proportion of those from Catholic schools with no GCSEs (9.4 per cent, compared with 6.3 per cent). However, when school type is considered, while there are only small differences between grammar schools, there are some intriguing differences between secondary schools. Thus, while those from Catholic schools are slightly more likely to leave with A levels (10 per cent compared with 6.8 per cent), those from non-Catholic schools are more likely to leave with 5+ GCSEs grades A★–C (19 per cent compared to 15.3 per cent). Additionally, boys leaving non-Catholic secondary schools are less likely to leave with no GCSEs (9.7 per cent) than those leaving Catholic schools (14 per cent).

Reviewing these data suggests that the biggest change in the past generation has been the improvement in the qualifications of those from Catholic schools relative to those from non-Catholic schools. Today, the outputs of the two broad systems are very similar. This represents a substantial change over the past generation. In the early 1970s, pupils from Catholic schools were less likely to leave with qualifications than leavers from other schools. Within this basic conclusion, there are some noteworthy differences. The first is the position of Catholic boys, who are more likely to leave school with no GCSEs.

Table 4.6

Destinations of school-leavers, boys, secondary schools, 2000–1

	Catholic-managed Schools		Other Managed Schools	
	No.	%	No.	%
HE institutions	274	6.8	176	4.3
FE institutions	742	18.4	1,172	28.5
Employment	776	19.3	916	22.3
Unemployment	222	5.5	282	6.9
Training	1,969	48.9	1,488	36.2
Unknown	43	1.1	75	1.8
Total	4,026	100	4,109	100

Source: DENI, special tabulations

Adding this group to those with low GCSE passes means that 28.4 per cent of Catholic boys have modest qualifications. The figure for non-Catholic male leavers is 25.4 per cent. The second point to note is the apparently more academic orientation of Catholic secondary schools, which are more likely to have leavers with A levels compared with the vocational orientation of non-Catholic schools. The conclusion that Catholic secondary schools are more academically orientated is sustained when the destinations of leavers is considered. Thus, in 2000–1, 20 per cent of girls leaving from Catholic secondary schools went to a higher education institution, compared to 9.7 per cent from non-Catholic schools; and for boys, while the figures are much lower, 6.8 per cent of Catholic leavers attend higher education institutions compared to 4.3 per cent of those from non-Catholic schools.[2] However, the big differences emerge in the proportions of boys moving on to further education colleges. The figures are shown in Table 4.6. Catholics are substantially less likely to go to further education institutions but are more likely to go into training, including the Jobskills programme, while those going into employment or unemployment are proportionately broadly similar between the two groups.

Curriculum differences
Religion and gender

One of the findings of initial research into the educational outcomes of the two school systems in Northern Ireland was that there seemed to be a lower emphasis on science-related subjects in Catholic schools. This difference was demonstrated by science subjects representing a lower proportion of passes at both GCE O level and A level (Osborne and Murray, 1978). At that time, three possible factors were identified as being potentially relevant: a response to prevailing patterns in the labour market which saw Catholics substantially underrepresented in areas where science qualifications were important; the effects of capital funding arrangements, where the fact that Catholic-managed schools had to raise a contribution may have indirectly inhibited science provision; and a dimension of the Catholic school 'ethos', which emphasised humanities rather than science subjects.

In the reforms of the late 1980s a common curriculum was introduced in Northern Ireland, which, it can be noted, had significant differences to the rest of the UK. It introduced a compulsory science element up to key stage 4 and the GCSE examinations. These changes, together with the increased funding for capital projects in Catholic schools, were assumed to have eroded the subject differences that had been evident thirty years before. Recent data, generated as part of a study of the flows into science and information technology jobs, generated data which enabled the subject to be re-examined (Osborne and Shuttleworth, 2003).

At GCSE, under the Northern Ireland curriculum mathematics is compulsory to key stage 4/GCSE, as is science. However, within science there is a choice between studying at three tiers, with triple award science the equivalent of studying three separate science subjects at GCE O level. Table 4.7 shows the representation of these subjects as a proportion of the cohort obtaining a pass at GCSE grades A*–C in 1996 and 2001. Here it can readily be seen that pupils at other schools are far more likely to take combinations of mathematics and two or three sciences than those at Catholic schools. The variation is especially striking for mathematics and three sciences, where the gap has slightly increased for females. That this difference should still be manifest some thirty years since it was first noted is rather unexpected in the light of the funding changes, capital improvements and changes noted above,

Table 4.7

Absolute number and percentages of year 12 cohort with GCSE passes at Grades A*–C by school management type and gender, 1996 and 2001

	1996				2001			
	Catholic-managed Schools		Other Managed Schools		Catholic-managed Schools		Other Managed Schools	
	No.	%	No.	%	No.	%	No.	%
Subject mix – male								
Maths and 1 science	317	14.9	337	11.4	333	14.3	275	8.7
Maths and 2 sciences	1,626	76.2	1,842	62.9	1,842	79.3	2,143	67.5
Maths and 3 sciences	190	8.9	789	26.6	149	6.4	757	23.8
Total	2,133		2,968		2,324		3,175	
Subject mix – female								
Maths and 1 science	533	20.1	435	13.0	442	16.0	399	11.2
Maths and 2 sciences	1,942	73.3	2,290	68.6	2,183	79.0	2,530	67.5
Maths and 3 sciences	176	6.6	612	18.4	140	5.0	650	23.8
Total	2,651		3,337		2,765		3,579	

Source: DENI, special tabulations

and the employment changes noted in Chapter 2. The reason for this difference in curriculum emphasis warrants further consideration. Osborne and Shuttleworth (2003) suggested that this difference, together with much larger gender differences at both second and third level education, were likely to restrict the flows into information technology and related occupations.

Higher education

Research on participation in higher education has covered the period from the 1970s through to the 1990s (Osborne, 1999). The evidence suggests that Catholic participation in higher education has increased over this period to the extent that it matches, if not exceeds, Protestant participation. As might be expected from the preceding sections, however, the class profile of the two groups shows a higher representation of Protestants from middle-class backgrounds and a higher representation of Catholics from the manual social classes. In addition, perhaps the most significant characteristic of higher education participation is the proportion of undergraduate entrants (which includes sub-degree and degree entrants) and degree level entrants who leave Northern Ireland. Approximately 35 per cent of entrants leave, although the figure is slightly higher for degree level entrants. The migration of entrants arises because the provision of places in Northern Ireland does not match the demand. However, amongst these leavers, two groups have been identified: the *determined* and the *reluctant* leavers. The *determined* leavers tend to be Protestant, from middle-class backgrounds, to be very well qualified and to attend the older universities. The *reluctant* leavers tend to be drawn more equally from the two communities, to be less well qualified, are less likely to be from the professional and middle classes and more likely to go to the former polytechnics. As we have seen before, the academic orientation of Catholic secondary schools has undoubtedly acted to boost Catholic participation levels overall and the representation of entrants from less well-off backgrounds (Osborne, 2001). As a result, the two Northern Ireland universities rank highly when compared with the rest of the UK in terms of widening access indicators (Osborne, 2003a). It is worth noting that parity in participation between Protestants and Catholics has been achieved without any of the innovations in admissions procedures which have, for example, developed in the US (Bowen and Bok, 1997). Nevertheless, without the migration of entrants it would have been much harder for parity of participation to be achieved and entry to higher education could have been a politically contentious issue.

If parity of entry has been achieved, what have been the experiences of graduates? Fortunately there have been a number of follow-up studies of graduates – up to six years after graduation – which suggest that once subject of degree is taken into account, there is no evidence of any discrimination in access to jobs or salary levels between Protestants and Catholics (Miller et al, 1991; Leith, Osborne and Gallagher, 2000). This statistical picture is confirmed by the views of graduates themselves, who indicated that they had not experienced religious discrimination. (It should be noted here that women graduates *were* in lower paid jobs compared to men, even when factors such as subject and class of degree were taken into account.) Another major finding of these graduate studies was that most of those who left Northern Ireland to study did not return, while most of those who remained in Northern Ireland were still located there. This means that the religious composition of graduates *in* Northern Ireland shows a higher representation of Catholics than amongst entrants overall.

There is no doubt that rising Catholic participation in higher education, together with the migration flows of students, has fed into the increasing representation of Catholics in professional, managerial and white collar jobs in general, and in the public services in particular, as is outlined in Chapter 2. The longevity of these trends means that graduates of fifteen or more years ago are now starting to appear in senior management positions and contributing to the positive outcomes in the labour market.

The stock of qualifications – evidence from the Census[3]

Thus far the flow of those entering the labour market has been examined with regard to performance in the education system. However, it is also important to examine the current *stock* of those in the total labour market. It follows that such an assessment requires an examination of the flows into the labour market stretching over forty or more years, and the measuring of the net effect of migration flows. Northern Ireland is an open society, in the sense that people leave and enter the region in substantial numbers. In the 1950s and 1960s, demographers noted that Catholics more than Protestants tended to migrate to find work. Latterly, during the 1980s, it was suggested that the Protestant propensity to migrate was more striking. Although it was noted that some people did return, it was the case that there was a net outflow of people, which resulted in a relatively stable population, notwithstanding the relatively high birth rates. The 2001 Census, however, found that migration was virtually in balance during the 1990s and this resulted in population growth, notwithstanding the decline in birth rates. In an examination of the information concerning the stock of those people with qualifications, it must be remembered that they are a net result of migration movements. As has been noted above, one of the most significant movements has been the migration, especially of Protestants, to attend universities and colleges in Britain, and graduate studies suggested that comparatively few returned in the 1980s and 1990s.

Although it is difficult to line up data with previous censuses, the information in Table 4.8 compares data from the 2001 Census with that from the 1971 Census. This basic table reveals the scale of change in the period 1971–2001. Thus in 1971, 6 per cent of Catholics recorded a qualification of degree level or higher, compared with 9 per cent of Protestants. By 2001, 16.9 per cent of Catholics recorded these qualifications, compared with 16.1 per cent of Protestants. Putting the data another way, Catholics accounted for 27.4 per cent of those with a degree or higher qualifications in 1971, compared with 46.2 per cent in 2001. These figures reflect not only the substantial increase in participation by Catholics in higher education in the past generation but also the long-term consequences of Protestant migration for higher education.

We can examine the 2001 Census data on qualifications in two ways.

Table 4.8

Degree and higher level qualifications, 1971 and 2001 Censuses

	Protestant (%)	Catholic (%)
1971 with degree qualification or higher*	9.0	6.0
1971 share of those with degree qualification or higher*	72.6	27.4
2001 with degree qualification or higher**	16.1	16.9
2001 share of those with degree qualification or higher**	53.8	46.2

*population aged 18–69; **population aged 16–64
Source: 1971 and 2001 Census data

First, we can examine the qualifications of the total population; and second, we can break the data down by age in order to see if patterns are changing for the younger age groups compared with the older groups.

Table 4.9 shows the qualifications held by the Catholic and Protestant population as whole, and gives the profile of the two groups in terms of the qualifications held at the time of the Census. The qualification profiles of Catholics and Protestants show relatively few differences. However, the evidence of few differences is itself evidence of change, as indicated above. The evidence of change producing parity or better for Catholics when compared with Protestants is further illustrated when the share of each qualification is compared with the relevant share of the total age group. Here, while Catholics represent 43.9

Table 4.9

Religion and qualifications of those aged 16–74, 2001 Census

| Level | Catholics | | | | | | Protestants | | | | | |
| | NQ | 1 | 2 | 3 | 4 | 5 | NQ | 1 | 2 | 3 | 4 | 5 |
Age	%	%	%	%	%	%	%	%	%	%	%	%
16–24	18.1	20.7	29.0	22.4	7.6	2.2	16.7	22.0	29.5	22.3	7.8	1.7
25–44	29.8	23.0	16.1	8.3	14.9	8.0	26.5	26.6	17.4	9.0	14.7	5.8
45–59	61.5	9.8	10.3	4.3	9.2	4.8	56.3	11.0	12.6	4.5	10.5	4.7
60–74	80.0	3.7	7.2	1.5	5.3	2.4	76.8	4.1	8.9	1.5	6.1	2.5

Note: NQ = no qualifications; Level 1 = GCSE grades D–G and equivalent; Level 2 = 5+ GCSEs and equivalent; Level 3 = 2 + A levels and equivalent; Level 4 = first degree and equivalent; Level 5 = higher degree and equivalent.

Source: calculated from 2001 Census

Table 4.10

Qualifications of those aged 25–44 by gender, 2001 Census

| | | Catholics | | | | | | Protestants | | | | | |
| | | NQ | 1 | 2 | 3 | 4 | 5 | NQ | 1 | 2 | 3 | 4 | 5 |
	Age	%	%	%	%	%	%	%	%	%	%	%	%
All	25–44	29.8	23.0	16.1	8.3	14.9	8.0	26.5	26.6	17.4	9.0	14.7	5.8
Female	25–44	25.1	23.2	19.2	9.0	15.4	8.0	22.6	27.1	20.4	9.9	14.7	5.4
Male	25–44	34.9	22.7	12.7	7.5	14.2	8.0	30.3	26.2	14.5	8.2	14.6	6.2

Note: as in Table 4.9

Source: calculated from 2001 Census

per cent of the population aged 16–74, they represent 49.4 per cent of those with Level 5 qualifications and 46.6 per cent of those with Level 3. All other qualification levels show proportions broadly in line with the population share. The 25–44 age group will have substantially completed the acquisition of educational qualifications and will be already using these credentials to move up the career ladder. The profiles show that Catholics record a slightly higher proportion of those with no qualifications, but taking Levels 4 and 5 together, record higher figures than Protestants (22.9 per cent compared with 20.5 per cent). Similarly Catholics record a higher share of those with no qualifications (49.1 per cent), and a higher share of those with Levels 4 and 5 qualifications (46.5 per cent and 54 per cent) compared with the population share of 46.1 per cent.

When gender is examined for the same 25–44 age group, Catholic males show a higher proportion with no qualifications compared to Protestant males (34.9 per cent compared with 30.3 per cent), but also a higher proportion with higher qualifications (Levels 4 and 5; 22.2 per cent compared with 20.8 per cent). The same differences are found for females: 25.1 per cent of Catholics have no qualifications compared with 22.6 per cent of Protestants, while 23.4 per cent of Catholics have higher qualifications, compared with 20.1 per cent of Protestants. See Table 4.10.

These stock figures from the Census reveal that a generation of change has resulted in the educational profiles of Protestants and Catholics now being very similar. The Catholic profile tends to show a slightly higher proportion of those with no qualifications and, at the same time, a high representation of those with the highest qualifications. The Protestant profile shows the impact of over two decades of outward migration of students for higher education and their failure to return in significant numbers.

Qualifications and the labour market – the labour force survey

It is a characteristic of meritocratic societies that educational credentials should receive a corresponding reward in the labour market. Put at its simplest and within the context of this chapter, there should be broadly similar evidence of labour market success for Catholics and Protestants who have the same level of qualifications. As reported above, there is evidence that this is probably the case for graduates, once subject of study is taken into account. In Table 4.11 are shown the unemployment rates for level of qualification held, as found in the LFS, 1999–2001. Unemployment rates are higher for those with no qualifications for all groups but substantially higher for Catholic than Protestants. Thereafter, Catholic rates of unemployment are also higher for each level of qualification for males and females, but the scale of difference is significantly smaller for the highest level of qualifications. This may reflect the subject difference noted in the study of graduates and may also be reflected in the much larger differences at intermediate qualification levels. This evidence implies that there are still differences in the capacity of Catholics to gain the same rate of labour market access as Protestants.

Social exclusion

This final section examines recent research evidence concerning the experiences of those who have few or no qualifications when leaving school. This group includes those who at age 16 and 17 are not in full-time education, employment or training. Those individuals who end up in these circumstances ('Status 0' in the literature) are likely to become discouraged about their chances of work and to become increasingly unattractive to employers and hence are likely to experience long-term unemployment. Research evidence has suggested that those who belonged to the Status 0 group at 16–17 years of age were likely to be so at aged 18+; they were more likely to be Catholic; they

Table 4.11

Unemployment rates by level of qualification (16–64 for males and 16–59 for females), Labour Force Survey, 1999–2001

	Protestant Males	Catholic Males	Protestant Females	Catholic Females
A level and higher qualifications	2.3	4.9	2.9	4.1
O levels/GCSE	5.1	10.6	4.4	6.8
Trade apprenticeship	5.2	7.2	8.3	15.6
No qualifications	12.4	20.0	7.3	14.3
Total	5.5	10.0	4.3	7.2

Source: LFS, special tabulation

are poorly qualified at 16; they come from disadvantaged areas and from families who experience unemployment; they come from single parent families (males) and have children (females). Often individuals suffer multiple disadvantages. Some do escape from Status 0 but there is also evidence that some people who have successful experiences at age 16–17 can fall back at 18+. Quantitative analysis has suggested that family employment status and social class, educational qualifications and initial labour market experiences are important, while qualitative evidence points to low self-esteem and aspirations and career confusion, helping to produce and reproduce social exclusion (McVicar, 2000).

These findings echo those found almost a generation ago when the then state-sponsored youth intervention programme was evaluated (McWhirter et al, 1987). Given these findings about an earlier state programme primarily aimed at young school-leavers with few or no qualifications, it is surprising and disappointing that the official published evaluations of the New Deal have not systematically examined equality issues to date (DEL, 2001; 2003)

Conclusions

Recent international research reveals that approximately a quarter of adults in Northern Ireland (as is the case in the rest of the UK and Ireland) are functionally illiterate (DENI, 1998). This is a measure of the failure of the education system over several generations and establishes the importance of adult and lifelong learning in Northern Ireland. On the other hand, another international study by the Organisation for Economic Co-operation and Development (OECD) suggests that Northern Ireland's current 15-year-olds do well, on average, in terms of their mathematical and scientific ability and use of English (National Statistics, 2001). The Northern Ireland scores, however, show the widest variations and, by definition, this implies that significant numbers are doing much less well than others. It is the need to enhance the performance of those at the bottom end of achievement, without unduly harming those at the top end, that lies at the heart of the debate over eleven plus selection.

The overwhelming message of this chapter, however, as it relates to the relative position of the two ethno-religious communities, is that the past generation has seen a substantial evening out in the patterns of qualifications held by the two communities. Educational inequalities, at the broadest levels, do not contribute to fair employment inequalities. Some of the evidence appears superficially contradictory, as Catholics are overrepresented amongst those with the highest qualifications and amongst those with no qualifications. But the scale of this latter differential is small, especially for current school-leavers. Within this general picture, a number of issues have emerged: the evidence of major underachievement of working-class Protestants; the apparent underrepresentation of science at GCSE level in Catholic schools, which could impact on particular growth sectors in the labour market; the higher experience of unemployment by Catholics for each level of qualification; and the cumulative impact of the migration of Protestants for third level education and their failure to return, which is likely to continue to have a significant impact on the religious composition of professional and managerial occupations as time goes on.

5

A place apart?
The Northern Ireland labour market in a wider context

IAN SHUTTLEWORTH AND ANNE GREEN

Introduction

It is tempting to assume that Northern Ireland is a 'place apart' and to understand and explain developments in the region's labour market in purely religious terms using a 'sectarian reading of sectarianism' (Anderson and Shuttleworth, 1998), in which the central feature of consuming interest is the balance of advantage between the 'two communities'. This viewpoint appears to have been dominant in public and political debates in Northern Ireland (see Chapter 1). However, many of the trends observed in Northern Ireland – changes in patterns of economic activity, occupational shifts, the altered role of the state, new labour market ideologies of skills and employability – have occurred to varying degrees in the UK, European and North American economies and are themselves symptoms of a wider change in how societies now operate in comparison with those of thirty years ago. This process of transformation has impacted upon the Northern Ireland labour market, altering the context for policy and changing the employment environment for both Catholics and Protestants, but these outcomes are not amenable to explanation in local, purely internal, Northern Ireland terms. Rather, they are part of a much bigger picture.

The task of this chapter, then, is to develop a wider conceptual overview by providing, firstly, a brief overview of some concepts of labour market change. It then goes on to outline how patterns of economic activity in advanced economies as a whole have changed in the recent past, before dealing, in turn, with occupational shifts, changed skill needs, and the altered role of government in the labour market. This 'macro context' sets the scene for Chapter 6, which considers the local manifestations of these general trends in Northern Ireland using empirical evidence to demonstrate how the labour market and its governance has changed in the recent past.

Concepts of labour market change

Older readers with memories of the economy and society of the 1960s and 1970s may well recall a very different world from that of today. It is difficult to encapsulate all the varied dimensions of these changes in a few words but, in identifying key features, it is true to say that a generation ago there was more manufacturing employment than now, less women's employment, greater government involvement in managing the economy (for example, the 'beer and sandwiches at No. 10' of the Wilson premiership in the UK, when trade union leaders were invited for discussions with the prime minister), more union involvement in economic management, and greater stability in the operation of the welfare state. These observations apply with greater or lesser force, according to national variations, to most other advanced economies.

Since then there have been a number of wide-ranging changes in the ways in which economies and societies work. Occupational change is one key dimension. For example, in 1971 there were jobs recorded in the Northern Ireland Census such as 'rope worker', which have since died out. Conversely, there are now job titles in Northern Ireland like 'call centre worker', which only came into existence in the 1990s. Other dimensions include the expansion of service sector work, the growth of women's employment, and changes in the role of government in the labour market, with a retreat from the attempted management of prices and incomes in the 1960s and 1970s to policies that currently emphasise terms like *flexibility* and *employability*. Again, most advanced economies, to a greater or lesser extent, have experienced similar changes to the UK.

These changes are apparent in the everyday lived experience of those with long memories, with the years between 1975 and 1980 being important in the transition from 'then' to 'now'. These years of crisis were experienced in the UK with particular severity, with the massive loss of manufacturing employment in a series of economic recessions, although other European and North American economies also went through the same type of transformation. The collapse of the British car industry in the West Midlands, for instance, is mirrored by the troubles of the Midwest 'rust belt' region of the US and the decline of its auto industry. It is clear that there have been far-reaching changes and the concepts of *crisis* and *transition* are generally accepted as being good descriptions of what has happened. However, there is less academic agreement on how this period of crisis and transition is to be interpreted and understood. Two useful notions (although not the only ones that are used) are the concepts of *globalisation* and *post-Fordism*. Both have much to say about how the world has changed and so they will be discussed in a little more detail.

It is often said that we now live in a global world characterised by the swift circulation of money, ideas, fashion, and growing competition for inward investment and jobs. The concept of globalisation is itself new, first coming into vogue around 1980. The internationalisation of economies is nothing new and there have been various global systems, such as that based on free trade with British world hegemony in the years before 1914. What is novel, however, is the growing intensification of global competition, so that Ireland now vies with India, for example, for call centre jobs, the increased role of computer technology which has speeded flows of information (and money) around the globe, and the inclusion of most parts of the world in this global system dominated by the US as the leading world power. One consequence in national labour markets brought about by these changes has been that competition between countries and companies has increased. Some of this competition has been expressed on cost grounds and growing demands for flexibility in wages and hours worked. But it can also be seen in the requirement for more skilled and qualified labour, where countries, to try to get their slice of the inward investment pie, compete in terms of labour quality rather than cheapness. Northern Ireland is part of this global system and neither its labour market nor its labour market policies can be fully understood without reference to it.

The idea of post-Fordism is the second overall interpretation of economic and social change that has often been used. This idea deals mainly with the concept of transition, since, as it is *post*-Fordism, it carries the implication of 'before and after'. The period 'before' was Fordism. This term is used in the literature to describe a social and economic system in its entirety. There are differing interpretations of what a Fordist system actually was and, as with all generalisations, it does not apply equally everywhere and at all times. However, there is agreement that the characteristics usually held to define a Fordist social and economic system would include large scale factory production, manufacturing, mass markets, a welfare state compact between labour and government, and a relatively regulated and protected mass workforce. Commonly, these features are said to define the economies and societies of advanced economies between 1945 and 1975 (although this periodisation is only approximate). The replacement of Fordism by post-Fordism after around 1980 implies that traditional large scale industrial production has been replaced by flexible 'just-in-time' production,[1] changes in the role and nature of the welfare state, and a growth in insecurity.

The concepts of globalisation and post-Fordism are, of course, complex, and can be challenged – there are many shades of opinion about their value. Despite these caveats, they provide interesting interpretations of socio-economic change in advanced societies, which draw together interrelated strands of social, economic and political change. However, they are rather abstract theoretical ideas and so, to show some of the concrete outcomes of economic restructuring and transformation, the selected aspects of unemployment, occupational change, and labour market policy and skills will be discussed in a little more depth to prepare the ground for the specific empirical material relating to Northern Ireland that will be considered in the next chapter.

The changing nature of unemployment in advanced societies

Unemployment seems to be a very straightforward concept with a clear binary distinction between those of working age (16–64 for men and 16–59 for women) who are in employment and those who are not. In fact, this twofold classification of labour market status (that is, the employed and the non-employed) is a thing of the past and has been increasingly called into question by the state of the labour market and institutional changes, which are part and parcel of the transition from Fordism to post-Fordism, a process that was under way during the years between 1975 and 1980 in the UK, as a series of recessions and crises hit the economy and many manufacturing jobs were lost.

In the 'old economy' of the Fordist era, which reached its height between 1945 and 1975, unemployment tended to be *cyclical* and of relatively *short duration*. It was cyclical in that, typically, unemployment peaked during recessions but fell during periods of economic growth. Joblessness tended to be short term because upturns in the business cycle meant that many unemployed people were quickly reabsorbed intot the labour market. Of course, this is a generalisation. Some regions of the UK, usually those in the North, for example, had worse unemployment records than others, but there is a germ of truth in this description for the 1950s and 1960s, despite being damned in retrospect, when years of economic decline were years of a 'full employment economy'.[2] The consequences of this were twofold. First, low unemployment levels, and the relatively high probability of being reemployed in the short term if a person became jobless, made it easier to support a simple 'employment/unemployment' binary distinction, because individuals were more likely to be continuously engaged with the labour market, either in work or looking for work which they would expect to find soon. Second, it was relatively easy for the welfare state to fund unemployment benefits in this scenario. Originally conceived as a short-term remedy to tide over jobless workers until an economic upswing gave an escape route back into work, unemployment benefits were never really designed to cope with individuals who had not worked for several years.

However, long-term unemployment was the challenge faced by many of the welfare states in advanced economies during the 1980s and 1990s. This was because the nature of unemployment had changed from being *cyclical* to being *structural* and from being *short term* to being, in many instances, *long term*. This is one of the key dimensions of the process of restructuring and the transition from Fordism to post-Fordism. Unemployment could be conceptualised as being structural because it arose from deep-rooted structural economic changes that saw whole economic sectors (for example, coal mining and steel production) lose their viability. The shake-out of manufacturing employment in most advanced economies around 1980 led to a variety of labour market mismatches. These included skills mismatches – the skills of those who had lost jobs meant that they could not be easily reabsorbed in the new service growth sectors – and spatial mismatches, where the economic bases of some regions were destroyed, while new jobs, created in other regions, were inaccessible unless households were prepared to move over long distances. As a rule, in these circumstances, unemployment tended to become more long term, as those who had become jobless had no easy escape route back into work because economic upswings were too feeble to reabsorb them or provided the 'wrong type' of jobs.

The implications of this transition are profound. First, many welfare states found it difficult to cope with enduring high levels of unemployment. Since, as a general rule, unemployment benefits had been designed to be a short-term fix, there was often a temptation to put unemployed people who had been jobless for several years on to other types of benefit, hence the many definitional changes of unemployment in the UK in the 1980s. This in itself made unemployment harder to define and to count (Royal Statistical Society, 1995), with the binary 'employment/unemployment' distinction being replaced by other categories as some people moved on to other benefits. Second, jobless people themselves sometimes withdrew from the labour market, particularly in areas of low labour demand, and stopped seeking work in a situation that they judged as being hopeless (MacKay, 1999; Beatty, Fothergill and MacMillan, 2000). Amongst the options they took were early retirement, withdrawal from the labour market, or avoidance of the state benefit system altogether.

The implication of these changes in Northern Ireland will be explored in the next chapter. For the moment it is sufficient to observe that the contemporary labour market has been variously characterised as 'fuzzy', 'complex' and 'fluid' (Bryson and McKay, 1994), with all kinds of 'grey areas' on the fringes of employment, unemployment and inactivity (Nicaise et al, 1995). This complexity makes it more difficult now to assess the meaning of features such as the unemployment differential than was the case in the past.

The changed nature of employment, and occupational restructuring

The altered nature and definition of unemployment is merely one part of a wider process of labour market restructuring. Another key element of this process, common to most advanced societies, has been the changed nature of employment. This changing nature itself has a number of aspects, one of which has been the loss of manufacturing jobs in a process that has been termed 'de-industrialisation' (Fothergill and Gudgin, 1982). De-industrialisation – the decline of 'traditional' employment, often full time, in sectors conventionally accepted as being the preserve of men – has been seen throughout North America and Europe, although its manifestations were particularly severe in the UK, which has seen the numbers of workers employed fall from their highpoint in 1966. The severity of job loss in the UK has been attributed to many different factors – outmoded technology, weak industrial relations, poor economic management – leading to high, uncompetitive exchange rates for sterling, and inflexibility in the labour market. However, since this process of industrial decline has been a general international trend, it is unlikely that purely national causes are sufficient to explain what has happened. Instead, recourse must be made to the operation of factors at a global level, such as broad shifts in patterns of investment.

Whilst the picture is bleak for the manufacturing industry, it would be untrue and unfair to say that the UK economic scene has been one of unremitting gloom. New jobs have been created but this process of change has involved substantial shifts in the balance of opportunities in the labour market. Part of this shift can be attributed to *sectoral* changes in employment – manufacturing jobs have declined and jobs growth in most European countries and North America has been in the service sector. There is some debate about the implications of this. One interpretation is that service sector employment is 'good', as it is based on high technology and the transmission and analysis of information. There are, however, critics of this relatively benign view of 'post-industrial society' (Bell, 1974), who argue that the label of 'service-sector employment' conceals a diverse range of jobs and that alongside the high quality service jobs there are many low quality service jobs (for example, in catering or personal services), which are often low paid and have poor conditions. This view points to polarisation in skill levels and opportunities in the labour market, with a 'primary segment' of high quality, high skill, knowledge-based employment, and a 'secondary segment' of rather uncertain, poorly paid work, for which 'flexibility' is perhaps shorthand for risk and insecurity.

Changes in the distribution of jobs by industrial sector have had the knock-on effect of altering the occupational structure of the workforce. Job titles such as 'foundry worker' have seen a fall in importance, whilst categories like 'call centre worker' have been newly created in the past ten years. This shift has also been matched by new opportunities for women and growing amounts of part-time work. Hakim (2000) has identified five separate historical changes in society and the labour market, which started in the late twentieth century and continue to produce a qualitatively different and new scenario of options and opportunities for women. First there is the contraceptive revolution, which has given sexually active women reliable control over their fertility for the first time in history. Second, the equal opportunities revolution has ensured that for the first time in history women have had equal access to all positions, occupations and careers in the labour market (although pay differentials between men and women remain). Third, there has been an expansion of white collar occupations, which are much more attractive to women than most blue collar occupations. Fourth, the expansion of opportunities for part-time work has meant the creation of jobs for 'secondary earners' – that is, those people who do not want to give priority to paid work at the expense of other life interests. Fifth, there is a trend towards the increasing importance of attitudes, values and personal preferences in the lifestyle choices of affluent modern societies.

Women are heterogeneous in their preferences and priorities, and not all women have chosen to, or have been in a position to, benefit equally from the new structure of employment opportunities. Hakim (2000) distinguishes three groups of women on the basis of their preferences and priorities regarding the (potential) conflict between family life and employment. First, there are 'home-centred' women, for whom family life and children remain the priorities throughout life and whose preference is not to work. At the opposite end of the continuum are 'work-centred' women, whose main priority in life is employment (or equivalent activities). This group is committed to work, and, typically, members make a large investment in qualifications and training. Childless women are concentrated in the work-centred group. Finally, there is a middle group of 'adaptive' women, who want to combine work and family. Members of this group typically obtain qualifications with the intention of working, but they are not totally committed to their work career. It was highly educated women and married women (many of them mothers) in households where the man was already in work that experienced the largest rise in women's employment during the 1980s and 1990s across the UK (McRae, 1997). In the terminology of Hakim's typology, these are the 'work-centred' and 'adaptive' women. This trend has helped fuel a growing polarisation between two-earner and no-earner households, and an associated increase in patterns of income inequality.

The labour market in Northern Ireland has reflected these general trends, which have affected, to a greater or lesser extent, most other advanced economies. The changes that have occurred as a result have transformed the context in which employment equality policy operates, as there are now new types of jobs being carried out by new categories of workers than was the case a generation ago. The local outcome of these changes and what they have meant in concrete terms for Northern Ireland will be explored in more detail in the next chapter.

Labour market policy and skills

Government has not been passive in the face of these changes and labour market policy has sought to adapt to them and to steer them where possible. Policy responses vary between nations – the concepts of the *free market* and *flexibilisation* are much more important in the UK and the USA than in many EU states – so most attention here will be focused on the trends in the UK as the immediate context for Northern Ireland. As a generalisation, it appears that changes in labour market policy mirror those in other aspects of social and economic life, with a current increased emphasis on flexibility and the individual and with a retreat of government from certain types of intervention. These can be interpreted in terms of the challenges posed by globalisation and the transition from Fordism to post-Fordism (Jessop, 2003), which created a very different social, economic and political environment. These developments mean that the policy environment in the first years of the twenty-first century is very different from that of the 1970s, which saw experiments with incomes policies, inflation targets, and increasingly problematic attempts to manage the economy to keep unemployment at an 'acceptable' level.

The transition from the types of government intervention used during the 1950s, 1960s and most of the 1970s is a consequence of the economic crisis of the 1970s. The implications of this transition were to discredit 'big government', as many of the social and economic crises did not seem to be manageable using the 'tried and tested tools' that had been developed since 1945. As a result, alternative approaches to government and labour market policy were sought, and the Thatcher years in the UK and the Reagan years in the US, with their emphasis on market solutions and more restrictive benefit regimes, are significant in setting the tone until the present day. Even the ostensibly more left-wing Blair and Clinton governments have continued with notions of 'welfare-to-work', 'workfare', and increasing attempts at compulsion directed at those who are deemed to be insufficiently involved in the 'world of work'. This transition has been described by Peck (2001) as a movement from a 'welfare state' to a 'workfare state', in which a key symptom is a change from the receipt of largely unconditional benefits to their receipt on the basis of certain conditions being fulfilled. There are, of course, other symptoms. In the UK, concerns with the impact of globalisation and the requirement to maintain an internationally competitive labour market has led to policymakers emphasising flexibility by increasing labour quality but also by attacking labour protection and workers' rights to ensure attractiveness to inward investment (see, for example, Jessop [2003] on UK attempts to weaken the EU Social Chapter). This, together with the advent of the workfare state, has created a climate in which labour market policy is much more about the individual – the assets and attitudes that they bring to the labour market – than was the case in the past (Jessop, 2003).

One outcome in the UK of some of these forces has been the introduction of the New Deal by the Blair government and the increased value attached to the notion of *employability*. The New Deal has sought to reduce the numbers of benefit claimants by getting jobless people into work by, amongst other things, improving their personal presentation, developing interview skills, and encouraging work experience with employers who have participated in the programme. It is significant because re-engagement with the labour market is seen by New Labour as being at the heart of tackling social exclusion and benefit dependency (Levitas, 1998). Allied to this philosophy is the concept of employability, which is based on a recognition that jobs for life are now gone and that the best way to achieve employment security is to enhance the adaptability and flexibility of individuals so they can adjust to a quick-changing set of opportunities. Implicit in the debate is the assumption that individuals should take responsibility for themselves because government cannot protect them in an economically insecure world; that they should augment their skills and education (hence the current emphasis on lifelong learning), and that they should learn to be flexible. As applied in the UK, these policies have been controversial because they have tended to emphasise the importance of the 'supply-side' (the assets an individual brings to the labour market) rather than the 'demand-side' (the availability of work), and so the point has often been made that increasing employability is not enough to get people into work when there are few local jobs for the population to secure when and if they become 'employable' (McQuaid and Lindsay, 2002; Sunley, Martin and Nativel, 2001). In Northern Ireland, there is the added twist that there could also be higher Catholic uptake of New Deal if earlier communal inequalities in training patterns have continued (see Chapter 4), although this is a grey area because of a lack of information. This, combined with low labour demand in some parts of Northern Ireland, might mean that Catholics are more likely than Protestants to be recycled between New Deal, other training options and joblessness.

Ideas about employability deal, implicitly, with concerns about skills in which labour market strategies have identified a 'skills gap' that restrains economic growth in the UK and the EU in comparison with competing economies (McQuaid and Lindsay, 2002). There is widespread recognition of the importance of education, training and skills to the competitiveness of local, regional and national economies. Moreover, in the face of globalisation and technological change, skill needs are changing rapidly. Given the dynamic nature of, and increasing pace of change in, skill requirements, the ability to adapt to and cope with change is paramount. This underlines the need for continual upgrading of skills throughout working lives; hence, the increasing policy emphasis on lifelong learning and skills enhancement and the growth of attempts at forecasting skills in the UK. The combination of technical change and organisational change has resulted in a changing nature of work, with new sets of skills required to meet new organisational configurations. These developments have occurred, to a greater or lesser extent, in most advanced economies including Northern Ireland.

There is a general consensus that skill demands are rising as a result of these changes. Morahan (2000) points to evidence of rising wage differentials between the skilled and unskilled as evidence for this trend, as well as results from employer surveys showing that skills needed by the average employee are increasing. A number of factors can be identified as causing such rising demand. These include the impact of globalisation, as labour intensive, lower skill jobs seek out lower cost locations and are replaced by more productive jobs with a higher skill content. A further factor is technological change, which can result in skills obsolescence as new technologies come on stream, and the pervasive impacts of information and communications technologies is felt across virtually all industrial sectors and occupations. This has led to a demand for computing skills at all levels, from the relatively elementary to the more specialised. At the same time, rising customer expectations also fuel rising skill demands. Management de-layering means that more individuals have greater autonomy over their workloads and have more responsibility for planning and undertaking their work. Again, some of these ideas will be explored in greater depth in the following chapter.

Conclusion

This chapter began by looking at some continuities between the Northern Ireland labour market of a generation ago and of the first years of the twenty-first century, but then looked at some of the broader factors that might be expected to lead to labour market change. Features like the Catholic/Protestant unemployment have persisted from the 1970s, and some aspects of contemporary debates have echoed from the 1960s until the present day. However, given the social, political, institutional and economic changes that have impacted upon most advanced economies, it would be naïve in the extreme to assume that Northern Ireland has somehow avoided these developments and is thus a 'place apart' which has remained unchanged. Within the conceptual framework that has been introduced, the task of the next chapter is to take these ideas forward and to show how the economy and society of Northern Ireland have evolved since the 1970s. It will show that there have been fundamental changes in the Northern Ireland labour market. These differences outweigh any similarities and they mean that employment equality policy now must operate against a very different background than a generation ago.

6

Labour market change in Northern Ireland
Unemployment, employment and policy

IAN SHUTTLEWORTH AND ANNE GREEN

Introduction

This chapter considers the 'local' outcomes in Northern Ireland of the
general processes of economic and institutional change introduced in
Chapter 5. The purpose of putting empirical flesh on these conceptual
bones is twofold. First, it provides concrete information on how the
Northern Ireland labour market has recently evolved. It is useful in its
own right to summarise recent developments, but the extent to which
Northern Ireland has shared in, or differed from, the trends that are
usually assumed to be shaping advanced economies can also be assessed.
Second, recent labour market developments in Northern Ireland have
changed the context for employment equality, creating new challenges, transforming the terms of debates, and perhaps providing new
opportunities for the reduction of inequalities.

Reflecting these priorities, the main part of this chapter is an empirical investigation of the ways in which unemployment and employment in Northern Ireland have changed through time. The focus will
be mainly on Northern Ireland as a whole, although geographical
variations will be considered where appropriate. This discussion will
then be used to inform an assessment of employment equality, where
it has been, where it is now, and where it might go in the future. To

keep the chapter manageable, and also because data constraints can make longer-term comparisons problematic, most attention will be devoted to developments in the 1990s. However, as a preliminary to these tasks, it is useful to provide a broad-brush picture to site the more detailed arguments. The chapter therefore commences with some observations on the Northern Ireland labour market's political significance and the extent to which it has been transformed.

The significance of the Northern Ireland labour market

The labour market, described by official data and the subject of pronouncements by economists, might be assumed to be one area about which it is easy to be objective, since 'facts are facts'. However, this is hardly ever the case – debates about the labour market can carry a lot of ideological, social and political freight in any society. This is especially so in Northern Ireland, where the labour market, against a background of civil conflict, has been seen at various times, and by various groups, either as a cause of violence or as a way of limiting conflict. These viewpoints have been intertwined with party political debates about the future of Northern Ireland and the extent to which the Northern Ireland economy can be judged a relative success or a relative failure. The interpretations advanced influence how the labour market, the present-day position of equality policy and its future directions are viewed. They are also significant since they give a backdrop for interpretations of the empirical labour market developments, which are the main subject of the chapter.

The causes of the Northern Ireland conflict remain a matter for debate, with differing perspectives influencing how current and historical events are viewed. Explanations, which have been suggested in various guises, in various places, include culture, the clash of competing nationalisms, history and religion (Ruane and Todd, 1996). Given the complex nature of the conflict and the legacy of social inequality in Northern Ireland, it is perhaps unsurprising that economic and labour market factors have also been advanced in some quarters as a cause of communal violence and division (McGarry and O'Leary, 1995). It is unlikely that any single explanation on its own is sufficient. Nevertheless, it is probable that the realm of the labour market and the economy has played some role in shaping the conflict and this belief has helped to form labour market and social policies in Northern Ireland during the

1970s, 1980s and 1990s. The legacy of these ideas is still important, although the terms of debate have gradually shifted as circumstances have altered during the 1990s.

Long-running communal differentials in the labour market and in access to economic resources have been suggested as at least a partial explanation of the recent conflict (Smith and Chambers, 1991). These differentials date at least to the early years of the twentieth century and encompassed occupational differentials (Hepburn, 1983) and differential access to the 'controlling heights' of the Northern Ireland economy (Ruane and Todd, 1996). More recent analyses from 1971 onwards have also drawn attention to continued differentials in occupation and unemployment (Aunger, 1975; Gallagher, Osborne and Cormack, 1994a). Inequalities in the labour market, it has been argued, have provided a material underpinning to the conflict (see McGarry and O'Leary, 1995), with the implication that the removal of unfair differences will remove (or reduce) the potential for conflict. Because of the political salience of labour market inequalities in these terms, their explanation and nature have become politicised on nationalist/unionist lines, with nationalists tending to emphasise the size of the inequalities and their cause in terms of discrimination and unionists tending to minimise their extent and to rationalise them as a result of factors other than discrimination.

The attractions of this economic perspective for policymakers are several. In the first place, the economy and the labour market represent an arena in which government has a history of intervention, and its problems are more tractable within existing policy frameworks than more 'difficult' topics such as culture, politics and contending nationalisms. Second, the economy and the allocation of resources can be portrayed as being technical and thus more amenable to rational solution. It is likely that this kind of focus has underwritten the 'equality agenda' and has been important in setting the terms for legislation (see Chapter 1) and the creation of institutions to intervene in the Northern Ireland labour market to encourage redistribution and equalisation.

Labour market conditions and the economy might also shape the political environment in other ways than through communal inequalities. Commonly, Northern Ireland in relative terms (compared to other UK regions) has been assumed historically to have had an underperforming economy, with higher rates of unemployment, lower rates of employment, and greater social deprivation (Smith and Chambers, 1991). In these circumstances it has been argued that absolute material deprivation is a significant cause of communal conflict (Whyte, 1990) and that reducing it could therefore also assist in reducing violence. This view was particularly credible in the crisis years of the 1970s and 1980s, given the loss of manufacturing jobs, soaring unemployment rates, problems of peripherality and high levels of violence, although the large public sector, in part a response to violence, helped to lessen the trend towards decline (Rowthorne and Wayne, 1988). A prescription following from this diagnosis is economic growth.

The crude application of these arguments to the contemporary situation is somewhat problematic, as the Northern Ireland economy, largely because of changes in the 1990s, differs in important ways from that seen in the 1970s and 1980s, though these perspectives remain influential in political discourses. Some headline statistics give an idea of the types of changes observed. Between 1992 and 2000, unemployment fell by around 40 per cent; the number of employee jobs grew by about 15 per cent over the decade (in comparison with a UK increase of 10 per cent); and the Gross Domestic Product (GDP) per capita gap between Northern Ireland and the rest of the UK decreased. Northern Ireland has made the transition from a high unemployment economy in the 1980s and 1990s, with labour shortages in some economic sectors and locales in the first years of the twenty-first century, although the extent to which they are 'real' is a matter for later discussion.

Communal inequalities in the labour market are also not what they once were in the 1970s and 1980s (see Chapters 1 and 2), with evidence of Protestant underrepresentation in some sectors rather than Catholic disadvantage, pure and simple. Northern Ireland is neither as absolutely disadvantaged as it once was, nor are Catholic/Protestant differentials the same as before, and this chapter will therefore explore how these changes in a rapidly transforming society have led to new conditions for employment equality.

Given these figures, it would be easy to paint a rosy picture of the Northern Ireland labour market but this would not be just, since substantial problems remain as a legacy of the past. Long-term unemployment persists, there are concentrations of social deprivation, rates of benefit dependency remain high (Morrissey and Gaffikin, 2001) and employment rates in some areas are low. Because of this, past arguments made about the contribution of the labour market and economic factors to communal divisions still have some resonance, although recent developments have changed their context. There are now new debates about an 'all-island' economy, in the context of the Irish Republic's 'Celtic Tiger', and there is contemporary discussion about the social distribution of the 'peace dividend'. The discussion of merits (or demerits) of an all-Ireland economy and North–South links has obvious nationalist/unionist dimensions, and the meaning of the peace dividend relates to older arguments about deprivation as a root cause of conflict. But despite this, the terms of these debates have moved on from those of the 1970s and 1980s. Part of this change is in response to new economic circumstances – including global changes of the kind identified in Chapter 5 – and part in response to new political and in- stitutional arrangements such as the Belfast/Good Friday Agreement. It is difficult to isolate cause from effect when looking at the changed political and economic scenes and it is perhaps best to consider these aspects as two sides of the same coin.

The remainder of this chapter builds on this general overview. First, it examines the changed nature of employment. It then considers how unemployment has changed in Northern Ireland. Finally, it synthesises these observations to make some comments about the changed context for employment equality policy with reference to labour market and economic changes and the contemporary policy environment.

Changing employment and economic activity in Northern Ireland

Official data show that employment increased in Northern Ireland throughout the 1980s and 1990s, rising by about 105,000 between 1984 and 1999. Over the 1990s there was a growth in the economically active population (people who are either in work or seeking work and are therefore 'engaged' in the labour market). But what underlies these headline figures? Who gained jobs by occupation and gender? In what parts of Northern Ireland was employment increase concentrated? How have patterns of engagement with the labour market changed? How does Northern Ireland compare with other areas? This section seeks to answer these and similar questions in the context of the broad patterns of restructuring identified in Chapter 5.

The patterns of change observed in Northern Ireland accord quite closely with those seen in other advanced societies, and they can be con- ceptualised in terms of the transition from Fordism to post-Fordism, which has seen occupational and gender shifts in involvement in the labour market, the rise of insecure employment, and uneven impacts, which have seen some groups lose out. Northern Ireland was not an exception to these trends, although outcomes there could be judged to be 'exceptional', in that they have changed the communal balance of the labour market and the context for employment equality policy in ways particular to Northern Ireland.

During the 1980s and 1990s there were substantial changes by gender in the balance of involvement in the Northern Ireland labour market. Male working-age economic activity rates declined while female rates increased. These developments can be attributed in part to the altered nature of employment. There were increases in employment for both men and women (with most of the increase in the late 1990s) but the growth was greater for women than for men. As in other economies, therefore, the Northern Ireland labour market has become more 'feminised'. Analyses by religion suggest that employment growth was experienced by both Catholic and Protestant females (although the growth was particularly marked for Catholics). The increase in working-age male employment might be largely attributed to increased Catholic employment (NISRA, 2001). This could be because the Catholic population tends to have a younger age structure than that of Protestants. This means, everything else being equal, that more Protestants would be eligible for retirement than Catholics. Protestant men may have also lost ground because of recent job losses in 'traditional', largely male, heavy industry, such as shipbuilders Harland & Wolff (Shuttleworth and Tyler, 2002). These patterns are, again, very much like those observed elsewhere. In the rest of the UK, for example, rates of economic activity have tended to fall for males aged over 50, although how much of the 'early retirement' is voluntary is a matter for debate.

These changes in the gender balance of employment and economic activity are part and parcel of other developments that have seen transformations in the status of work and the types of jobs that have been done. Much of the growth in female employment in Northern Ireland, as elsewhere, has been in part-time work and it has been accompanied by a growth in service sector employment. Occupationally, women remain concentrated in clerical and secretarial and personal and customer service occupations, while men are highly represented in craft and managerial occupations. The 1990s saw female employment grow in clerical and secretarial work and fall in the plant and machinery operative category, whereas most male gains were in managerial employment. The balance also favoured females in higher-status professional and associate professional work in the 1990s. Catholic employment in the 1990s grew most markedly in service and professional occupations. Occupational forecasts (IER, 2001) suggest that jobs in these categories will increase in the medium term in the UK and Northern Ireland. It is possible that this will mean increased female and Catholic participation in the labour market.

Despite this complex pattern of 'winners and losers', it is probably fair to conclude that the Northern Ireland labour market has performed well during the 1990s. But how well has it performed relative to elsewhere? The answer to that question depends on the choice of comparator. Relative to the heady performance of the Celtic Tiger of the Irish Republic in the 1990s, Northern Ireland's performance, despite increases in employment and economic activity, has not been outstanding. Compared with other regions of the UK, it is probable that various labour market 'gaps' remain, although they were diminished during the 1990s. The Northern Ireland working-age employment rate is higher than the EU mean, although by UK standards it is amongst the lowest, since the UK's rates are higher than most other European states. Northern Ireland's economic activity rates are also somewhat lower than the rest of the UK. These lower Northern Ireland economic activity and employment rates are probably the result of the interaction of a number of factors, including the demand for labour, wage rates, the benefits system, and historical factors. Because these rates are lower, it is likely that there remains considerable 'slack' in the Northern Ireland labour market, even after a relatively successful economic performance in the 1990s, and that there could be considerable reserves of 'hidden unemployed', that is to say, people who are not involved in the labour market and who do not count in conventional official statistics but who might want work if other circumstances were different. The *Employability Scoping Study* (Deloitte and Touche, 2001) observes that, if Northern Ireland had the same employment and economic rates as the UK average, there would be some 75,000 more people seeking work and about 14,000 more benefit claimants would be in employment.

It is also worthwhile to note that the Northern Ireland LFS shows that Protestants usually have higher economic activity and employment rates than Catholics, and that this differential exists for males and females. These measures may now be better labour market indicators than the standard measure of unemployment customarily used. As was noted in Chapter 5, there are a number of questions about the statistical and conceptual meanings of unemployment data, and these doubts mean that discussions of unemployment, and the unemployment differential, are now much more problematic than in the 1970s, 1980s, or even the 1990s. These rates are not only determined by the supply and demand for labour, but also by a variety of institutional and cultural factors, which may range from perceptions of the quality of job opportunities in the local labour market, in comparison with other avenues, such as education and training, to institutional factors such as access to childcare. The factors that underlie the decision to become economically active when entering the labour market, or to become inactive when withdrawing from it. However, it is interesting in a wider comparative context to observe that relatively high rates of participation by Catholic young people in education and training are

Map 6.1

Employment rate in Northern Ireland, 2001

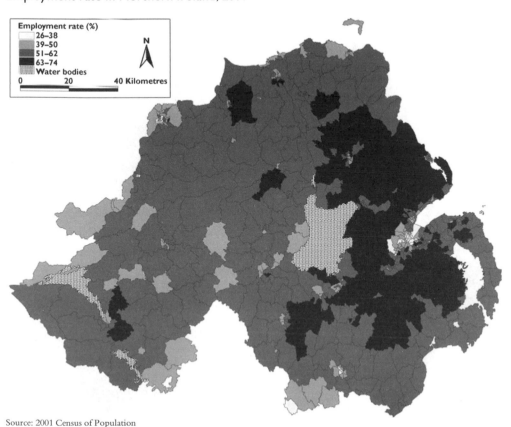

Source: 2001 Census of Population

mirrored by similarly high rates for some ethnic minority groups in Britain, and that minority populations with histories of discrimination, such as African Americans in the US, have comparatively low levels of economic activity (Bound and Freeman, 1989; Shuttleworth, 1999). It would be interesting to examine how views about perceived or actual discrimination act to influence decisions about education, training and labour market participation and also achievement in these spheres.

There are also major differences within Northern Ireland at district council level. Map 6.1 shows these patterns with regard to employment rates using information from the 2001 Census of Population, and indicates higher employment rates in an arc around Belfast. This might reflect a 'Belfast commuting belt' whose residents have high levels of employment. There is an east–west pattern with generally

Map 6.2

Economic activity rates in Northern Ireland, 2001

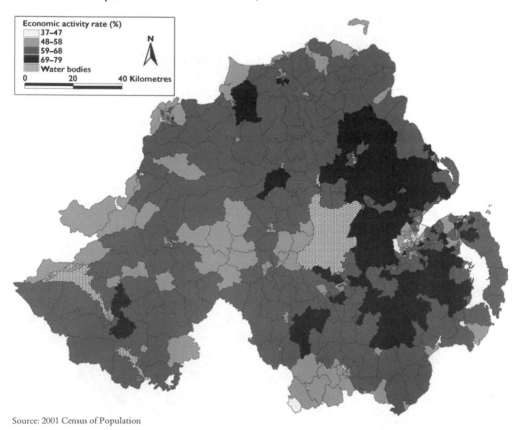

Source: 2001 Census of Population

lower employment rates in the west. These patterns are largely replicated in Map 6.2, where the picture for economic activity is examined
using the 2001 Census. Again, there are usually higher rates of employment in the east, with lower rates in the west, in district councils such
as Strabane and Derry. It is likely that there are 'hidden labour
reserves' in these areas. This general east–west division, with lower employment and economic activity rates in the west and higher in the
east, may reflect the geography of employment and labour demand.
To examine geographical variations in employment, information
from the government's Census of Employment was used. This records
where jobs are located, unlike the Census of Population, which records
where workers live. The Census of Employment data are not fully
comprehensive (they are a count of 'employee jobs' and exclude the

Map 6.3

Number of jobs within a 10 km radius, 2001

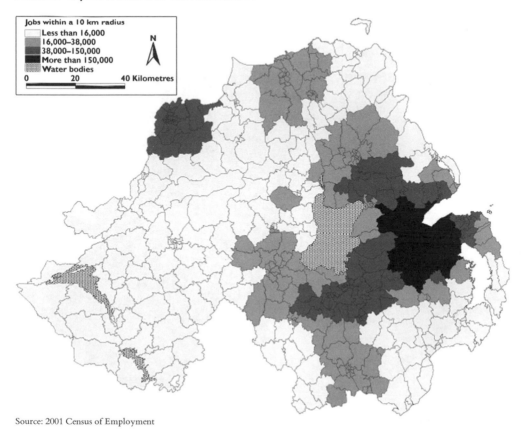

Source: 2001 Census of Employment

self-employed, for example) but they nevertheless cover a substantial part of the labour market and they give a good geographical picture of employment. These data are outlined in Maps 6.3 and 6.4, which show, respectively, the location of jobs in 2001 and the pattern of employment change between 1995 and 2001.

Map 6.3 indicates that job-rich areas are mainly in urban areas such as Belfast, Derry and Newry. However, the major employment location in Northern Ireland is the Belfast Urban Area, although there appears to be a 'Greater Belfast Employment Region' with a hinterland of high employment levels throughout the east of Northern Ireland and encompassing towns such as Antrim and Ballymena. The pattern revealed suggests strong continuities with the past, since the long-

Map 6.4

Pattern of employment change in Northern Ireland, 1995–2001 (jobs within a 10 km radius)

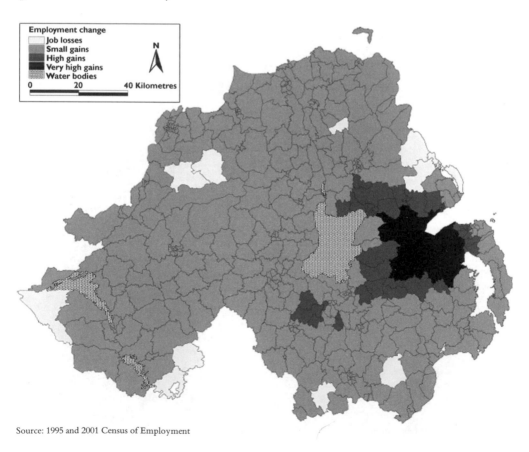

Source: 1995 and 2001 Census of Employment

established 'east of Bann/west of Bann' division noted, for example, by Smith and Chambers (1991) appears to have persisted, although this is not altogether surprising, given the dominance of Belfast in Northern Ireland and its continuing social and economic advantages.

Map 6.4 shows the pattern of change in the late 1990s. Very few areas lost employment but most growth was concentrated in urban areas and especially Belfast and its wider hinterland. This implies that the big gainer of the employment expansion of the 1990s, which saw growth in service employment numbers and women workers, was the Belfast region. The concentration of growth where there were already high numbers of workers also might suggest that active measures to encourage economic decentralisation from the Greater Belfast area might be needed in some circumstances.

Trends in unemployment and non-employment

Unemployment has long been one of the most widely used measures of economic and social disadvantage. The long-standing 'gap' in unemployment rates between Northern Ireland and the UK has been a key headline indicator of structural weakness in the Northern Ireland labour market. Changes in the structure of the labour market and the associated 'blurring of boundaries' between unemployment and inactivity, as seen in Chapter 5, has, however, led to increasing debate about the need for broader measures of unemployment and non-employment, in order to accurately measure the true extent of joblessness (Beatty and Fothergill, 1996; Green and Owen, 1998). Analyses have shown that it is in regions characterised by long-standing disadvantage, where non-participation becomes more entrenched, that pressures causing a diversion from recorded to 'hidden' unemployment are greatest (MacKay, 1999; Beatty, Fothergill and MacMillan, 2000), although analyses by Gregg and Wadsworth (1998) suggest that Northern Ireland has shared less in the increase in inactivity than some other UK regions. Nevertheless, in a Northern Ireland context, Armstrong (1999) has estimated that, if the hidden component of joblessness is accounted for, total male unemployment in Northern Ireland would be more than one-third higher than the official figures suggest. Hence, when interpreting the 'conventional' unemployment statistics, it is important to bear in mind that they understate the extent of joblessness.

Across the UK there was a steady decline in the International

Labour Organisation (ILO) unemployment rate,[1] from levels of nearly 12 per cent in the mid-1980s, when unemployment levels exceeded 3 million, to under 7 per cent in 1990, as the level of unemployment fell below 2 million. Unemployment increased once again in the early 1990s, peaking at just under 3 million (over 10 per cent) in spring 1993, before declining steadily to 1.75 million in spring 1999. In Northern Ireland, there was a similar marked reduction in unemployment levels in the late 1980s, as the number of ILO unemployed contracted from over 100,000 to 80,000 (an unemployment rate of just under 12 per cent) in 1990. The subsequent increase in unemployment in the early 1990s was much less marked in Northern Ireland than across the UK as a whole, leading to a narrowing of the Northern Ireland:UK unemployment gap. From 1996 onwards, there has been a decline in the perception of unemployment as the 'most important problem' in Northern Ireland (Kennedy, 2000), underlining the 'tightening' of the labour market, and this has been matched by continuing falls in unemployment counts.

The number of males unemployed still exceeds the number of females unemployed by a factor of around 2:1, with the unemployment rate for males consistently exceeding that for females. There are also marked differences in unemployment rates between Catholics and Protestants, with higher rates for the former than for the latter. LFS data show that Catholic unemployment rates were consistently higher than those for Protestants, particularly amongst males (where unemployment rates are twice as high for Catholics as for Protestants). Analyses have shown these differentials[2] to remain relatively constant – averaging 2.2 for males and 1.6 for females over the period 1990 to 1999 – despite changes in the level of unemployment. Various explanations have been put forward for Catholic:Protestant unemployment differentials. 'Structuralists' see high levels of Catholic unemployment as being the product of structural factors, such as poor location, labour market segmentation, differences in education and skill levels, differences in work commitment, and so on. Conversely, others see Catholic disadvantage, as measured by higher unemployment rates, as being the product of discrimination – whether direct or indirect. On the basis of analyses of data from the 1991 Census of Population Sample of Anonymised Records, Borooah (1999) concludes that there is evidence for a 'religion penalty', with a great deal of the overrepresentation of Catholic males amongst the jobless being attributable to *who* they were, after controlling for *what* they were (Borooah, 2000). Evidence was also found for a 'religion penalty' in 'explaining' the over-representation of Catholic females amongst the jobless, although the size of the penalty was smaller in the case of females than of males. The lower unemployment levels of the late 1990s and early twenty-first century, however, may mean that the unemployment differential is less significant now in absolute terms than it was in the past. The focus for the equality debate, as already indicated, might also be better directed to the themes of employment rates, economic activity rates and joblessness, given the queries raised about the conceptual meaning of unemployment data (see Chapter 5).

Substantial local variations in labour market conditions are reflected in local unemployment and long-term unemployment rates, as is shown in Map 6.5. This uses 2001 Census of Population data and

Map 6.5

Unemployment rates in Northern Ireland wards, 2001

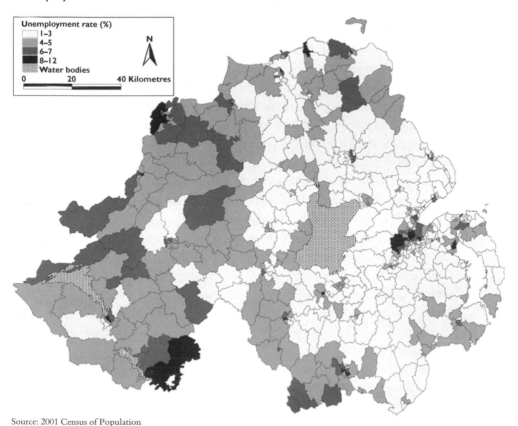

Source: 2001 Census of Population

shows that areas in the west tend generally to have higher unemployment levels. However, this picture is not straightforward. A case in point is Dungannon District Council. This area had a growing working-age population through the 1990s and it could be argued that jobs growth in that period had failed to keep pace with the expansion in working-age population, thus explaining its relatively low economic activity and employment rates (see Map 6.1), even by Northern Ireland standards, which indicate a large 'hidden' labour supply. Yet recently, a large and growing Portuguese community has located in the area to supply labour for manufacturing employment, because employers claim that there is a shortage of local labour, jeopardising production and expansion plans. Some signs therefore indicate near 'full employment'; but others suggest that there is a substantial unmet labour demand in the area that could support growth in local employment and an expansion in economic activity rates. At a smaller spatial scale, there are much more extreme variations in unemployment – with 'hot spots' of high unemployment within areas with relatively low unemployment rates, as well as neighbourhoods with relatively low unemployment within high unemployment rate districts (Social Disadvantage Research Centre, 2001).

Certain groups are overrepresented amongst the unemployed: notably, young people, single parents, disabled people, older people, and those with no qualifications. Long-term unemployment tends to be a bigger problem among people coming to the end of their working life than it is among younger people. The proportion of the economically active who are long-term unemployed is highest for those aged in their late fifties and early sixties (ONS, 1998). However, young people are not immune from long spells of joblessness. The young jobless often face a combination of disadvantaged family background, poor school experiences and qualifications, and come from the most disadvantaged areas of Northern Ireland (McVicar, 2000).

Despite the fall in unemployment, there remains a substantial problem of long-term unemployment – although the numbers of long-term unemployed have declined also. Indeed, the long-term unemployed may be increasingly marginalised at a time of economic expansion. In Northern Ireland at least half of the stock of ILO unemployed were unemployed for at least one year throughout the period from spring 1985 to spring 1999 (with the exception of spring 1998).

While much of the debate on unemployment focuses on the stocks of unemployed, there is increasing interest in unemployment flows.

While there has been a reduction in the stocks of unemployed, on-flows and off-flows to the unemployment count have remained at a more stable level, despite monthly variations. At a time when off-flows exceed on-flows, there is a reduction in the unemployment stock. Conversely, there is an increase in the unemployment stock at a time when on-flows exceed off-flows. More buoyant local labour markets tend to be characterised by a greater than average likelihood of ceasing to be unemployed, and also a greater than average likelihood of becoming unemployed. This reflects a greater tendency for 'turnover' in buoyant labour markets, as those in the labour force are willing to move from one job to another. On the other hand, areas of entrenched unemployment tend to be characterised by a lower than average likelihood of ceasing to be unemployed.

Since 1996, information has been made available on reasons for claimant off-flows. In Northern Ireland the proportion of claimants finding work has remained consistently below the UK average: on average, in the year 2000, two-thirds (66 per cent) of those leaving the claimant count in the UK found work, compared with less than 61 per cent in Northern Ireland. At the Travel-to-Work Area (TTWA) level there are more marked differentials in the numbers finding work, with the average percentage in the year 2000 from 55 per cent in Derry to over 64 per cent in Ballymena, Dungannon and Mid-Ulster. Differences are also evident between sub-groups in the percentages of count leavers finding work, with younger people being more likely to make a transition to employment and older people to other types of benefit. The evidence on unemployment flows therefore suggests that those who have been unemployed longest, and those living in areas of highest unemployment, are least likely to find work. Gordon (1999) contends that concentrated unemployment is fundamentally a reflection of the experience of long periods of demand deficiency – though not necessarily local job losses. Over time, he suggests that the form of chronic joblessness may be shaped by a number of other processes operating within labour markets and housing markets, such that demand-deficient unemployment may be transformed into structural unemployment. Where workers from low-skilled jobs, particularly at risk of unemployment, are concentrated together, disadvantage may be further fuelled by attrition of informal information networks, which might once have offered access to more stable employment, and a lowering of educational aspirations amongst young people and of expectations amongst adults. Those most disadvantaged in the labour market tend to have a more 'local' orientation than more advantaged groups, and have least locational flexibility in seeking employment. For some of the most disadvantaged in the labour market, 'spatial mismatches' (that is, an insufficiency of jobs in accessible locations) and 'skills mismatches' (i.e. a lack of skills to meet the requirements of available jobs) may create a 'double barrier' to job access (Green, 2001).

Implications for equality policy

The changes seen in employment and unemployment in Northern Ireland are far from being the exception, since they largely conform to the 'rule' observed in other advanced economies. However, their local outcomes are not reducible to a 'rule', since few European countries have had Northern Ireland's social and political history. Given this background, and repeated state attempts to intervene in the labour market to reduce Catholic/Protestant community differentials dating back to the 1970s, what is the likely implication of these labour market developments for equality policy? It is difficult to attribute what changes are due to policy and what to other developments, given the complexity of the factors in play. Nevertheless, it remains worthwhile to attempt to construct a balance sheet of the impact of the fundamental societal transformations that have been observed to make some general comments about the changed context for employment equality policy. This task is the focus for the remainder of the chapter.

Reviewing the evidence for employment growth in the 1990s, a reasonable judgement is that the relatively good performance of the Northern Ireland economy helped to reduce community differentials and was a favourable environment for the operation of employment equality policy as it stands at present. This is because the legislation operates during the hiring process by seeking to ensure fair recruitment. Given this, new employment opportunities should offer routes out of unemployment, and an expanding labour market, with plenty of hiring, could be expected to allow the legislation much scope to operate. Everything else being equal, therefore, it would be expected that the 1990s would see progress towards equality being made as a result of job creation during the period.

Although the overall conditions during the 1990s were likely to have eased moves towards equality, the pattern of employment change might also have posed some challenges. Some of these have been met.

For example, recognising that many of the 'new jobs' were part time, monitoring was extended to include employment in this category. But there are other challenges that perhaps have attracted less attention. The growth of female employment might have consequences for the distribution of work amongst households. Because of the ways in which the benefit system operates, it is sometimes uneconomic for a woman to work in a household where her partner is not in work. As a result, it is probable that some of the new female jobs have been taken by women who are now in 'two-job households'. The cost of this is the growth of 'no-job households' and the polarisation of access to the labour market between those households with multiple access to employment and those with none. A further challenge is posed by the rise of insecurity in the labour market and the increase of short-term, temporary, part-time and contracted jobs. This is a trend noted elsewhere with the rise of 'economic risk' and Northern Ireland is unlikely to buck this trend. This means that there might be substantial churning (turnover) between unemployment and low-paid irregular work

Figure 6.1

Community background and unemployment rate, 2001

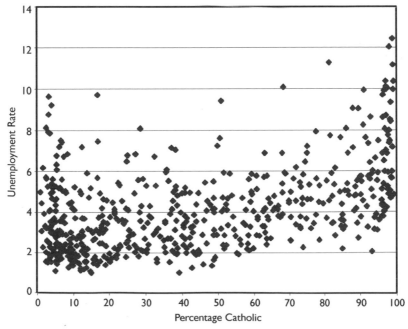

Source: 2001 Census of Population

(Deakin and Reed, 2000). Very little is known about this, since in the case of redundancies, other dismissals, or termination of employment there is no monitoring. So it is not known whether each 'step forward' in the labour market is associated with a 'step back'. Finally, Northern Ireland, in common with some other regions of the UK, appears to be becoming a country of immigration. This is a very recent trend and is historically unprecedented in the context of population out-migration from the mid-nineteenth century. Because of the newness of the immigration, evidence is hard to collect but it appears that many immigrants – the number is far from precise – are employed in low-grade employment and the irregular work discussed above. This state of affairs, and the likely increase in the importance of this type of work in restructured economies, will mean that issues associated with immigration (for example, workers' rights and pay) will come more and more to the fore.

The ECNI, with religion, gender, race and disability under one roof, could be in a good position to meet these challenges, since they are interrelated. Gender issues and female employment, for instance, have obvious interrelations because of the probable trends towards the polarisation of economic activity into work-rich and work-poor households. There is clearly opportunity in this, and in similar issues, for 'joined-up government'.

The new situation for employment equality arising from the changed nature of employment is also reflected in the fundamental transformation in the nature of unemployment. There are some features in the early twenty-first century that are the same as those observed in the 1970s, 1980s and 1990s – the unemployment differential remains and, as Figure 6.1 shows, there is still a positive relationship between the percentage of a ward's residents with a Catholic community background and the ward's unemployment rate. But the fall in unemployment since the days of the 'high unemployment' economy of the 1970s and 1980s means that the unemployment differential is unlikely to be the centrepiece of the political and academic debate about employment equality that it once was. This changed environment shifts concentration to other issues. One theme is the continued gap in employment and economic activity rates between Catholic and Protestant – the 2001 Census of Population showed that 73 per cent of Catholics aged 16–74 were economically active as compared to 79 per cent of Protestants; and 44 per cent of Catholics were employed against 50 per cent of Protestants. This might be a more suitable indicator since it measures involvement in the labour market. Unemployment, because of the growth of 'hidden unemployment', and the shift of people to other kinds of benefit, is no longer the indicator it once was and might thus be questioned for the reasons outlined in Chapter 5. A focus on the dichotomy between those in jobs and the jobless (far more inclusive than a count of individuals on benefit or who are explicitly seeking work) is sensible because of the complexity of labour market states, which make it more difficult to count somebody now as 'unemployed' than was the case thirty years ago. It also has the added practical virtue of tying employment equality more closely into mainline UK labour market policy.

Since the inception of the New Labour government in 1997, labour market policy has had the aim of increasing the ties of marginalised groups with the labour market on the assumption that the best way to overcome social exclusion and poverty is through work. The main concept pressed into service in pursuit of this objective is 'employability'. This has formed a central plank of policy in Britain but also has been used in Northern Ireland (Deloitte and Touche, 2001). The links between policies of this type and employment equality could be particularly close, given the changed labour market environment. This has seen employment growth, falls in unemployment, and a move away from a high unemployment economy, but not everyone has benefited from this. Some people, and some areas, have not become included in the labour market. A policy to increase economic activity rates and employment rates would help to increase social inclusion (following the premises of New Labour thinking), would help to boost the output of the Northern Ireland economy, and would also help the operation of employment equality policy. Remembering that the legislation operates at the moment of hiring, its effectiveness would be enhanced if more people were applying for jobs and being appointed, since those who are long-term unemployed, or economically inactive and thus not taking part in the labour market, are unlikely to benefit from the present legislation.

Action on these lines would again benefit from the crossdepartmental thinking of joined-up government. It would be complex, as themes such as the operation of the benefits system, the types of job on offer, job search practice, and employers' recruitment practices would all become pertinent. But it would locate employment equality practices more centrally within official policy and accord them greater priority than in the 1980s, for example, when the dominant free-market paradigm made labour market interventions of the type seen in Northern Ireland much more exceptional.

Future trends and concluding comments

Forecasting the future is always a dangerous business. At the moment, however, it looks as if the changed economy of the 1990s and the altered political environment following the 1998 Belfast/Good Friday Agreement has fundamentally changed the circumstances for equality policy. Politically, it has increased in importance. At the same time, labour market change has meant that the debate about equality has moved on even from the early 1990s. The unemployment differential still has some importance, and will doubtless continue to have political significance, but it is now not the only show in town. New issues that have emerged are encouraging greater economic activity and employment, coping with part-time and temporary work, protecting immigrants' rights, and making links between the various arms of equality policy such as religion and gender. Occupational forecasts point to the continuation of past trends, and economic forecasts do not suggest that the Northern Ireland economy faces imminent problems. Therefore, on the basis that the best guide to the future is the immediate past, it seems safe to assume that most of the trends identified in Chapters 5 and 6 will continue into the foreseeable future. So in this relatively benign scenario, there could be a gradual evolution of employment equality and slow but sure expansion of its scope.

But a major caveat concerns the future trajectory of the economy. As part of a globalised world, Northern Ireland is sensitive to external shocks. Major investors basing themselves in Eastern Europe, Russia or Asia and leaving Northern Ireland could put the brakes on growth. Another war or 9/11-style terrorist attack could harm the international economy. And the continued political uncertainty in Northern Ireland could mean that internal factors on their own could prove to be serious economic checks. In this more pessimistic frame of mind, Northern Ireland could easily slide back towards the high unemployment economy of old. This would provide a much less favourable environment for equality policy and, as people's economic expectations failed to be met, could even lead to a revival of the 'war of the dispossessed' thinking about the causes of conflict that was prevalent in the 1970s and 1980s.

Only time will tell which of these general forecasts proves most accurate. At present, however, it seems safe to say that the radical changes seen in Northern Ireland in the recent past will not be easily undone and that the terms of debate have altered. This means new challenges for equality policy as old ones become less relevant: the need for new types of thinking and the requirement for institutional flexibility. In this context, it will be interesting to see how the political and public debate about equality will reflect these changed circumstances which mean that the world of the twenty-first century is very different from 1971 or even 1991.

7

The impact of affirmative action agreements

CHRISTOPHER McCRUDDEN, ROBERT FORD
AND ANTHONY HEATH

Introduction

The 1990s were a decade of rapid change in the Northern Ireland labour market. The previously dominant public sector declined, industry stagnated and services boomed. In the monitored labour force, both religious communities saw employment growth, but Catholic employment growth was consistently stronger. Catholic labour force participation rose throughout the economy; although Catholic under-representation remained a problem, the gap has narrowed. Segregated employment declined in all sectors of the economy, and integrated employment rose.

In this chapter we focus upon the activities of the Fair Employment Commission (FEC) during the period 1990–2000.[1] During this period, the FEC pursued an evolving strategy towards achieving the goal of fair participation in the labour market. In the early period, the Commission focused upon large public sector and private sector employers and sought legally enforceable Article 13 agreements, particularly in the private sector. As the 1990s progressed, the emphasis gradually shifted towards the private sector and towards smaller concerns. With these smaller firms, the FEC was more likely to seek informal, voluntary affirmative action agreements, which could not be legally enforced.

We examine two possible goals the FEC pursued through affirmative action agreements to achieve fair participation: increased employment growth of the underrepresented group, and increased integration of workplaces. In both respects we find that firms reaching agreements show significant evidence of change over the decade. Employment growth was rapid for underrepresented groups at firms with agreements throughout the 1990s. Although the patterns of change varied considerably depending upon which community was underrepresented and what type of agreement was reached, in all cases the overall trend is towards greater employment of the underrepresented group. We also find that agreement firms have become more integrated over the decade; although the pace of change has been slow, given such characteristics as the size, sectoral distribution and past history of many firms, it remains an important shift. Again, there have been differences between communities and between agreement types, but in all cases the trend is moving in the direction of increased integration. We should note that employment growth for underrepresented groups and increased workplace integration have both apparently been achieved simultaneously at agreement firms.[2] While we are using aggregate figures, and it is therefore possible that one target is being pursued at some sites while the other is being pursued elsewhere, this initial analysis does suggest there is no definitive trade-off between pursuing greater employment growth and pursuing integration as strategies for achieving fair participation.

Methodology

The database we have examined is based upon the monitoring returns provided by Northern Ireland employers from 1990 to 2000. Firms with less than 25 employees did not provide monitoring returns prior to 1992, and to avoid any discontinuities these firms have been excluded from the following analysis. The total number of firms with 25 or more employees in the database was 1,850 in 1990 and rose to 2,338 in 2000. At several points in the analysis, again to ensure continuity, we have focused only upon those firms which provided monitoring returns throughout the decade. Throughout the analysis, we adopt the following convention used by the Commission and Northern Ireland Statistics and Research Agency (NISRA) in their reporting: unless specifically indicated, all community proportions reported in the analyses are the proportions of those whose religion has been determined as Protestant or Catholic; the non-determined portion is excluded.

The analysis will proceed in two sections. In the first, we examine the overall pattern of agreement activity, and how this relates to the strategies pursued by the FEC. In the second section, we analyse the association between agreements and changes occurring at monitored firms, placing this in the broader context of trends emerging from the monitoring returns. This is the first statistical analysis to be undertaken examining these relationships and, as such, it is subject to numerous constraints. The aim of the 1989 legislation, and the work undertaken by the FEC, was to achieve fair participation in employment, although the meaning and scope of this term is contentious. For the purposes of this chapter, we have considered two targets associated with achieving fair participation: combating the underrepresentation of Catholics or Protestants at particular workplaces, and promoting integration of workplaces.

1: Trends in agreement activity, 1990–2000[3]

The agreements database provided to us by the ECNI details 366 agreements reached between 1988 and 2002 with the FEA (1988–90), the FEC (1990–9) and the ECNI (2000–2); we consider only the 322 agreements reached with the FEC between 1990 and 2000,[4] the period covered by the monitoring returns. Around 40 agreements were reached in this period with firms that have since deregistered, due to insolvency, mergers, or public sector reorganisation; these firms are included in this analysis of agreement activity but are excluded from subsequent sections. Table 7.1 shows the agreement activity in the three major economic sectors, the number of agreements reached and the mean size of the concerns involved. The graphs on the following pages depict the agreements by community underrepresented, by economic sector, and by the type of agreement set up. They also show the number of agreements reached in each year, and the number of employees at the firms covered by these agreements.

The Fair Employment (Northern Ireland) Act 1989 placed affirmative action on a statutory footing for the first time, with new statutory duties being placed on employers and the FEC. In deciding whether a firm was meeting the requirements of fair participation, the FEC recognised the complexities inherent in a mature and diverse economy, with different labour markets operating in different locations, or for different jobs in the same location. An assessment of imbalance, therefore, needed to be more sophisticated than a simple comparison of workforce composition with local or Northern Ireland-wide community balance. Overall workforce compositions were also disaggregated to take into account the differing compositions in the various occupational categories and locations, which often differ.[5] Specific or overall underrepresentation are both possible, as is underrepresentation within one firm of both communities, in different job groups or locations. The majority of agreements dealt with overall underrepresentation of one group, although several of the largest agreements in both the public sector and the private sector were concerned with local or internal underrepresentation.

Two provisions of the 1989 Act, Section 11 Investigations and Section 31 Reviews, were the cornerstones of the FEC strategy on the promotion of affirmative action with public sector and private sector employers. More recently, the Fair Employment and Treatment (Northern Ireland) Order 1998 has replaced the former Fair Employment Acts. The investigation provision is set out in Article 11 of the Order and the review provision is set out in Article 55. The 1998 Order also includes special provisions permitting employers to recruit directly from those not in employment and for religion-specific training.

The FEC divided the agreements reached with firms into three main categories. Article 13 agreements are legally enforceable formal undertakings, detailing the action firms intend to take. Failure to take the agreed action could lead to legal enforcement action from the FEC. Voluntary and formal agreements are not legally enforceable, and are distinguished by the level at which they are concluded. Formal agreements were approved by the FEC executive, while voluntary agreements were negotiated by Commission staff. There have not been many formal agreements, around 15 in total, and for the purposes of this chapter they will be grouped with voluntary agreements.

The predecessor to the FEC, the FEA, conducted a large number of investigations during the period 1978–1990. Investigations ranged widely, including banks and financial institutions, district councils, the NICS, Northern Ireland Housing Executive (NIHE), NIE, the health sector, and car retailing and engineering companies. The FEC and ECNI strategies have focused on private sector concerns. Analysis of the first series of monitoring returns in 1990 suggested to the Commission that the major labour market problem was male Catholic underrepresentation. The Commission had learnt from the early monitoring returns that private sector employment in Northern Ireland was concentrated in large concerns; in 1990, 7 per cent of employers with a workforce above 250 people accounted for almost 50 per cent of total monitored private sector employment. Catholic participation amongst this group of large firms was also lower in 1990, at 32.5 per cent, than in the private sector overall, at 34.1 per cent.

The FEC identified for investigation a group of 47 large private sector concerns, each employing more than 250 employees at that time. This group of concerns was selected to represent different industrial sectors and geographic locations. The purpose of the investigations was to assist the Commission in considering what, if any, action for promoting equality of opportunity ought to be taken by the investigated concerns. Of the 47, 39 resulted in Article 13 agreements, 2 had formal Commission agreements and the remaining 6 companies deregistered in the course of the investigations. Many investigations continued for a number of years, resulting in an ongoing pattern of agreements amongst the investigated firms, with the most co-operative firms signing agreements early on, and less co-operative firms signing agreements as late as the mid-1990s.

Table 7.1

Summary of agreements, 1990–2000

Year	Industry		Economic Sector Services		Public Sector		Annual Total	
	No. of Agmnts	Mean Size*	No. of Agmnts	Mean Size	No. of Agmnts	Mean Size	No. of Agmnts	Mean Size
1990					2	14,490	2	14,490
1991					1	162	1	162
1992	3	4,149			3	4,021	6	4,085
1993	5	346	2	1,427	1	292	8	610
1994	10	444	4	237	2	139	16	354
1995	13	469	4	962	10	497	27	552
1996	13	406	8	1,066	10	226	31	519
1997	39	268	21	273	8	2,526	68	535
1998	40	309	12	190	5	1,169	57	360
1999	30	161	27	151	13	537	70	227
2000	22	211	11	90	3	1,670	36	296
Sector totals	175	356	89	328	58	1,501	322	555

*The average number of workers employed by firms signing agreements in that year

Source: FEC and ECNI

We can see this activity reflected in Figures 7.1 to 7.6 and in Table 7.1; in the early years, roughly 1990–4, Commission activity was focused upon the public sector and large private sector firms. The earlier FEA investigations may be related to the large public sector agreements reached at the time, including the 1988 agreement with the NICS which continued under the FEC,[6] and the 1992 agreement with the RUC. FEC investigation activity is reflected in the Article 13 agreements reached in this period with large private sector employers. Three agreements were reached in 1992 with very large industrial employers, averaging over 4,000 workers each, which are presumably among the largest of the firms targeted by the early FEC investigations. Agreements in this period were focused particularly upon Catholic underrepresentation, with the majority reached in the traditionally male-dominated industrial sector.

Under Section 31 of the 1989 Act, and later under Article 55 of the 1998 Order, employers had a duty to complete a triennial review of employment composition and practices, to establish whether members of each community were enjoying fair participation and, if they were

Figure 7.1

Agreements reached – by community underrepresented, 1990–2000

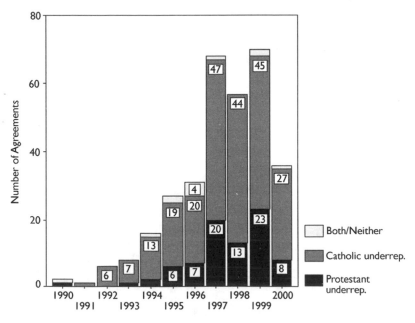

Source: FEC and ECNI

not, to establish with the FEC what steps would be taken to remedy this. The first reviews, from all public sector bodies with over 10 employees and all concerns employing more than 100 people (excepting those concerns under investigation), were received in 1993. The FEC examined reviews from selected employers to establish that they were using a reasonable determination of fair participation and taking appropriate affirmative action measures. Reviews were selected from a range of employers and evaluated to decide how best to target resources in accordance with the FEC's overall policy aims of proportionate representation for both communities in all types of employment, and the removal of segregation in the labour force. The reviews were evaluated to identify areas with both the need and the potential for change.

The FEC prioritised large companies in its activities responding to

Figure 7.2

Workforce covered by agreements – by community underrepresented, 1990–2000

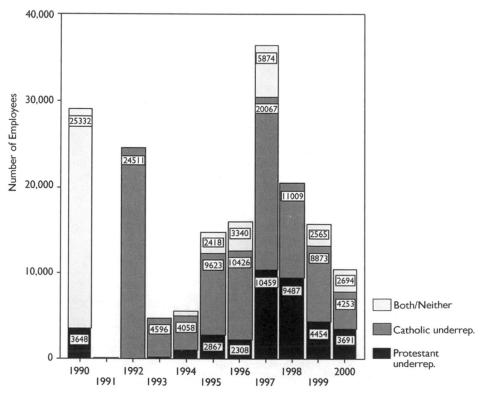

Source: FEC and ECNI

review reports, targeting those companies with high staff turnover, potential for change and where there was clear evidence of underrepresentation. Targets were established for the promotion of affirmative action in 78 private sector concerns with more than 250 employees. The public sector was also a priority, owing to its continuing importance within the Northern Ireland economy and labour market; affirmative action targets were established at 58 public sector concerns. The FEC moved down the size hierarchy through the 1990s, reviewing 100 concerns in the 101–250 employee band in 1995 and then targeting groups of employers in the 51–100 employee band in 1998. The FEC decided to focus upon securing voluntary agreements with these smaller employers.

For public sector organisations, affirmative action recommendations were made as follow-ups to their first reviews, and they were requested to respond in their second reviews. The majority of the resulting agreements were voluntary. In the private sector, Article 13 agreements were generally sought in order to promote openly the importance of affirmative action generally. Undertakings were also sought from

Figure 7.3

Agreements reached – by agreement type, 1990–2000

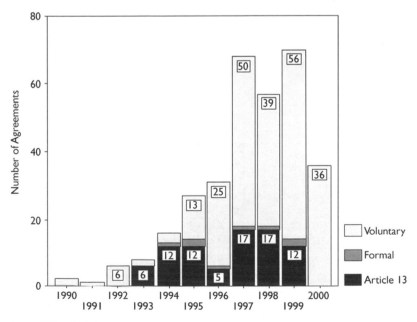

Source: FEC and ECNI

employers for other reasons, including size, strategic importance or lack of previous experience of working with the FEC. Some employers were willing to enter into Article 13 agreements to demonstrate their commitment to the principles of equality.

All affirmative action agreements included similar enforcement provisions, regardless of whether they were legally enforceable. In particular, agreements included a 'review of progress' clause, a provision for FEC staff to liaise with the employer and ensure that the agreed action was being undertaken, and to review regular reports on employment trends. For voluntary agreements, FEC staff reviewed the reports to ensure that good faith efforts were being implemented, and considered whether a legal undertaking should be sought if they were not. In the

Figure 7.4

Workforce covered by agreements – by agreement type, 1990–2000

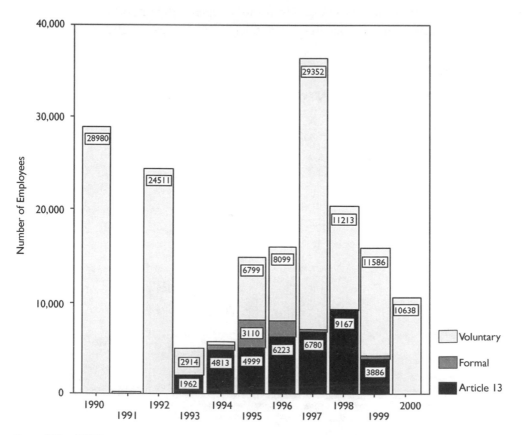

Source: FEC and ECNI

case of Article 13 agreements, an FEC committee reviewed reports to consider whether any further action was appropriate under the 1998 Order. As time progressed, the FEC resources became more engaged in ensuring the effective implementation of existing agreements than in reaching further new agreements.

The patterns of review–driven activity are clearly visible in Figures 7.1 to 7.6 and Table 7.1. The pace of new agreements accelerated after 1993, the year the first reviews were conducted, rising from 8 agreements in 1993 to 27 in 1995 and 68 in 1997. The three-year period 1997–9 was a time of intense activity, with approximately 60 agreements reached each year. Over half of the agreements under examination were reached in this period. The number of employees in firms covered by agreements also rose rapidly, from 4,876 in 1993 to 36,400 in 1997. The initial focus of private sector activity was in industry, where 44 agreements were signed before 1997, although the service sector was not neglected, with 18 agreements reached there between 1993 and 1996, including a group of 8 very large employers, with an average of over 1,000 employees each, in 1996. We can see the strategic

Figure 7.5

Agreements reached – by economic sector, 1990–2000

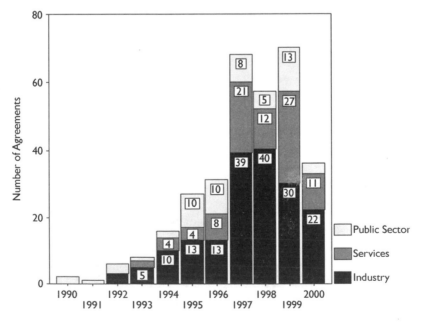

Source: FEC and ECNI

focus upon the largest firms; firms signing agreements in the mid-1990s employed on average over 400 workers each, compared with an average workforce of under 100 amongst firms without agreements. The majority of these early private sector agreements were legally enforceable Article 13 agreements. The continuing importance of the public sector is also visible; although activity was subdued here in 1993–4, while first reviews were being given consideration, larger numbers of agreements were reached in all years thereafter, including an important group of large public bodies in 1997.

In the latter half of the 1990s we see two trends reflecting the Commission's changing strategic priorities; the average size of private sector firms signing agreements fell rapidly from over 400 employees in 1996 to around 100 employees in 2000, while the total number of employees brought in under agreements fell rapidly from 1998 onwards. This

Figure 7.6

Workforce covered by agreements – by economic sector, 1990–2000

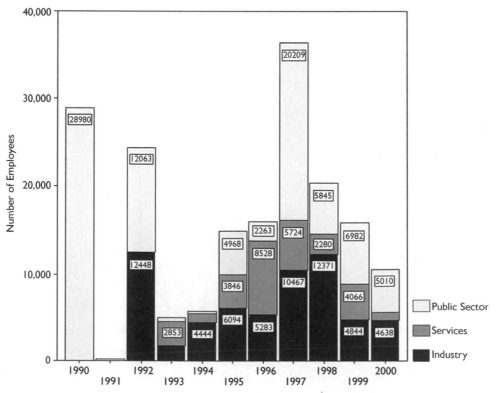

Source: FEC and ECNI

rapid fall in size, resulting from a shift in new agreement activity towards smaller firms, is accompanied by a growing emphasis upon voluntary agreements; while the majority of public sector agreements were voluntary throughout the decade, in the private sector voluntary agreements only predominate after 1996. In 2000, all agreements reached were voluntary. While new agreement activity shifted towards smaller firms, contact was maintained with the larger companies where agreements had been reached earlier, to ensure the continuing progress towards fair participation.

2: Is there an association between agreements and change?

Before we examine the impact agreements may have had, it is necessary to strike a cautionary note concerning the limitations of our statistical analysis. Any assessment we make is based upon aggregate data, which cannot take into account the varying conditions faced by individual firms. We have made no assessment of the population balance in local catchment areas, which varies very considerably between parts of Northern Ireland, such that a workforce with over 50 per cent representation from one group may still be considered underrepresented relative to the local population. Such an assessment will be an obvious priority for future research. Nor have we examined the geographical distribution of employment within individual firms; whilst some firms may possess many small sites spread across Northern Ireland, others of similar size may be concentrated in one site. There may be problems of internal segregation at some companies, or problems associated with the 'chill factor'– the various social and psychological factors that may discourage individuals from an underrepresented group from applying to a firm – such as historical associations with a different group, real or expected discrimination from workmates in the opposite community, or disapproval from friends and family. Chill factors may be more prevalent in firms working with the FEC than in the employer population as a whole, as many of the firms signing agreements were selected precisely due to their history of underrepresentation of one community. As a result, chill factors may depress the overall rates of change within the agreement firm population, although not necessarily because agreements are not working; small shifts in employment balance at such firms may reflect much larger shifts in practices and perceptions.

The statistical analysis of the possible effects of agreements will proceed in three stages. We initially analyse the distribution of agreement firms and employment, and how this has changed over the decade. We then examine patterns of employment growth, to see if firms signing agreements follow a distinct employment growth pattern. Finally we examine how the proportions employed from each community have altered over the past decade at firms with agreements. As we have seen, the great majority of agreements reached between firms and the Commission are one of two types: Article 13 agreements, which are formal, legally enforceable arrangements, and voluntary agreements, which are informal and non-enforceable. At several points, we will examine these two types of agreement separately to see if differences result in differing patterns of association with change.

The distribution of agreement firms: segregation and integration

The histograms in this section show the distribution of the firms who reached either Catholic or Protestant underrepresentation agreements, compared with the distributions in the overall monitored workforce. A more detailed analysis of trends in monitoring returns can be found in Chapter 2. To limit the effects of a changing firm population, only those concerns that have provided monitoring returns for the whole decade have been included; firms which signed agreements and subsequently deregistered are excluded from the analysis. Examining Figures 7.7 to 7.10 we can see similar changes in both distributions: large declines in the number of highly segregated firms and a gradual movement towards more integrated employment. We calculated the total number of firms employing less than 25 per cent of one community by adding together the number of firms in the most segregated parts of the distribution; the five columns on the far left of each figure and the five columns on the far right. Amongst monitored firms without agreements, the total, shown in Figures 7.9 and 7.10, fell from 561 in 1990 to 484 in 2000, a fall of 8 per cent, from 57 per cent to 49 per cent of the total. The firms reaching agreements with the FEC, shown in Figures 7.7 and 7.8, started with higher segregation, but saw it fall further over the decade. In 1990, 203 of these firms, 73 per cent of the total, employed less than 25 per cent of one community. By 2000, this had fallen to 177 firms, 63 per cent of the total; a 10 per cent drop. This is impressive when we consider that the agreement firms were also on average much larger employers, so changes in community proportions involve larger numbers of jobs.

Most of this decline was concentrated in the most segregated sections of the distribution. Again the change in the distribution of firms with agreements was significantly larger. The number of monitored firms employing less than 10 per cent of either community, calculated by adding the two columns on the far left and the two on the far right of Figures 7.9 and 7.10, fell from 252 in 1990 to 192 in 2000, a fall of over 6 per cent, from 26 per cent to under 20 per cent of the total. The number of agreement firms in similar circumstances fell from 85 in 1990 to 49 in 2000, a fall of 12 per cent, from 30 per cent to 18 per cent of the total. Extreme segregation was more common in 1990 among agreement firms than in the general monitored population, but fell twice as far over the decade. By 2000, extreme segregation was less common amongst firms with FEC agreements than in the monitored workforce. As is noted in Chapter 2, segregation is declining generally in the Northern Ireland labour force. Amongst both monitored and

Figure 7.7

Distribution of agreement firms, 1990

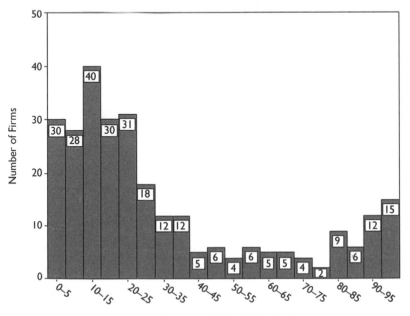

Percentage Catholics Employed

Source: FEC and ECNI

agreement firms, underrepresentation of one community remains a common phenomenon, although the severity of this underrepresentation has declined considerably. The declines were more rapid amongst the firms that had reached agreements with the FEC, suggesting that agreements may have had an impact in reducing underrepresentation. We should note, however, that firms with agreements remained significantly more segregated in 2000 than the monitored workforce. Despite this, the overall trend is clear: movement towards a more representative mix of communities in the workplace. Affirmative action agreements certainly do not hinder this trend, and seem to accelerate it.

Employment growth at agreement firms

Northern Ireland's population is growing more rapidly than the UK average, and the total working-age population grew by 9 per cent between 1990 and 2000 (NISRA, 2001). The region enjoyed strong employment growth in the 1990s, with employment rising 13 per cent

Figure 7.8

Distribution of agreement firms, 2000

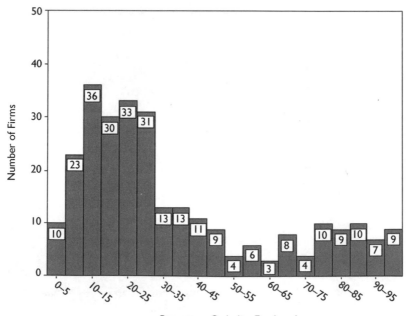

Source: FEC and ECNI

over the decade. The monitored workforce grew roughly in line with the general economy, with employment rising by 42,350, or 12 per cent. Catholic employment rose more rapidly, by 32,700 (28 per cent), than Protestant employment, which rose by 10,300 (4.8 per cent). The firms with agreements behaved very differently from the monitored firms.[7] The agreement workforce grew far more slowly than the over-all monitored workforce, rising by 2,800, or 2 per cent, over the entire decade. There was a large divergence between the two communities: Catholic employment in the agreement workforce rose rapidly, by 8,000 (18.8 per cent), while Protestant employment declined, falling by over 4,000 (4 per cent). There were also large differences between the two main agreement groups. Employment at Article 13 firms grew a little more rapidly than in the overall monitored workforce, rising by 3,800 (or 13 per cent) over the decade. Growth was roughly divided between the two communities, as it is in the monitored work-force more generally: Catholic employment grew rapidly, by 2,800 (32 per cent); Protestant employment grew much more slowly, by

Figure 7.9

Distribution of monitored firms without agreements, 1990

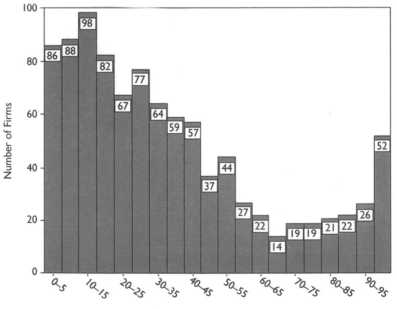

Source: FEC and ECNI

700 (3.7 per cent). In contrast, at voluntary agreement firms, overall employment levels stagnated over the decade, falling by 900 (0.8 per cent), perhaps due to the number of large voluntary agreements in the shrinking public sector. This overall pattern masks divergent trends: strong Catholic employment growth, rising by over 5,200 (15.4 per cent); and declining Protestant employment, falling by over 4,700 (6.1 per cent).

Figure 7.11 shows annual employment growth in the monitored workforce. We can see the brisk progress of the Northern Ireland economy in the 1990s: after a sharp decline in 1993, the monitored workforce grew steadily by an average of over 5,000 per year between 1994 and 2000. Employment growth in the two communities has diverged, as we would expect given different rates of demographic change, and the efforts to correct for previous Catholic underrepresentation in the labour force. Catholic employment growth continued through the early 1990s recession, with 2,000 new employees added in 1993, when overall monitored employment shrank by 4,000. Since 1994,

Figure 7.10

Distribution of monitored firms without agreements, 2000

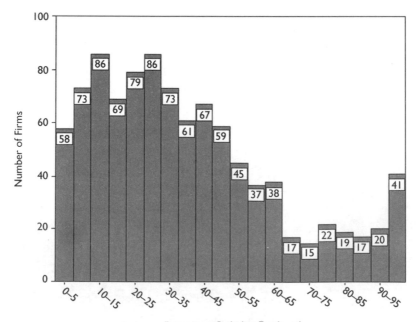

Percentage Catholics Employed

Source: FEC and ECNI

employment growth has averaged over 4,000 per year, with a dip to half this level in 2000. Protestant employment fell sharply in 1993, declining by over 6,000, and has grown more slowly, by an average of under 2,000 per annum between 1994 and 1997; growth accelerated in the last years of the decade, rising to over 3,000 in 1999. Although it has narrowed in the last years of the series, there has thus been a consistent gap in monitored employment growth between the two communities throughout the 1990s, reflecting the steady gains Catholics have made in the labour market. By the end of the decade, the Catholic monitored workforce had risen from 116,096 (33.0 per cent of total monitored employment) to 148,763 (37.8 per cent).

Figures 7.12 and 7.13 show the corresponding trends at firms with Catholic and Protestant underrepresentation agreements. In Figure 7.12, employment growth at firms reaching Catholic underrepresentation agreements was slower than in the overall monitored workforce, perhaps because many of these agreements were focused in the slow-growing manufacturing sector, and the public sector, where employment declined. Total employment at these firms, which stood at 77,607 in 1990, declined sharply in 1992, and did not begin to recover

Figure 7.11

Employment growth in the monitored workforce, 1990–2000

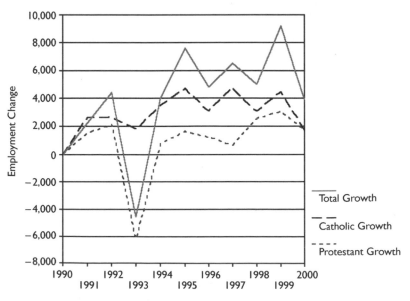

Source: FEC and ECNI

until 1995. Employment growth was slow and unsteady in the late 1990s, with further declines in 1997 and again in 1999–2000. Total employment in 2000, 76,245, was lower than in 1990. By contrast, Catholic employment in these firms grew strongly throughout the decade. Total Catholic employment was 12,612 in 1990, and grew by over 500 per year throughout the decade, with two dips in 1992 and 2000, when employment declined by around 100 in each case. By 2000, Catholic employment had grown to 16,177, a rise of over 3,500, or 28 per cent, despite stagnation in total employment. Protestant employment, by contrast, declined nearly continuously during the period. Beginning the decade at 62,163, employment fell by nearly 3,000 in the 1992 recession, and continued to decline there-after, with periods of very mild growth in 1995–6 and 1998. Protestant employment at these firms in 2000 was 57,074, over 5,000 lower than in 1990, an 8 per cent drop. Firms with Catholic underrepresentation agreements have seen rapid Catholic employment growth, despite a decline in total employment. Catholic employment proportions rose

Figure 7.12

Employment growth at Catholic underrepresentation agreement firms, 1990–2000

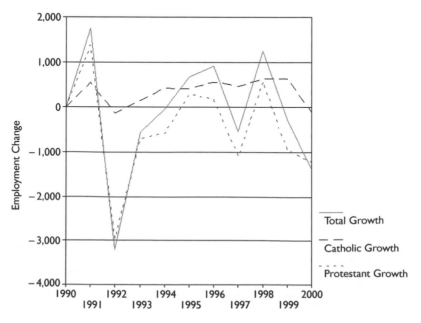

Source: FEC and ECNI

from 16.9 per cent to 22.1 per cent of total employment at these firms. The evidence here suggests that Catholic underrepresentation agreements have had a significant impact on Catholic employment growth in the 1990s. Catholic employment rose as fast in agreement firms as in the monitored workforce, despite declining total employment at these firms.

The pattern among Protestant underrepresentation agreements, shown in Figure 7.13, is rather different. The total employed by these firms was much lower, standing at 23,078 in 1990. Total employment growth, although erratic, was more positive, with employment rising every year from 1995, at an average of over 400 per annum; employment at the end of the decade had risen to 25,475. For most of the decade, Catholic employment growth at these firms was consistently faster than Protestant employment growth. After 1997, a year when Catholic employment rose by 834 and Protestant employment fell by 61, Catholic employment growth dropped sharply and was overtaken by Protestant employment growth. The figure suggests that in the

Figure 7.13

Employment growth at Protestant underrepresentation agreement firms, 1990–2000

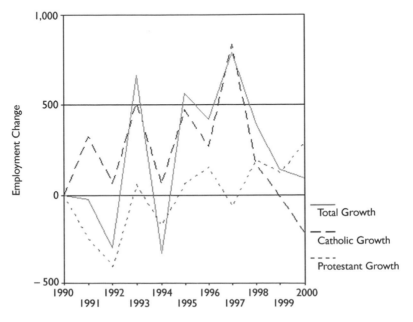

Source: FEC and ECNI

late 1990s progress has been made in correcting hiring disparities; Protestant underrepresentation agreements were reached on average later than Catholic underrepresentation agreements, which may explain the persistence of disparities into the mid-1990s. There remains, however, a growing disparity in employment proportions; the Catholic proportion of employment at these firms has risen from 62.7 per cent in 1990 to 66.5 per cent in 2000. Despite this, there has been a clear reversal in employment growth trends over the 1990s, with a considerable acceleration in Protestant employment growth in the latter half of the decade, when most of the firms considered here were reaching or had reached agreements.

Figures 7.14 and 7.15 illustrate the changes in employment at firms with Catholic underrepresentation agreements only.[8] We can see some important differences between the two groups. The Article 13 agreement firms are the smaller group: in 1990, employment at these firms totalled 23,032, compared with 49,808 for voluntary agreement firms. They had a very difficult start to the decade, with total employment

Figure 7.14

Employment growth, Article 13 Catholic underrepresentation agreements, 1990–2000

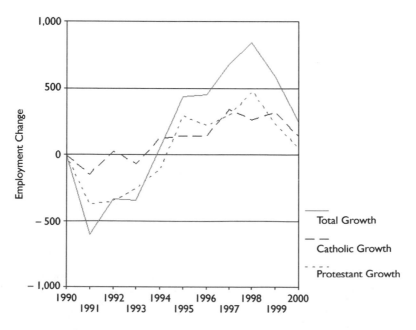

Source: FEC and ECNI

levels declining for three years running in 1991–3 (see Figure 7.14). In the second half of the decade, firms enjoyed strong employment growth, with employment levels rising by more than 500 a year in the period 1996–9; the growth rate then slowed again in 2000. Total employment rose by 2,049 (8.9 per cent) over the decade. The growth in employment was shared between the two communities. Catholic employment fell less severely during the recession, falling by less than 200 between 1990 and 1993. After 1993, Catholic employment growth ran at around 140 per year in 1994–6, accelerating to over 300 per year in 1997–9, decelerating again to 143 in 2000. Total Catholic employment rose by over 1,300 (27 per cent), from 4,937 in 1990 to 6,257 in 2000. Protestant employment declined by over 1,000 between 1990 and 1994. Since then, employment growth has been strong, averaging over 250 per year in 1995–2000, with a peak in 1998 when 477 Protestants were hired. Total Protestant employment rose by over 500 (3 per cent) over the decade, from 17,488 to 18,010. The total numbers of Catholics and Protestants hired by these firms in the later 1990s were

Figure 7.15

Employment growth, voluntary Catholic underrepresentation agreements, 1990–2000

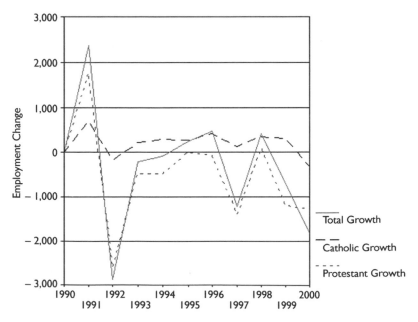

Source: FEC and ECNI

roughly similar, although this represents a larger proportional increase for the previously underrepresented Catholics. The overall proportion of Catholics employed at Article 13 firms rose from 22.0 per cent of the workforce in 1990 to 25.8 per cent in 2000.

A very different pattern is visible amongst the voluntary agreement firms (see Figure 7.15). Here, total employment has grown very slowly; after a very sharp drop in 1992, total employment was effectively stagnant, with years of slow growth offset by sharp declines in 1997 and 1999–2000. Total employment fell by 3,400 (6 per cent), from 54,575 in 1990 to 51,164 in 2000, possibly due to the predominance of voluntary agreements in the public sector, where employment levels fell through most of the 1990s. While total employment stagnated, Catholic employment grew consistently; after a very sharp rise in 1991 and a shallow fall in 1992, growth averaged about 280 per year between 1993 and 1999, before declining by over 300 in 2000. Catholic employment rose by nearly 2,200, or 28.5 per cent, over the decade, from 7,675 to 9,860. By contrast, after a sharp rise in 1991, Protestant employment fell nearly continually throughout the decade, falling by over 5,600, or 12.5 per cent, from 44,675 in 1990 to 39,064 in 2000. The overall proportion of Catholics employed in these firms rose from 14.7 per cent of the workforce in 1990 to 20.2 per cent in 2000.

In both sets of Catholic underrepresentation agreements we can see a consistent rise in the number of Catholics employed, although the groups of firms involved seem to be facing rather different economic circumstances. The growth rates for Catholic employment were as strong or stronger than those seen in the overall monitored workforce, despite considerably slower overall growth amongst both groups of firms. Thus, if Catholic employment growth is a goal of Catholic underrepresentation agreements, then aggregate figures suggest the Commission strategy has met with some success.

Workplace integration at agreement firms

The other goal the Commission may pursue is increased workplace integration, which may lead to a greater degree of contact between individuals from the two communities. The histograms we have previously analysed provided some evidence indicating that greater integration may be occurring – the number of firms with highly segregated workforces has been declining, as has the number of workers working in segregated workplaces. Table 7.2 shows the changes in the mean percentage of Catholics working for each firm, for all firms with underrepresentation agreements and a full eleven-year set of monitoring returns; a total of 208 firms with Catholic underrepresentation agreements and 72 firms with Protestant underrepresentation agreements. We should expect the firms with agreements to move in the direction of the overall population mean, and for this movement to accelerate in the second half of the decade, when the majority of firms sampled were reaching or had reached agreements.

In Table 7.2, we can see that the mean proportions employed are in both cases moving in the direction of increased integration over the decade. At firms with Catholic underrepresentation agreements, the average percentage of Catholics employed rose consistently through the decade, by a total of 4.2 per cent, from 17.5 per cent in 1990 to 21.7 per cent in 2000. The rate of change accelerated slightly in the second half, with a 1.7 per cent change in 1990–5 and a 2.2 per cent change in 1996–2000. At firms with Protestant underrepresentation agreements, the average per cent of Catholics falls 1.9 per cent over the decade, from 78.8 per cent in 1990 to 76.9 per cent in 2000. There were, however, very different trends in the two halves of the decade. In 1990–5, the mean percentage of Catholics employed rose slowly, by 0.5 per cent over five years, peaking in 1995 at 79.3 per cent. In 1996–2000, this proportion fell by 1.8 per cent in total.

Table 7.2

Workplace integration

| | AGREEMENT TYPE | |
Year	Protestant Underrepresentation Mean Percentage Catholics Employed	Catholic Underrepresentation Mean Percentage Catholics Employed
1990	78.83	17.49
1991	79.38	17.76
1992	79.29	17.95
1993	79.42	18.36
1994	79.11	18.84
1995	79.25	19.24
1996	78.66	19.50
1997	78.41	20.27
1998	77.70	20.65
1999	77.18	21.17
2000	76.88	21.68

Source: FEC and ECNI

There has clearly been change at the agreement firms in the direction one might expect; namely, towards greater integration. The pattern of change also seems to be as might be expected: change accelerates in the second half of the decade, when most firms have reached agreements, as compared with the first half. The rate of change, however, is quite slow: 2 to 4 per cent over a decade. There are at least three important factors that may be contributing to this. First, the FEC sought to sign agreements with the most segregated and slowest changing firms. This creates a 'selection bias' problem: the agreement and non-agreement firms are not the same. Firms with agreements are often precisely those that were less likely to change in the first place, therefore any change at all may be significant, while the firms without agreements were often passed over precisely because they were more likely to change without specific attention. We cannot quantify the effect of such a bias without detailed information on the individual firms, although we can say that such a bias would become more severe the more successful the FEC was at identifying and reaching agreements with slow-changing firms. The FEC could have thus become a 'victim of its own success': the better it was at selecting hard cases, the harder it became to achieve rapid rates of change.

The firms selected by the FEC were chosen on the basis of size as well as segregation; high priority was given to the largest employers, particularly in the earlier agreements. As a result, the agreement firms were on average very considerably larger than the non-agreement group; the average workforce at agreement firms is above 300, compared with under 100 in non-agreement firms. This makes it much more difficult to shift the proportions employed; achieving a proportional shift is harder at large firms, as it means a much larger change in numbers hired. If one employs 50 workers – 5 Catholic and 45 Protestant, and one hires 10 Catholics, the proportion of Catholics employed will rise from 10 per cent to 25 per cent. If one employs 500 workers in the same ratio, achieving the same shift in proportions means hiring an extra 100 Catholics (and no Protestants). The large average size of agreement firms may explain the disparity between the previously noted consistent growth in employment and the relatively slow shifts in proportions employed. Even if considerable numbers of the under-represented group are being hired year on year, their proportion of total employment at large employers will rise only slowly, due simply to their size; just as a large bath will fill only slowly even if the taps are fully open.

The agreement firms were not only larger, they also had a different sectoral balance to the non–agreement firms. Agreements were focused in the slow-growing industrial sector and the declining public sector, particularly in the first half of the decade. The service sector, the source of most recent employment growth in Northern Ireland, was under-represented in agreements, and barely represented at all in early agreements. If, as would seem reasonable, shifts in proportions are more easily achieved at firms with rapid employment growth, due to greater workforce turnover, hiring and so on, then the underrepresentation of the service sector within the agreement firm population is likely to act as a brake on shifts in employment proportions.

Table 7.3 compares the two major agreement types for Catholic underrepresentation agreements only. Voluntary agreements appear to be associated with a greater rate of change in average Catholic proportions than Article 13 agreements; the proportion of Catholics employed rose by 1.9 per cent at Article 13 firms, and by 5.1 per cent at voluntary agreement firms. There were divergent trends of change in the two major agreement types. At Article 13 firms, the share of Catholics employed remained roughly stable until 1995, then rose

Table 7.3

Workplace integration, by agreement type, Catholic underrepresentation agreements

| | CATHOLIC UNDERREPRESENTATION AGREEMENTS – BY AGREEMENT TYPE | |
| | Article 13 | Voluntary |
Year	Mean Percentage Catholics Employed	Mean Percentage Catholics Employed
1990	19.07	16.87
1991	18.99	17.29
1992	18.93	17.56
1993	18.76	18.21
1994	19.32	18.66
1995	19.09	19.29
1996	19.43	19.52
1997	20.33	20.25
1998	20.54	20.69
1999	20.86	21.28
2000	20.96	21.96

Source: FEC and ECNI

steadily. At voluntary agreement firms, share of Catholics employed rose continuously through the decade, with no major shift in the pace of change in the second half. Much of this pattern of change is related to the trends we have already examined in employment growth. We see a greater adjustment in Catholic proportions in voluntary agreement firms than in those with Article 13 agreements because, while Catholic numbers were increasing in both agreement groups, overall employment was rising at Article 13 firms but declining at voluntary agreement firms. In the former, Catholics have become a larger share of a growing pie, in the latter a larger share of a shrinking pie. The latter group of firms will see a larger shift in community employment proportions, but this may be because of economic circumstances rather than the relative effectiveness of the two agreement types.

It is not clear whether the divergences between the two main types of agreement are a result of differences in the effectiveness of agreement enforcement methods, or differences in the characteristics of the firms under agreement. Much of what we have said in the previous section concerning selection and sectoral biases could also apply to the two agreement types. Article 13 agreements were mainly reached with larger and/or less co-operative firms; the Commission employed these criteria explicitly in the selection of firms for these agreements, while aiming primarily to secure voluntary agreements with smaller firms. A different range of sizes and different attitudes towards employment reform may have played a role in the slower rate of change, as well as differing economic circumstances. The two groups of firms may therefore not be strictly comparable. It remains possible, however, that the relative success of voluntary agreements is related to the strategies employed by the FEC in enforcing these agreements; perhaps agreements that emphasise informality and co-operation are more likely to induce co-operation from firms.

Conclusions

The preliminary statistical analyses presented here provide indications that significant changes occurred in the employment growth and community balance of firms with agreements, with trends towards more balanced and integrated employment. There are three main areas where research is needed to build on these findings: changes outside the monitored labour force, changes within the monitored labour force, and institutional changes within the ECNI. We were unable for reasons of time to pursue these issues. We hope to address them in further research.

There were important economic, social and political trends that we have not been able to examine adequately, including the economic transformations driving shifts in employment patterns, and what these may mean for the achievement of fair participation. Examples include the underlying causes of the boom in service sector employment, for example the rise of call centres as large employers, and the reforms responsible for the decline in public sector employment, which appears recently to have been reversed. The major improvements in Catholic educational performance outlined in Chapter 4 will have contributed significantly to Catholic employability and reduction in the unemployment gap. We have not considered the shifts in the geographical distribution of firms and employment, or how these were related to employment growth and to shifts in employment balances. Similarly we have not considered the residential distribution of the two communities through Northern Ireland, how this has changed and what the implications of these changing distributions might have been for employment growth and employment integration. We have not analysed the chill factor operating in certain firms, industrial sectors or geographical areas. We have also not been able to incorporate the impact of the changing political environment of Northern Ireland in the 1990s, in particular any effects upon the social and economic environment arising from the Good Friday Agreement and the absence of sustained violence by most paramilitary groups since 1994. Nine years of more peaceful relations between the two communities may have had a considerable cumulative impact upon the political and social environment.

There are potential problems with excluding the workforce whose community background remains undetermined – we do not know whether this group remained roughly constant in its relative size and community balance or changed as the decade went on.[9] If the undetermined proportions of the monitored workforce were changing, it would have considerable effects on the trends analysed. Where we see changes in employment, we also have no information about the quality of jobs taken up; representation might have been growing at firms where the underrepresented group simply took up positions on the lowest rungs of the career ladder and did not advance. Where it appears that employers are becoming more integrated, we must make this observation without possessing information concerning internal segregation, and how this has changed. Internal segregation, between different geographical locations or between different employment levels within a single firm, might have been a crucial element of employment segregation, particularly at the largest employers. We also do not know how working practices changed at various employers; it may be that many firms made genuine reforms to their working practices, but these reforms had not resulted in any visible change in employment levels or proportions up to 2000. Such genuine efforts at reform would not be visible using our current methods of analysis.

There is, finally, a great deal we do not know about the changing priorities and institutional structure of the FEC. We know little concerning the approaches taken by the FEC towards enforcement, and how these approaches were affected by the type of agreement being enforced or by the various other factors affecting individual firms. It would be valuable to learn more about the day-to-day policies and priorities employed by former FEC employees in working with firms. We also do not know how the activities of the FEC were affected by the creation in 2000 of the ECNI, which took over the FEC's employment responsibilities, but has a much broader remit.

However, taking all these factors into account, we may tentatively point towards links between the activity of the FEC and changes in the patterns of employment growth and community balance at firms. The analysis suggests a move towards greater employment of the under-represented community and greater overall employment integration in firms reaching agreements concerning both Protestant and Catholic underrepresentation. While further research is needed to confirm and clarify these trends, the evidence from monitoring returns data does suggest the FEC enjoyed some success in its attempts to achieve fair participation through the negotiation and maintenance of affirmative action agreements with private sector firms and public sector concerns. It is likely that the work of the FEC was an integral part of the processes driving change in the Northern Ireland labour market in the 1990s.

8
Review of fair employment case law[1]

BARRY FITZPATRICK

Introduction

The purpose of this chapter is to examine the contribution of the Fair Employment Tribunal to the development of fair employment law in Northern Ireland. It was through the Fair Employment (Northern Ireland) Act 1989 that the FET came into existence as a specialist tribunal dealing with religious and political discrimination cases in employment. At the same time, an 'individual litigation' route was established, whereby complainants could bring their applications to the FET. This chapter is largely concerned with the extent to which this case law has contributed to the redistributive objectives of the legislation, but also considers wider issues of religious and political discrimination law.

The original Fair Employment Act 1976, through the establishment of the Fair Employment Agency (FEA), envisaged an 'agency investigative' model (Magill and Rose, 1996: 9–13), reminiscent of the model adopted in the Race Relations Act 1965. It was only after the 1987 SACHR report on fair employment (SACHR, 1987: 133–53) that the Northern Irish 'fair employment' model, through the 1989 Act,[2] undertook a *legal* 'metamorphosis' into the same 'individual litigation' model which had been adopted in relation to sex and race discrimination in Great Britain in the mid-1970s (Hepple, 1990). It must also be noted that the 1989 Act continued to adopt a less adversarial investigative model than that encountered in the sex and race discrimination models.[3] What is now the 'FETO model' also contains what McCrudden has described as the 'statutory novelties' of monitoring and review, 'fair participation' and affirmative action, which are not found in the other regimes (McCrudden 1992, 184). It is these factors which mark out religious and political discrimination law in Northern Ireland as having more of a focus on a 'redistributive approach' towards labour market composition than the other equality law regimes (Fitzpatrick, Hegarty and Maxwell, 1996: 153; Hepple, 1990, 412; McCrudden, 1992: 199–200).

It was with the establishment of a specialist FET in the 1989 Act that any review of fair employment case law could commence (SACHR, 1987: 142–7).[4] As part of a second SACHR review of fair employment (SACHR, 1997), Bell undertook an extensive and incisive review of the case law of the FET between 1990 and 1996 (Bell, 1996). Many of the basic principles of religious and political discrimination law in Northern Ireland were established during that period. It is proposed in this chapter to build on the work which Bell has already undertaken to chart the further development of FET case law in the second half of the 1990s and into the twenty-first century. As with Bell's analysis, this is not an empirical analysis of the FET's work but rather its purpose is 'to provide information about current interpretations, and also to analyse their implications for the legislation's remedial and strategic ambitions' (Bell, 1996: 71).[5] Bell divided her work into two main parts: the first, 'The Interpretation and Application of Key Definitions in the Acts', and second, 'Employers' Liability: Influencing Employment Practices'. Since Bell's analysis was published, the major development in religious and political discrimination law has been in the FETO, which consolidated and revised the earlier Acts. Compared to the recommendations of SACHR, let alone earlier proposals by the Committee on the Administration of Justice, the FETO 'reforms' were very modest (Fitzpatrick, 1999).[6] By way of conclusion, some thought will be given to the extent to which the 'agenda' of religious and political discrimination law in Northern Ireland has been advanced since the 1989 Act and, in particular, since the mid-1990s, and to the extent to which the prospect of single equality legislation may affect this agenda.

The interpretation and application of key definitions in the Acts and Order

In what is now the FETO, the 'individual litigation' model of religious and political discrimination law follows closely the model in sex and race discrimination law. Although there are other features of the FETO that distinguish it from the model prevalent in discrimination law in Great Britain, and imported into Northern Irish discrimination law, the enforcement of individual rights is not one of them. The policy appeared to be that the provision of innovations in the legislative structure could be portrayed as specific to Northern Ireland but that the traditional concepts of discrimination law had to be protected from 'read across implications' into discrimination law in Great Britain (Hepple, 1990: 411). So also it is arguable that, in contrast to the sex and race equality regimes, the non-discrimination principle was not the primary focus of the fair employment regime but rather the 're-distributive' principles of 'fair participation', 'affirmative action' and 'equality of opportunity' (McCrudden, 1992: 191). Hence, we find provisions on direct discrimination, interpreted to include harassment, victimisation and indirect discrimination. So also we find a range of exceptions, two identified by Bell as of particular note, namely affirmative action and security certificates.[7]

Direct discrimination

The principle of direct discrimination lies at the core of the FETO model. In a redistributively focused regime, it can be anticipated that very many cases will concentrate on whether members of the perceived disadvantaged group are denied employment opportunities by reason of their religion or political opinion. The manner in which the definition of direct discrimination is couched in the FETO has allowed for its extensive use and some (but not all) of the difficulties encountered in sex discrimination law have been avoided.

At the core of the British definition of direct discrimination lies a comparative method. Discrimination is established when it can be shown that the applicant has suffered 'less favourable treatment' on one of the prohibited grounds. Article 3(1) of the Sex Discrimination Order 1976 (SDO) provides that '[a] person discriminates against a woman in any circumstances relevant for the purposes of any provision of this Order if (a) on the ground of sex he treats her less favourably than he treats or would treat a man'. It is indicative of the subtle distinctions between statutory regimes that ostensibly similar terminology in what is now the FETO can result in a significant, more wide-ranging provision in the FETO than in the SDO. Hence, Article 3(2) of the FETO provides that '[a] person discriminates against another person on the ground of religious belief or political opinion in any circumstances relevant for the purposes of this Order if (a) on either of those grounds he treats that other less favourably than he treats or would treat other persons'. Both regimes then set out the 'basis of comparison' as in Article 3(3), namely, 'A comparison of the cases of persons of different religious belief or political opinion under paragraph (2) must be such that the relevant circumstances in the one case are the same, or not materially different, in the other.'[8]

Although both definitions are symmetrical, in that the regimes apply equally to discrimination against men as much as women (Article 4 of the SDO), and Protestants and unionists as much as Catholics and nationalists, the comparison in the SDO must be between a woman and a man, while the comparison in the FETO can be between the applicant and any other person, and the ground of religious belief or political opinion does not even have to be that of either party to the comparison. Hence, in *Re Northern Ireland Electricity Service's Application* (2 September 1987 QBD, per Nicholson J) it was established that the phrase 'on grounds of religious belief or political opinion' was capable of covering the belief or opinion of the alleged victim, the alleged perpetrator or of some relevant third party. As Bell points out, earlier decisions of the FET established that the belief or opinion at issue could include that of a third party such as the wife of the applicant (*Meek* v. *Fire Authority for Northern Ireland*, 22 July 1992 FET) or of a client or customer (*Neely* v. *Duncan*, 29 November 1991 FET). Even within the statutory framework, the definition of 'religious belief or political opinion' is broadened still further by way of Article 2(3) of the FETO, which provides that these terms 'include references to (a) his supposed religious belief or political opinion and (b) the absence or supposed absence of any, or any particular, religious belief or political opinion'.

Nonetheless, the 'relevant circumstances' test has caused difficulties in both Northern Irish 'fair employment' and sex equality law. In *Chief Constable of the Royal Ulster Constabulary* v. *Sergeant A* ([2001] NI 261 (NICA)) and *Chief Constable of the Royal Ulster Constabulary* v *Shamoon* ([2001] IRLR 520 (NICA)), the Court of Appeal adopted a narrow approach to suitable comparators, reversing tribunal findings of direct discrimination. On appeal to the House of Lords in *Shamoon* (*Shamoon* v. *Chief Constable of the RUC* ([2003] IRLR 285 (HL)), the House sustained a narrow approach to the 'relevant circumstances' test in Article 7 of the SDO. However, it also promoted extensive use of the 'hypothetical comparator' approach, thereby encouraging a wide-ranging examination of whether employment decisions have been taken on grounds of sex or, in this context, belief or opinion.[9]

The vast bulk of the FET's case law has concerned anticipated issues of Northern Irish religious beliefs and political opinions specific to Northern Ireland. For example, in *Paisley* v. *Arts Council of Northern Ireland and others* (28 July 1998 FET), the FET concluded that the manner in which the applicant was interviewed was discriminatory on grounds both of her membership of the Free Presbyterian Church and the Democratic Unionist Party. In relation to 'religious belief', it has also been non-contentious that the definition could include a 'Born Again Christian' (*Kennedy* v. *Gallaher Ltd*, 17 December 1991 FET)[10] and a Hindu (*Sudhir Kumar Tundon* v. *James P Corry (Holdings) Ltd*).[11] Greater controversy has surrounded the scope of the definition of 'political opinion'. Within the context of political opinion specific to Northern Ireland, the legislation only provides a limitation to the scope of 'political opinion' in relation to the 'approval or acceptance of the use of violence for political ends connected with the affairs of Northern Ireland' (FETO Article 4(4)). Kerr J concluded, in *In the Matter of Seamus Treacy and Barry Macdonald* ([2000] NI 330 (QBD)), that claims of discrimination on grounds of political opinion had to be treated with a sensitivity that might not be required in relation to other 'immutable' discrimination grounds. Hence, not every requirement with which an applicant disagreed on political grounds, in this case a refusal by two barristers to make the then necessary affirmation in order to become Queen's Counsel, could form the basis of a finding of political discrimination.

The scope of 'political opinion' is not restricted to the Northern Irish context. In *McKay* v. *Northern Ireland Public Service Alliance* ([1994] NI 103, [1995] IRLR 146 (NICA)), the applicant successfully claimed unlawful discrimination on grounds of his 'broad left' political opinions. Kelly LJ concluded that 'political opinion envisaged by the fair employment legislation is that which relates to one of the opposing ways of conducting the government of the state'. However, in *Gill* v. *Northern Ireland Council for Ethnic Minorities* (27 June 2001, [2001] IRLR 74 (NICA)), the Court of Appeal, relying on its judgment in *McKay*, rejected the conclusion that 'cultural values' could be encompassed within the definition of 'political opinion'. Nonetheless, the FET, in a preliminary ruling in *McKay* in *Neill* v. *Belfast Telegraph Ltd* (4 July 2002), accepted that a 'political opinion' that 'workers should have the right to collectively organise . . . and to engage in collective bargaining with management to promote workers' rights and interests' came within the statutory definition. These judicial pronouncements in *Treacy and Macdonald*, *McKay*, *Gill* and *Neill* reflect potentially significant difficulties in limiting the scope of 'non-immutable' grounds of discrimination such as 'religious belief' or 'political opinion'.

Those anticipating the scope of 'religion or belief' in the implementation of the Framework Employment Equality Directive 2000 (FEED) in their jurisdictions will find few examples of the limits of their scope in the Northern Irish case law. Even if any attempt to limit the scope of 'religious belief or political opinion' to their Northern Irish context failed, the extensive case law of the Northern Ireland courts and tribunals indicates that it has been the employment (and non-employment) of Protestants/unionists and Catholics/nationalists that has dominated the work of the FET.

Indirect discrimination

What appeared to be a major development in religious and political discrimination law in the 1989 Act was the inclusion of a definition of indirect discrimination, well established in the sex and race equality regimes, but not included in the 'agency investigation' model in the original 1976 Act (SACHR, 1990: 56–60). However, while the SACHR had proposed a 'modernised' definition, the formula in the 1989 Act strictly followed that already well established in sex and race discrimination law (Hepple, 1990: 411). Bell (1996: 75–78) engaged in a detailed discussion of the seminal decisions of the FET (and the Court of Appeal) in the convoluted litigation in *McCausland* v. *Dungannon District Council* (16 September 1992 FET; 30 June 1993 NICA; 21 October 1993 NICA; 20 December 1993 FET), a case concerning an 'internal trawl' for the position of chief works manager with the council, in which Catholics were underrepresented in employment. By adopting a pool of comparison of all those in the Northern Irish labour market potentially able to apply for the post, the resultant percentages of those who could satisfy the requirement were both very small, 2.1 per cent in the case of qualified Protestant workers and 1.5 per cent in the case of qualified Catholic workers. Nonetheless, given that the percentage for qualified Catholics was 71 per cent of the percentage for qualified Protestants, it was concluded that the 'Catholic' percentage was 'considerably smaller'. The FET then adopted the accepted test from race discrimination law of 'objective justification' (*Hampson* v. *Department of Education and Science* [1989] IRLR 69 (CA)), namely striking a balance between the 'discriminatory effect of the requirement against the reasonable needs of the employer and that only if the discriminatory effect could be effectively justified by those needs would the requirement be met' (*Briggs* v. *North Eastern Education and Library Board* ([1990] IRLR 181 (NICA)), and concluded that the practice was not justified.[12]

Another rare indirect discrimination case, *Hall & Others* v. *Shorts Missile Systems* (8 March 1996 FET), exhibits an interesting interaction between indirect discrimination and affirmative action issues. The FET had concluded that a decision to ignore service scores in a redundancy situation was indirectly discriminatory against a number of Protestant workers, but was justified in order to provide some protection for the company's affirmative action programme, a conclusion with which a majority of the Court of Appeal concurred (26 November 1996 NICA).[13]

It was clearly anticipated, when the 1976 Act was amended in 1989, that the introduction of the concept of indirect discrimination into religious and discrimination law in Northern Ireland would precipitate challenges to structural or systemic discrimination. That only five cases have come to hearing[14] is a reflection of the polycentricity of the indirect discrimination principle. While sex and race discrimination law have developed a more 'diagnostic' approach towards equality issues, and arguably the introduction of a concept of 'reasonable accommodation' in disability discrimination law has had a similar effect, indirect discrimination claims have not been widely utilised to advance the 'fair employment' agenda. Developments in the law on indirect discrimination may encourage greater use of the concept in religious and political discrimination cases. A powerful disincentive to the pursuit of an indirect discrimination case, namely the non-availability of compensation in the absence of 'intentional' indirect discrimination (Bell, 1996: 77–8), has now been replaced by a discretion to award compensation in such circumstances where it is 'just and equitable' to do so (Article 39(3) FETO). More pertinently, a new definition of indirect discrimination has been introduced, in the employment field, in the proposed Fair Employment and Treatment Order

(Amendment) Regulations (Northern Ireland) 2003 (Article 3(2A)).[15]

First, the 'requirement or condition' criterion is replaced by 'a provision, criterion or practice', effectively bringing to an end the 'absolute bar' approach adopted by the Court of Appeal in *Hall*. Second, an attempt is made to move away from the predominately statistical approach in the previous definition through the utilisation of a concept of 'particular disadvantage when compared with other persons'. Third, the justification test is now articulated as being 'a proportionate means of achieving a legitimate aim', a vague formulation which may not be as strong as the previous test of balancing 'reasonable needs' and the discriminatory effect. Whether a more accessible concept, but one which might be more easily open to justification, will encourage a more diagnostic challenge to religious and political discrimination, be it on labour market composition questions or otherwise, remains to be seen.

Exceptions

Bell (1996) picks out two areas of exceptions for particular comment, namely affirmative action and national security certificates. *Hall*, discussed above, was decided shortly after Bell's commentary was completed and reflects a trend, in the very limited number of cases in which these issues are addressed, to protect affirmative action programmes both in discrimination and other employment law cases.

National security certificates, on the other hand, have been the subject of great controversy. In sex discrimination law, the 'blanket' coverage of national security certificates had been breached in one of the most significant cases to be assisted by the former equality agencies, Case 22/84, *Johnston* v. *Chief Constable of the Royal Ulster Constabulary* ([1986] EC R 1651, [1986] IRLR 263 (ECJ)), in which the European Court of Justice concluded that a national security certificate could not be an absolute bar to a sex equality case under the Equal Treatment Directive 1976. After a series of cases in the FET and the Court of Appeal, which eventually concluded that what were then Section 42 certificates could not be challenged in the Northern Irish courts, two successful challenges were made before the European Court of Human Rights. In *Tinnelly & Sons Ltd* v. *United Kingdom* ((10 July 1998), Reports 1998-IV p. 1633 ECHR), the Court decided that the conclusive nature of the certificate issued in those cases, which pre-empted claims that the awarding of building contracts was discriminatory, contravened Article 6 of the European Convention on Human Rights on access to judicial process. The Court noted that there had been no scrutiny of the facts behind the certificates and no evidence produced before the FET to indicate why the applicants were perceived to be security risks. In deciding that the issuing of 'blanket' certificates was disproportionate to the aim to be achieved, the Court took into account the severity of the effect of the certificates on the applicants' right of access to the tribunal.

The particular issue of national security certificates in relation to public employment has exercised the Strasbourg institutions on two occasions. In *Quinn* v. *United Kingdom* ((33694/96) (23 October 1997) EComm HR), the European Commission on Human Rights dismissed an application by a worker whose FET case over his dismissal was excluded by a Section 42 certificate. This was on the basis that his dismissal from public employment did not determine a 'civil right' within the meaning of Article 6. However, in *Devlin* v. *United Kingdom* ([2002] IRLR 155 (ECHR)), the Court effectively reversed the outcome in *Quinn* by taking into account its judgment in *Pellegrin* v. *France* ((28541/95), Reports 1999-II ECHR), in which it concluded that 'civil rights' did not include the employment of public servants 'whose duties typify the specific activities of the public service in so far as the latter is responsible for protecting the general interests of the State or other public authorities'. As *Devlin* concerned an application to work as an administrative assistant in the Civil Service, the Court had no difficulty in applying Article 6 to the case.[16]

As Bell (1996: 82) points out, more Section 42 certificates were applied to Catholics than Protestants. More particularly, significant aspects of what ought to have been the jurisdiction of the FET were insulated from the pursuit of claims by the use of certificates. Hence, the eventual application of the European Convention to the controversy ensured that this outcome did not prevail.[17]

Employers' liability
Influencing employment practices

In this section, some consideration will be given to proving discrimination and to remedies available to the FET.

Proving discrimination: inferences and the Code of Practice

Given the overwhelming preponderance of direct discrimination cases in the FET, the issue of proof of discrimination has proved to be central to the operation of the Tribunal. The Northern Irish courts have always been sympathetic to the difficulties which applicants encounter in proving direct discrimination.[18] For example, in a recruitment or promotion, the burden would initially be on the applicant to establish a prima facie case that discrimination had taken place. The primary method of doing so would be by establishing that applicants were at least as well qualified as successful candidates. The 'onus' is then on the employer to provide an 'innocent explanation'. Failing that, the Tribunal is entitled to draw an inference of discrimination. An effective 'reversal of the burden of proof' has been introduced into the FETO by the Amendment Regulations (Article 38A), which already reflects FET practice. Central to these considerations is the Fair Employment Code of Practice (DED, 1989). Given that the FET is a specialised Tribunal dealing with 'fair employment' cases, it is hardly surprising that the Code of Practice has played a powerful role in the considerations of the Tribunal. There is a consistent pattern of references to the Code by the Tribunal.[19] Even if the Court of Appeal has been a little more circumspect in its support for the Code,[20] it is clear that a failure to follow it renders it more difficult for an employer to provide an 'innocent explanation' of its conduct.

It is through references to the Code that the FET has established a clear and coherent regime governing issues such as 'systematic and objective recruitment' (DED, 1989: §§5.3.2–5.3.5), 'selection and promotion' (DED, 1989: §§5.3.6–5.3.7) and 'good and harmonious working environment' (DED, 1989: §5.2.1). Bell (1996: 83–8) sets out an extensive discussion of the important FET decisions in which the 'ground rules' for the great bulk of the FET's case law were established. An entirely Protestant shortlist in *Belfast Port Employers' Association* v. *Fair Employment Commission for Northern Ireland* (29 June 1994 NICA) was held to amount to prima facie evidence of discrimination for which the employers could provide no 'innocent explanation'.[21] So also the use of 'subjective' criteria has proved to be problematic (*Duffy* v. *Eastern Health & Social Services Board* [1992] IRLR 251 (FET)). The development of the extensive use of marking schemes obviously provides greater protection for the recruitment process. Nonetheless, the FET will still look behind such processes to establish whether the best qualified candidate was appointed and the extent to which emphasis on interview performance masked a case of discrimination.[22] So also promotion processes have come under close scrutiny. For example, in *Willis* v. *Police Authority for Northern Ireland and others*, the FET concluded that it was a discriminatory arrangement for the Chief Constable both to provide assessments on candidates for promotion and to advise a lay panel in the decision-making process.

The FET has been particularly active in developing the Code's approach to a 'neutral working environment' in relation to harassment cases. The most significant decision was in *Neeson* v. *Securicor Ltd* (21 December 1993 FET), a case in which a young woman, the first Catholic to be employed in a particular office, was subjected to a 'shameful, mean and sectarian' campaign of harassment. There was both 'management participation' and 'total indifference' to the applicant's plight. In another influential decision, *Brennan* v. *Shorts Bros plc* (20 November 1995 FET), the failure of an employer to protect an employee in a sectarian workplace was held to be discriminatory. In particular, the FET commented that '[a] neutral working environment is one where employees can work without contemplating their own or any other person's religious beliefs or political opinions' (see DED, 1989: §5.2.1). As a counterpoint, a Protestant working in an otherwise exclusively Catholic environment was similarly successful in *Shaw* v. *Greenan Inns Ltd t/a Balmoral Hotel* (22 May 1998 FET). In *Smyth* v. *Croft Inns* (16 November 1994 FET; [1996] IRLR 84 (NICA)), a failure to allow the transfer of an employee who was the subject of harassment from *outside* the workplace was still held to be the responsibility of the employer. In particular, both the FET and the Court of Appeal rejected what (the then) Hutton LCJ described as a 'fallacious' argument that the respondent would have equally refused to transfer a Protestant barman in a predominantly Catholic area. More recently, in *Brannigan* v. *Belfast City Council* (16 January 2002 FET),[23] the FET concluded that the manner in which a 'flags and emblems' policy was introduced itself engendered sectarian harassment which the employer failed to take adequate measures to prevent.[24] Unlike tribunals and courts considering other regimes,[25] the FET has never exhibited any doubts about the applicability of the principle of direct discrimination to harassment situations.[26]

Remedies

As in the other areas of equality law, the remedies available to the FET (Article 39) are made up of a declaration of rights, a compensation order and a recommendation 'for the purpose of obviating or reducing the adverse effect on the complainant of any unlawful discrimination to which the complaint relates'.[27] The declaration of rights need not detain us, as this amounts to nothing more than a finding of discrimination. In the absence of standing for the ECNI, trade unions or interest groups and a range of proactive remedies, the focus of the remedial structure has been upon compensation. It is significant that, while the maximum compensation award in discrimination cases under the other regimes in Northern Ireland and Great Britain was limited at the time to about £10,000, the maximum under the 1989 Act was set at £30,000.[28] Hence arguably the most important FET decision was made in *Duffy* v. *Eastern Health & Social Services Board* ([1992] IRLR 251) in March 1992. In what the editor of the *Industrial Relations Law Reports* described as an 'eloquent decision' ([1992] IRLR 249), the President of the FET outlined acts of blatant discrimination, suppression of evidence and the 'sending to Coventry' of the applicant after the initial finding of discrimination in her case. The FET decision reflected what was then perceived to be the different aspects of compensation which might be awarded, namely financial loss, injury to feelings, aggravated damages and exemplary damages.[29] The applicant in *Duffy* had suffered no financial loss in that she had applied for a permanent position in place of a temporary one and was indeed granted a permanent post upon launching her FET application. She was, however, awarded £15,000 for injury to feelings, in itself 50 per cent more than an industrial tribunal could award in an equivalent sex discrimination case and, in practice, at least double what might have been anticipated in such a case.[30] However, this influential decision did not stop at this exceptional award. It is open to tribunals and courts in calculating tort damages to take into account the 'aggravated' nature of the act of discrimination or subsequent acts of the part of the perpetrator. The FET in *Duffy* concluded that the manner in which the applicant had been treated, particularly after the finding of discrimination in her case, justified an award of a further £5,000. The FET proceeded to award the applicant a further £5,000 in 'exemplary' or punitive damages, a conclusion which the Court of Appeal effectively overruled in the later case of *O'Gara* v. *Limavady Borough Council* (6 April 1995 NICA).

The significance of *Duffy* for the centrality of 'fair employment' law to employment practices in Northern Ireland cannot be underestimated. There can be little doubt that, in one of its first decisions, the FET revolutionised Northern Irish discrimination law by inflicting on the employer a compensation award which dwarfed any equivalent award in sex discrimination law, then the only other discrimination law regime. Previously mentioned decisions also resulted in some substantial compensation orders by the FET. For example, in *Neeson*, the FET made a compensation order for £25,157, including £10,000 for injury to feelings and £10,000 as aggravated damages.

Contemporaneously with a 'backlash' against substantial discrimination law awards in the tribunals and courts in Great Britain (*Armitage, Marsden and HM Prison Service* v. *Johnson* [1997] IRLR 162 (EAT)), the Northern Ireland Court of Appeal sought to 'reign in' compensation awards in the FET. In *McConnell* v. *Police Authority for Northern Ireland* ([1997] IRLR 625 (NICA)), the Court of Appeal (by a majority) reduced the compensation of a Catholic who failed to win the position of an armourer in the RUC from £10,000 for injury to feelings to £5,000 and set aside an award of £5,000 for aggravated damages. The rationale of the Court of Appeal was, first, that awards for religious and political discrimination in Northern Ireland should not be higher than equivalent awards for sex and race discrimination in Great Britain, and second, the surprising conclusion that since aggravated damages were merely an aspect of 'injury to feelings', the aggravation should be included in the calculation of damages for 'injury to feelings' and should not be an independent head of compensation.

The recent English Court of Appeal judgment in *Vento* v. *Chief Constable of West Yorkshire (No 2)* ([2003] IRLR 102 (CA)) will no doubt re-establish some element of stability in the calculation of compensation awards. The Employment Tribunal had awarded the applicant, harassed out of a probationary position which was not made permanent, £257,844. The Court of Appeal reinstated an award of £165,829 for future loss of earnings but sought to constrain the awards for injury to feelings and aggravated damages. In *Vento (No. 2)*, the Tribunal had awarded £50,000 for injury to feelings, £9,000 for psychiatric damage[31] and £15,000 in aggravated damages. The Court of Appeal reduced the first and third sums to £18,000 for injury to feelings and £5,000 for aggravated damages.[32] The Court of Appeal, most helpfully for all equality law tribunals including the FET, indicated 'three broad bands of compensation for injury to feelings'. 'Most serious cases', involving 'a lengthy campaign of discriminatory harassment', should precipitate injury to feelings compensation of between £15,000 and £25,000. Such compensation should rarely exceed this limit. A middle range of 'serious' cases justified awards between £5,000 and £10,000, and a range of £500 and £5,000 was appropriate for 'less serious cases'. The Court of Appeal was content with awards of aggravated damages depending 'on the particular circumstances of the case and on the way in which the complaint of discrimination was handled', as long as there was not 'double recovery'.

This extensive analysis of *Vento (No. 2)* is necessary to illustrate that what might be perceived as a 'restraining' judgment for tribunals in Great Britain sets out significantly higher figures as appropriate compensation than those determined by the Northern Ireland Court of Appeal, albeit some five years earlier, in *McConnell*. Given the legislative intent in relation to the 1989 Act, particularly the initial setting of a higher limit for compensation orders than in the other regimes, it was clear that compensation in religious and political discrimination cases, as calculated in deeply influential FET decisions such as *Duffy*, was intended to reflect a public policy stance sternly against sectarian discrimination in the sensitive circumstances of Northern Ireland. Certainly, in the spirit of 'equality of the inequalities', FET assessments of compensation should not be inconsistent with awards in race, sex or disability discrimination cases. Nor should compensation awards in these regimes be inconsistent with those of the FET. Nonetheless, the impressive development of compensatory awards in the FET is broadly within the guidelines in *Vento (No 2)*. This is not to say that *McConnell* was wrongly decided on its facts, merely that the deeply influential approach of the FET towards compensation calculations should not be constrained by limiting interpretations of compensation principles.

Conclusions

In the context of this volume, the case law of the FET, largely supported but sometimes limited by the higher courts, has been to develop a rigorous enforcement regime, directed largely at 'labour market composition' issues of recruitment and selection, dismissal and harassment, augmented by dramatic and innovative approaches towards the calculation of compensation, which has focused the attention of Northern Irish employers upon extensive recruitment, promotion and harassment processes and policies. It can hardly be doubted that the case law of the FET was highly influential in these developments. Indeed, it is appropriate to appreciate the courage and decisiveness of early decisions of the FET. On issues such as inferences of discrimination, the necessity of a neutral working environment and the need for significant, intrusive compensation orders, it cannot be doubted that the FET set an agenda for Northern Irish employers which has significantly augmented the efforts of the FEC (and now the ECNI) to maximise the potential of a unique 'fair employment' regime in Northern Ireland.

This commentary has indicated that religious and political discrimination law is increasingly integrated into a broader equality law agenda. The creation of a single ECNI, some degree of even minimalist 'harmonisation' of equality law through EU implementation and the genesis of a Single Equality Act can only hasten this process. The ECNI is proposing a definition of direct discrimination, which focuses on whether a 'disadvantage' was 'on grounds of' a prohibited factor, rather than the essential reliance on a comparative method. It also wishes to see a definition of indirect discrimination, which incorporates a more 'user-friendly' definition of indirect discrimination but with a more rigorous test for 'objective justification' than that provided for in the FETO Amendment Regulations. It wishes to see the application of the disability discrimination concept of 'reasonable accommodation' applied to all grounds, including religious and political discrimination cases. So also a more permissive system of affirmative action would promote a range of 'inclusionary' measures at present of doubtful legality.[33]

Hopefully, the future case law of the FET, in an era of an integrated Commission and of a Single Equality Act, will provide opportunities for a more diagnostic approach towards religious and political discrimination in Northern Ireland, feeding off and learning from the extensive experience of challenges to systemic discrimination in sex, race and disability law regimes. Nonetheless, in relation to these other regimes, courts and tribunals can only learn from the determination and dedication of a specialist equality tribunal in resolutely adjudicating upon the more obvious forms of discrimination on grounds of religious belief or political discrimination in Northern Ireland. Rather than allow the FET to be subsumed into a generalist employment tribunal system, the ECNI proposes that the precedent of a specialist FET[34] should be used as the basis of a Single Equality Tribunal in Northern Ireland, so that the accumulated expertise of the FET (and of the Northern Irish industrial tribunals in sex, disability and race cases) should be exploited in the furtherance of a perceptive and strategic attack on discrimination across all the grounds in a Single Equality statute.

9

Attitudes towards equality in Northern Ireland
Evidence of progress?[1]

JOANNE HUGHES

Introduction

Since 1989 the Northern Ireland Life and Times Survey (NILT) and its predecessor, the Social Attitudes Survey, have monitored the attitudinal climate in Northern Ireland towards a range of current and ongoing socio-political issues. Following the signing of the Belfast Agreement in 1998, and consistent with the rolling programme of equality enshrined within the Agreement, a number of new questions were developed for the survey. These items are intended to measure perceptions of disadvantage in the post-Agreement period and to understand the population's attitudes towards equality reform. Some questions are 'time series', appearing in the same format on consecutive surveys between 1998 and 2000, and offer a unique opportunity for longitudinal analysis. Others, some of which replace or revise time series questions, were first included in the 2001 survey.[2] Taking the Agreement as a starting point, and reflecting the aim of the book to examine 'where we are now' in terms of fair employment, responses to those questions in the Northern Ireland survey that relate to employment opportunity and related equality concerns are examined in this chapter. In order to set the context, the following section outlines the key legislative and policy developments from the time of the

Agreement that constitute government's current equality agenda. These are presented against the background of constitutional and political reforms that, it is argued, may have mediated the nature of Catholic and Protestant responses to equality issues in recent years.

The Belfast Agreement

The Belfast Agreement represented the convergence of what were hitherto considered two separate processes: the search for political settlement in Northern Ireland and the pursuit of equality. It heralded a fundamental transition in governance, intertwined with a clear commitment to mainstream equality in policymaking. The Agreement became possible following a protracted multi-party talks process, involving the British and Irish governments and the main political parties in Northern Ireland, and the declaration of ceasefires by loyalist and republican paramilitaries. It outlined a range of measures that were aimed at the creation of a more equitable society in Northern Ireland and at protecting the interests of the two main communities. These include the following:

- devolution to a 108-member local assembly and its Executive Committee of Members;[3]

- arrangements to ensure that key decisions made by the Assembly are on a cross-community basis either by parallel consent or through a weighted majority;

- the adoption of the European Convention on Human Rights, which neither the Assembly nor any other public body can infringe, and the establishment of a Human Rights Commission;

- the establishment of an Equality Commission to monitor a statutory obligation to promote equality of opportunity and parity of esteem between the two communities and to investigate individual complaints against public bodies;

- the extension and strengthening of anti-discrimination legislation through a single Equality Commission, and a new and more focused approach to combating unemployment and eliminating the differential in employment rates between the two communities;

- arrangements for promoting, facilitating the use of, and protecting the Irish and Ulster/Scots language traditions, and;

- a programme of policing reform to include the implementation of 50:50 (Protestant/Catholic) recruitment; provision for the review of flags and emblems associated with the Police that could be construed as offensive to either community; and a new oath, affirming commitment to fundamental human rights and according equal respect to the legitimate and democratic beliefs and traditions of all individuals. (The Agreement, 1998)

In stressing the importance of these reforms, the Northern Ireland Executive's first *Programme for Government* stated:

> Only if we are confident in our rights and responsibilities, only if we create security for the individual from poverty and communities from disadvantage, only if we can help the confidence of a community to express its needs can we build a firm foundation for tackling divisions in our society. (Office of the First Minister and Deputy First Minister, 2001:1)

Before examining in detail the survey data that attempt to isolate and measure attitudes towards the equality agenda in particular, it is worth considering community responses to the Belfast Agreement in general.

Support for the Agreement

Although the signing of the Belfast Agreement was greeted with some degree of enthusiasm by both Protestants and Catholics, research has shown that the Protestant community has become increasingly disillusioned (Aughey, 2001; Hughes and Donnelly, 2002; MacGinty and Wilford, 2002; O'Neill, 2000). In an analysis of political attitudes, MacGinty and Wilford (2002) found that, by the time devolution 'went live' in November 1999, the majority of Protestants (56 per cent) had come to believe that nationalists were the prime beneficiaries of the Agreement. In addition, Catholics were more than twice as likely to perceive the Agreement as having bestowed equal benefits on both communities than Protestants. Reflecting Protestant grievance, parliamentary and local elections in the post-Agreement period have seen a shift in voting preference amongst Protestants from the pro-Agreement Ulster Unionist Party to the more extreme anti-Agreement Democratic Unionist Party (Carmichael and Knox, 1999).

The increasingly negative stance of the Protestant community towards reform has been attributed to the nature of the compromises made by the unionist and nationalist communities in order to make the

Agreement possible (Aughey, 2001;[4] MacGinty and Wilford, 2002). Referencing the zero-sum nature of Northern Ireland politics, MacGinty and Wilford (2002) make the point that nationalist and republican compromises were 'aspirational and academic', including, for example, the recognition of a Northern Ireland state that was already in existence. Unionist compromises, on the other hand, were of a different and altogether more tangible order. The reform of the RUC and the early release of republican and other paramilitary prisoners were particularly hard for Protestants to accept. Resentment was compounded by the failure of the Irish Republican Army (IRA) to comply with the deadlines set for decommissioning (Aughey, 2001). The depth of Protestant feeling is evident in the findings of a 2003 poll cited in the pro-union newspaper, the *News Letter*. The poll found that only 27 per cent of Protestants supported the institutions of government, though 57 per cent said that they would support a return to devolution if the IRA made a serious gesture towards decommissioning, and 71 per cent indicated that, if the IRA declared that the war was over, they would support devolution (*News Letter*, 16 May 2003).

Although the kernel of Protestant resentment is the concessions made to republicans, the theme of Catholic gain and Protestant loss is also recurrent in attitudes towards equality. The data presented below show increased confidence within the Catholic community that equality reforms are having some impact and suggest some concern amongst Protestants that the pendulum has begun to swing in the other direction and that they (Protestants) are becoming victims of discrimination. That said, the zero-sum argument in relation to equality is tempered somewhat by the finding that Protestant and Catholic communities each perceive some benefits from reform measures.

Survey analysis

The analysis is presented in three sections, reflecting categories of equality questions in the Northern Ireland surveys. In broad terms these relate to perceptions of equal treatment, fair employment and the value of legislation. In the case of time series questions, the content of some survey items is often vague so that analysis focuses on the perceived relative position of Protestants and Catholics on some unspecified scale such as 'equal treatment'. These questions are complemented by some that are more clearly focused and less open to interpretation by respondents.[5]

Equal treatment

The most recent figures (2000) indicate that, while more than half of all Protestant respondents and just less than a third of Catholics believe there is equal treatment for both communities in Northern Ireland, the figures were higher in 1998 (see Table 9.1). The negative trend in the period following the signing of the Agreement is slightly more pronounced for Catholics, with 43 per cent in 1998 against 32 per cent in 2000 indicating a belief that Protestants and Catholics are treated equally, a decrease of 11 percentage points over the three-year period $(p<0.01)$.[6] The Protestant response during the same period decreases by 6 percentage points, from 61 per cent in 1998 to 55 per cent in 2000 $(p<0.01)$. In a parallel though more marginal trend, the numbers of those who believe that the two communities are not treated equally increases between 1998 and 2000, from 21 per cent to 26 per cent for Protestants $(p<0.01)$ and from 33 per cent to 36 per cent for Catholics $(p<0.05)$.

A partial explanation for these findings begins to emerge when data generated by a more loaded, though essentially similar, question on perceptions of equality are interrogated (see Table 9.2). When asked the question 'who is usually treated better – Protestants or Catholics?', many more Catholics in 2000, 42 per cent, responded that 'it depends' than was the case in 1998, 25 per cent $(p<0.01)$. There was also a substantial decrease between 1998 and 2000 in the number of Catholics who believe that Protestants are treated better than Catholics, from 70 per cent in 1998 to 54 per cent in 2000 $(p<0.01)$. Thus, it would seem

Table 9.1

Do you think that, in general, Protestants and Catholics in Northern Ireland are treated equally?

	Protestant %			Catholic %		
	1998	1999	2000	1998	1999	2000
Yes	61	64	55	43	38	32
No	21	21	26	33	40	36
It depends	15	11	13	21	18	27
Don't know	4	3	6	3	3	4
Other	0	0	0	0	1	1

Source: Northern Ireland Social Attitudes Survey/Northern Ireland Life and Times Survey

that, for Catholics at least, the decline in the numbers of those who believe that there is equal treatment for Protestants and Catholics can be explained not as might be expected by an increase in the numbers who believe that Catholics are less well treated, but rather by an increase in the perception that Protestants less frequently receive preferential treatment – depending on the issue. To illustrate just how far confidence amongst Catholics has grown, it is worth considering findings from the first Northern Ireland Social Attitudes Survey. Although referring only to treatment in the labour market, Osborne (1991) reported that, in 1989, 89 per cent of Catholics believed that Protestants were 'favoured' and 87 per cent believed that this was because employers discriminated against Catholics.

Interestingly, the Protestant response to the question of who is treated better reveals little change over time in the period from 1998 to 2000. There is a small but relatively insignificant increase of 2 percentage points amongst those who believe that experience of better treatment 'depends', from 35 per cent in 1998 to 37 per cent in 2000 (p>0.05), and a decrease of 2 percentage points in those who believe that Catholics are treated better, from 48 per cent in 1998 to 46 per cent in 2000 (p>0.05). It is worth pointing out that these marginal trends, taken together with the more seismic shift in Catholic opinion, represent a narrowing of the gap between the Protestant and Catholic response. In 1998, for example, 35 per cent of Protestants against 25 per cent of Catholics respond in the 'it depends' category, while in 2000 the figure for Protestants is 37 per cent and for Catholics is 42 per cent. The response differential has reduced by half, from 10 percentage points in 1998 to 5 percentage points in 2000.

Table 9.2

Who is usually treated better – Protestants or Catholics?

	Protestant %			Catholic %		
	1998	1999	2000	1998	1999	2000
Protestants	12	11	11	70	73	54
Catholics	48	52	46	1	1	3
It depends	35	29	37	25	24	42
Don't know	6	6	4	4	2	2
Other	*	2	1	*	0	0

Note: * indicates that the 'other' category was not included in the year of data collection.
Source: Northern Ireland Social Attitudes Survey/Northern Ireland Life and Times Survey

A buoyant Catholic response is also evident in a series of questions included for the first time in the 2001 survey. When asked to compare the treatment received by each group now *vis-à-vis* five years before, 40 per cent of Catholics thought that they were currently receiving *better* treatment (see Table 9.3). By comparison, only 8 per cent of Protestants thought that Protestants were getting a better deal than before (see Table 9.4). Of particular significance, though, is that almost 40 per cent (39 per cent) of Protestants believed that they were treated *worse* than five years before, whereas just 4 per cent of Catholics thought that in 2001 they were treated less well. Furthermore, only 16 per cent of Catholics thought that Protestants were treated better,

Table 9.3

Thinking about each of these groups in turn, do you think they are generally treated better than they were five years ago, worse, or are they treated the same as they were five years ago: Catholics?

	Protestants % 2001	Catholics % 2001
Treated better than 5 years ago	64	40
Treated worse than 5 years ago	0	4
Treated the same as 5 years ago	30	53
Don't know	5	3

(p<0.01)

Source: Northern Ireland Social Attitudes Survey/Northern Ireland Life and Times Survey

Table 9.4

Thinking about each of these groups in turn, do you think they are generally treated better than they were five years ago, worse, or are they treated the same as they were five years ago: Protestants?

	Protestants % 2001	Catholics % 2001
Treated better than 5 years ago	8	16
Treated worse than 5 years ago	39	2
Treated the same as 5 years ago	48	77
Don't know	6	5

(p<0.01)

Source: Northern Ireland Social Attitudes Survey/Northern Ireland Life and Times Survey

compared to 64 per cent of Protestants who thought that Catholics were treated better. The widely held perception amongst Protestants that Catholics were currently treated better may help explain why Protestants are increasingly negative in their view that there is equal treatment for Protestants and Catholics (see Table 9.1).

On a more optimistic note, it is relevant to point out that, despite the degree of negativity in the Protestant response, 8 per cent believed that they were actually treated better than five years before and 48 per cent believed that they were treated the same as five years before. For the majority of Protestants (56 per cent) then, the perception was that their position had either improved or remained static.

Fair employment

Other interesting trends emerge in relation to views on the areas in which there should be equal treatment (see Table 9.5). In 2000 fewer Protestants and Catholics believe that equal treatment in job opportunities is as important as was the case in 1998. Indeed, the numbers of Catholics who attribute importance to this issue more than halved between 1998 and 2000, from 54 per cent to 21 per cent (p<0.01). The decline in the number of Protestants who attribute importance to job opportunities is relatively more conservative at 8 percentage points, from 41 per cent in 1998 to 33 per cent in 2000 (p<0.01). It would appear that in the case of both Protestants and Catholics these downward trends can, at least in part, be explained by increasing numbers in favour of treating both communities equally in relation to all areas. Amongst Protestants there has been an increase of 17 percentage points between 1998 and 2000 amongst those who believe that this should be the case, from 25 per cent to 42 per cent (p<0.01). For Catholics the increase is even more impressive, with more than twice as many in 2000 (50 per cent) than in 1998 (22 per cent) favouring equal treatment in all areas (p<0.01). It is important to note, however, that this general transference of opinion conceals a more subtle trend. In 2000, 12 per cent more Protestants than Catholics believe that equality in employment is important, contrasting with the 1998 figures, where the differential is reversed (13 per cent more Catholics than Protestants think that job opportunity is an important equality issue). An analysis of a series of questions that focus specifically on employment and were included in the 1994 and 2001 surveys may assist in the interpretation of these trends.

The questions designed to access data on actual experience of disadvantage/discrimination in the workplace ask respondents to indicate whether or not they have experienced unfair treatment in relation to applying for either a new job or promotion (see Tables 9.6 and 9.7). Interestingly the data reveal that the total proportion of Catholics and Protestants who believe themselves to have been refused a job because of their religion has remained fairly stable since 1994 (at between 3 per cent and 6 per cent). However, the proportion of Protestants who indicate that they have not been refused a job because of their religion has fallen by 3 percentage points between 1994 and 2001, from 84 per cent to 81 per cent ($p<0.05$). Figures for the Catholic response, on the other hand, indicate an increase of 4 percentage points during the same period, from 81 per cent to 85 per cent ($p<0.05$). Protestants were also more likely to record a 'don't know' response in 2001 than in 1994 (see Table 9.6). When asked about promotion, the same trend applies (see Table 9.7). Whilst the majority of respondents (95 per cent) continue to feel that they have not been treated unfairly, there appears to be more uncertainty amongst Protestants in 2001 than in 1994. The proportion of Protestants who recorded a 'no' response to the question 'have you been treated unfairly when applying for promotion for reasons to do with your religion?' fell between 1994 and 2001, from 98 per cent to 94 per cent ($p<0.01$). In addition, the 'don't know'

Table 9.5

In which ways is it important that Protestants and Catholics should be treated equally?

	Protestant %			Catholic %		
	1998	1999	2000	1998	1999	2000
Job opportunities	41	37	33	54	31	21
Housing	4	3	2	2	4	2
Expressing their own culture	16	13	11	4	8	5
Treatment by the police	5	4	7	13	15	16
Educational opportunities	7	6	3	4	4	4
Other	1	0	2	0	0	0
Should be treated equally in all these areas	25	34	42	22	37	50
Don't know	1	3	2	1	1	1

Source: Northern Ireland Social Attitudes Survey/Northern Ireland Life and Times Survey

response increased from 0 per cent in 1994 to 4 per cent in 2001. Mirroring this, the proportion of Catholics indicating that they have been treated unfairly when applying for promotion fell marginally, from 5 per cent to 3 per cent (p>0.05).

A possible interpretation of these findings is that Protestants perceive themselves to be experiencing a negative impact of legislation that was originally designed to tackle discrimination experienced most acutely by the Catholic community. If this is the case, it might help explain why, in 2000, Protestants were more likely than Catholics to consider job opportunity an important equality concern.

Affirmative action

Despite some evidence of concern amongst Protestants that discrimination in the work environment is becoming more of a reality than was previously the case, Protestants are much less predisposed towards

Table 9.6

Have you been refused a job for reasons to do with your religion?

	Protestant %		Catholic %	
	1994	2001	1994	2001
Yes	3	2	6	4
No	84	81	81	85
Have not worked in last 10 years	13	15	14	11
Don't know	0	2	0	1

Source: Northern Ireland Social Attitudes Survey/Northern Ireland Life and Times Survey

Table 9.7

Have you been treated unfairly when applying for promotion for reasons to do with your religion?

	Protestant %		Catholic %	
	1994	2001	1994	2001
Yes	2	3	5	3
No	98	94	95	96
Don't know	0	4	0	1

Source: Northern Ireland Social Attitudes Survey/Northern Ireland Life and Times Survey

supporting the notion of affirmative action than Catholics (see Table 9.8). Indeed more than twice as many Catholics (31 per cent) as Protestants (15 per cent) agreed that firms *should* ensure that under-represented religions are given preferential treatment (p<0.01).[7] To set this finding in context it is important to note that at the time of data collection the reform of the RUC was receiving much media attention and the 50:50 recruitment pattern applying to the new PSNI was the subject of unionist outrage. Underlining Protestant fears at the time, Lord Laird (an Ulster Unionist peer), in an interview with the *Belfast Telegraph*, referred to the recruitment policy as 'a ridiculous piece of religious discrimination' (*Belfast Telegraph*, 2 November 2001). Taken together with the sense of political disenchantment experienced by unionists in 2001 (see MacGinty and Wilford, 2002), it is perhaps more surprising that almost 30 per cent of Protestants either agree with preferential treatment for underrepresented religions (15 per cent) or are unsure (14 per cent).

The significance of this finding is further endorsed when responses to a similar (though not identical) question included in the 1994 question are considered. When asked, 'If a particular religion is underrepresented in a firm, do you think the firm should give preferential treatment to people from that religion when filling posts?', 61 per cent of Catholics and 81 per cent of Protestants in 1994 disagree with the statement (Miller, 1996). Compared with the 2001 data, the number of Catholics who oppose positive discrimination has remained unchanged (61 per cent), while there has been a significant decline in the Protestant response (from 81 per cent to 72 per cent). Based on findings suggesting that Protestants perceive themselves to be

Table 9.8

Should firms give preferential treatment to people from underrepresented religions?

	Protestants 2001 %	Catholics 2001 %
Yes	15	31
No	72	61
Don't know	14	8

Source: Northern Ireland Social Attitudes Survey/Northern Ireland Life and Times Survey

experiencing more unfair treatment, these data could be interpreted as an acknowledgement by some Protestants that fair employment legislation has the potential to protect both communities.

Other equality concerns

Employment is clearly the most important equality concern for both Protestants and Catholics (see Table 9.5). It is worth highlighting, however, some of the ostensibly less noteworthy data presented in Table 5. Interestingly, only small percentages of Protestants and Catholics attribute importance to housing and education as relevant equality concerns and the numbers have either remained static or declined since 1998. Of particular note is the decline in the numbers of Protestants who see educational opportunities as important (from 7 per cent in 1998 to 3 per cent in 2000). This is somewhat surprising given the appointment of a Sinn Féin Minister for Education in 1999 and the ongoing debate about the number of controlled (Protestant) schools transforming to integrated status.[8] The latter has sparked some concern amongst Protestants regarding diminishing employment opportunities, a problem that is compounded by the fact that the appointment of teachers in Northern Ireland is currently exempted from fair employment law.

Other findings that merit a mention are the facts that, relative to Protestants, Catholics consider treatment by the police a more important concern, and that, relative to Catholics, Protestants consider the issue of cultural expression to be more important. Both of these trends can be explained in the context of concerns voiced by each community during recent years. For Catholics the reform of the RUC was considered central to progress in the search for peace. At the time of data collection in 2000 there was an ongoing debate about the extent to which the reforms outlined in the Patten Report had been fully implemented. The general perception amongst republicans was that the Belfast Agreement incorporated only a 'watered down' version of Patten's key recommendations. For Protestants, concern about the status of Protestant culture was fuelled by a perception that community relations providers in Northern Ireland consistently accorded Irish (Catholic) language and tradition greater priority than the Ulster/Scots (Protestant) heritage and tradition (see Hughes, 2001). The fact that due recognition was given to the culture of both communities in the Belfast Agreement may help explain the decline in importance attached to this issue by Protestants in the period from 1998 to 2000 (see Table 9.5).

Rights

Given the apparent consensus amongst Protestants and Catholics that Protestants are in general less well treated, and the growing concern that both communities should be treated equally in all areas, it is interesting to consider responses to a question that attempts to gauge perception of whether Catholic rights are accorded more legitimacy than Protestant rights. The question asks whether or not respondents agree with the statement that there is 'always talk of the rights of Catholics but never of the rights of Protestants' (see Table 9.9). Not surprisingly, in each year that the item was included in the survey the majority of Protestants agree with the statement and the majority of Catholics disagree with it. When the data are considered over time, however, an interesting pattern emerges. Between 1998 and 2000 there is a decline in the number of both Protestants and Catholics who disagree that the rights of Catholics are accorded greater priority than the rights of Protestants. Collapsing the 'disagree' and 'strongly disagree' response categories reveals that the Protestant response has decreased from 22 per cent in 1998 to 15 per cent in 2000 (p<0.01) and the Catholic response from 66 per cent in 1998 to 59 per cent in 2000 (p<0.01). Although this finding is in line with a more general perception of improving treatment for Catholics (see Table 9.3), a parallel trend

Table 9.9

How much do you agree or disagree with the following statement? There is always talk about the rights of Catholics but never about the rights of Protestants.

| | Protestant % | | | Catholic % | | |
	1998	1999	2000	1998	1999	2000
Strongly agree	23	19	25	1	2	1
Agree	35	34	32	10	8	8
Neither	16	25	21	19	18	24
Disagree	19	14	13	51	47	42
Strongly disagree	3	3	2	15	19	17
Can't choose	5	5	6	5	5	7

Source: Northern Ireland Social Attitudes Survey/Northern Ireland Life and Times Survey

discernible in Table 9.9 suggests that over time more people accept that the rights of both communities are accorded legitimacy. Between 1998 and 2000 there is an increase of 5 per cent in the numbers of both Protestants, from 16 per cent in 1998 to 21 per cent in 2000 (p<0.01), and Catholics, from 19 per cent in 1998 to 24 per cent in 2000 (p<0.01), who perceive that the rights of neither community feature more prominently in everyday discourse. It is significant that in 2000

Table 9.10

How much do you agree with the following statement? Equality laws protect Protestants at the expense of Catholics.

	Protestants 2001 %	Catholics 2001 %
Strongly agree	0	1
Agree	3	6
Neither agree nor disagree	24	13
Disagree	44	54
Strongly disagree	15	12
Don't know	14	15

(p>0.01)

Source: Northern Ireland Social Attitudes Survey/Northern Ireland Life and Times Survey

Table 9.11

How much do you agree with the following statement? Equality laws protect Catholics at the expense of Protestants.

	Protestants 2001 %	Catholics 2001 %
Strongly agree	17	1
Agree	21	4
Neither agree nor disagree	22	12
Disagree	24	58
Strongly disagree	2	12
Don't know	14	14

(p<0.01)

Source: Northern Ireland Social Attitudes Survey/Northern Ireland Life and Times Survey

more than 20 per cent of both Protestants (21 per cent) and Catholics (24 per cent) believe that the rights of neither community are prioritised.

Equality laws

In the 2001 survey a series of questions was included that aimed to assess the extent to which equality legislation was perceived to be having an impact and to ascertain the perceived value of such legislation. As Tables 9.10 and 9.11 demonstrate, the main finding was the degree of consensus amongst both Protestants and Catholics that legislation has less to offer Protestants. When respondents were asked to indicate their views on the statement 'Equality laws protect Protestants at the expense of Catholics', only 3 per cent of Protestants and 7 per cent of Catholics agreed or strongly agreed that this was the case. Interestingly, more Catholics (66 per cent) than Protestants (59 per cent) disagreed or strongly disagreed with the statement. It cannot be assumed from their responses that either community is confident that the inverse – that is, that the legislation protects Catholics at the expense of Protestants – necessarily applies (see Table 9.11). Indeed only 5 per cent of Catholics believe this to be the case and 70 per cent disagree. The figure for Protestants who believe that equality laws favour Catholics is higher (38 per cent). It is worth pointing out, though, that 36 per cent of Protestants either record a neutral response (22 per cent) or indicate that they don't know (14 per cent), and that more than a quarter (26 per

Table 9.12

There is no need for equality laws in Northern Ireland

	Protestants 2001 %	Catholics 2001 %
Strongly agree	4	2
Agree	15	9
Neither agree nor disagree	16	6
Disagree	43	44
Strongly disagree	11	32
Don't know	12	7

(p<0.01)

Source: Northern Ireland Social Attitudes Survey/Northern Ireland Life and Times Survey

cent) either disagree or strongly disagree that equality laws protect Catholics at the expense of Protestants.

In the light of these findings it is interesting to note the degree of support for equality legislation in Northern Ireland. When respondents were asked in the 2001 survey to consider the statement 'there is no need for equality laws in Northern Ireland', a majority in both communities disagreed (54 per cent of Protestants and 76 per cent of Catholics). Although the figure for Catholics is significantly higher ($p<0.01$), the fact that the majority of Protestants accept the need for equality legislation is perhaps further endorsement that they (Protestants) perceive themselves to be in a more vulnerable position than may have previously been the case (see Table 9.12).

Conclusions

The value of social attitudes survey data lies in its potential to provide reliable indicators of public opinion at particular time points. To this extent the longitudinal analysis presented above facilitates an understanding of how attitudes towards efforts to tackle discrimination and disadvantage have evolved over time. At one level, the findings are reasonably positive, with both communities indicating some gain from policy and legislative reform. Fair employment, for example, is less of a concern for Protestants and Catholics now than it was five years ago. There is also evidence in regard to issues that have in the past fuelled the equality debate (such as housing) that only a residue of concern persists of the need to accord continuing importance. Moreover, majorities in both communities accept the value of equality legislation and, post-Agreement, there have seen sizeable increases in the numbers of both Protestants and Catholics who believe that equality should permeate every aspect of social and political life. It could be argued that these findings reflect the positive influence, on attitudes at least, of an institutional environment that has sought to promote equality as the norm.

That said, a comparison of responses between the two communities also reveals some significant differences. Relative to Protestants, Catholics are, for example, clearly more confident that their rights are given due expression and that the legislation currently in place protects Catholic interests. Moreover, in the post-Agreement period Catholics perceive themselves to be more favourably treated than Protestants and there is evidence to suggest a growing belief amongst Catholics that this may be at the expense of preferential treatment for Protestants. When considered against survey findings in the late 1980s, which reported a majority perception amongst Catholics of discrimination and social disadvantage against the Catholic community (Osborne, 1991), the extent of attitudinal change is irrefutable. The response to the equality agenda by Protestants is a little more complicated. At one level there is evidence that Protestants perceive themselves to be in a less privileged position than was the case five years before, yet on other measures of equality it would seem that Protestants are not necessarily threatened by the relatively improved position of Catholics. Indeed, on some scores, increasing Catholic confidence serves to narrow the gap in the perception of equal treatment between Protestants and Catholics, not, as might have been expected, to promote greater insecurity amongst Protestants (see Table 9.2).

From an objective standpoint, these are positive findings, given that the need for equality legislation and policy was prompted by an acknowledgement of unfair treatment for Catholics in Northern Ireland (see Chapter 1). The fact that Catholics perceive an improvement in their position and that Protestants are somewhat ambivalent about this points to the success of the legislation. The data suggest, however, that there is potentially a fly in the ointment. Although the evidence is fairly weak, trends indicate that Protestants are increasingly likely to perceive discrimination in the area of employment. Taken together with evidence suggesting that employment is now more of an equality concern for Protestants than it is for Catholics, and the fact that a substantial minority of Protestants (38 per cent) believe that legislation protects Catholics at the expense of Protestants, this is an area that raises some cause for concern.

The relevance of these findings should not be underestimated. For many years the Catholic response to government efforts aimed at tackling discrimination and disadvantage was characterised by scepticism (Gallagher, 1995). Catholic perception of an improvement in their lot and implications for perceived parity of esteem within the context of Northern Ireland may form an important plank in the fragile search for peace. In the absence of the security and confidence that is engendered by a sense of equal status, Catholic support for devolved government, which is currently strong (ESRC, devolution briefing paper, 2003), could so easily be undermined, prompting in the worse-case scenario a return to violence. By the same token, neither should the seeds of Protestant concern about employment patterns be allowed to flourish. Miller (1996) makes the point that there is an inverse correlation between perceived experience of discrimination and positive attitudes towards the notion of equity in the labour market. Social attitudes are not reflective of objective facts, and whether or not there is any evidence to support a perception of increased discrimination against Protestants is an entirely different issue. People's actions, however, are determined by perception (objectively erroneous or not) and, taken together with the fact that Protestants already feel marginalised at the wider political level, it is important that policymakers should not become complacent in the light of the more positive findings reported here.

Methodology

The survey is administered annually on a face-to-face basis by trained interviewers. It is designed to yield a representative sample of adults aged 18 years or over, with respondents drawn as a simple random sample of all households listed on the ratings list. Until 1998 approximately 1,400 addresses were drawn in the anticipation of achieving 1,000 completed interviews. In 1999 the sample size was increased to 2,200. The interviewers referred to a Kish grid to select one respondent from those eligible for inclusion in the survey living in the household. Because the selection of an individual respondent at each address could not be conducted with probability proportionate to household size, the sample was weighted before analysis. For each year of the survey, fieldwork took place between October and December, although this was extended to mid-January 2000 for the 1999 survey. All interviews were conducted in the respondents' homes and interviewers made up to a maximum of five calls before the respondent was deemed to be non-attainable. The response rate to the survey varied each year but averaged around 68 per cent. Full technical details for each year are available in the annual reports (see http://www.ark.ac.uk/nilt/techinfo.html).

10
Concluding remarks

IAN SHUTTLEWORTH AND R.D. OSBORNE

Introduction

The chapters in this book have examined employment equality from a variety of perspectives, including education, social mobility, employment and the labour market, law, and public opinion. In discussing different themes, each chapter has drawn its own specific conclusions. But what general conclusions can be drawn and what are the main messages of the book as a whole? Readers will doubtless place their own interpretations on the different contributions. Nevertheless, it is worthwhile for the editors to extract the main themes they feel to be important, both as a guide for readers and as something to spark further critical debate. In looking across the context of the book, it was felt that three clear summary messages emerged: the changed positions of the Catholic and Protestant communities; the transformed context for employment equality policy; and the need to set new policy agendas for the future.

The changed positions of the Catholic and Protestant communities

Chapter 2 showed that the 1990s saw 'substantial progress towards a more equitable distribution of employment and employment opportunities'. The evidence presented in Chapter 3 reinforces this conclusion by indicating that, unlike a generation ago, religion ceased in the 1990s to have a direct independent effect upon an individual's social position. In the realm of education (Chapter 4) there is further evidence that indicates that 'the past generation has seen a substantial evening out in the patterns of qualifications held by the two communities'. Viewing these contributions in combination, a major conclusion of the book is that there has been increasing equalisation between Catholics and Protestants and that Northern Ireland society has become increasingly meritocratic. As ever, this basic generalisation requires elaboration. Catholics continue to experience higher rates of unemployment but at a time when absolute unemployment rates are at a historic low and measuring unemployment is increasingly problematic as an accurate indication of labour market participation. Other studies also find a substantial decrease in the differential experience of social disadvantage between Catholics and Protestants.

The relative contribution of equality legislation to greater equality in the labour market, as opposed to other developments, is difficult to measure precisely. Equality legislation and the work of the FEC plainly had a substantial effect on the labour market, with Chapter 7 concluding that 'the statistical analyses presented here provide indications of significant changes occurring in employment growth and community balance of firms with agreements', whilst Chapter 8 argues that 'the case law of the FET has been to develop a rigorous employment regime'. It is also clear that, while the legislation provided a framework, it required effective implementation. The evidence suggests that the FEC had a clear strategic approach to the use of its legal and other powers. However, it is difficult to isolate the precise independent contribution of institutional and legal factors to employment outcomes from the effects of the educational, economic and social trends identified in Chapters 4, 5 and 6. Although this attribution might be of theoretical interest, it is in practice impossible because of the conceptual and methodological problems of comparing alternative 'what if' situations, such as 'what if there had been no employment legislation?' or 'what if there had been no decline in manufacturing employment?' However, it is true that the effective implementation of legal and other powers by the FEC took place in an economic environment, particularly in the employment growth decade of the 1990s, that was favourable to change, and it is highly improbable that progress would have been as rapid as it was if there had been no legislation. Moreover, the relatively peaceful environment from the early 1990s undoubtedly assisted in creating a positive environment. A major conclusion of the book, therefore, is that the greater equality seen in the 1990s and the early twenty-first century could be explained by strong legislative initiatives effectively implemented in a highly supportive economic, political and social context.

The changed context for employment equality policy

Despite these favourable conclusions, it should not be forgotten that some inequalities persist despite the general tendency towards educational and labour market equality. In employment, Catholics remain underrepresented in the security-related jobs and also more widely in the private sector. Protestants are now underrepresented in parts of the public sector, such as education and health. In education, the poor educational performance of the Protestant working class remains a concern, and the continued emigration of highly educated Protestant young people is likely to have a negative impact on the Protestant community's future access to higher level jobs. And although there is evidence for greater integration of workforces (see Chapters 2 and 7), residential segregation (and social exclusion) in some highly socially deprived areas means that not everyone has a day-to-day greater experience of equality and opportunity. These complexities mean that old certitudes (and old terms of debate) about Catholic/Protestant differentials should be qualified, and a major conclusion is that political and policy debates should reflect these developments. A particular challenge, identified in Chapter 9 in the light of Protestant perceptions, and the reality of Protestant underrepresentation in some sectors, is to encourage engagement of the Protestant community with equality policies.

The economic changes noted in Chapters 5 and 6, besides contributing to changed patterns of inequality, have altered the context for employment equality in other ways. Arguments in the past about community balance in the labour market have tended to fixate upon the unemployment differential. The future use of this indicator can be challenged on two counts. First, declining headline figures for unemployment throughout the 1990s, which meant that unemployment, as reported in the 2001 Census, was much lower than that seen earlier, directed attention towards other indicators. Second, increasing questions about the meaning of headline unemployment data cast doubt on the present and future use of the unemployment differential. Changes in benefit regulations and the tendency for some groups, particularly older men in areas of low labour demand, to withdraw from the labour market and to cease searching for work, mean that many individuals who would have formerly been counted as 'unemployed' are not classed in this way now. Instead, they may now be grouped with the long-term ill or the retired. Because of this, better measures of labour market conditions might be employment (or non-employment) rates. Moreover, the increasing complexities of the types of job and economic activity that exist pose problems for accurate monitoring regimes. Therefore, a conclusion of this book is that new ways are needed to measure and to describe the labour market to reflect changed times, so as to provide more suitable targets for employment equality policy.

New policy agendas for the future

Some of the trends alluded to above suggest new policy challenges and agendas for the next decade. In the short term, the unemployment differential could be augmented or even supplemented by other indicators such as the employment rate or the economic activity rate, suggesting the use of a wider range of labour market measures to guide policy. Wider realisation that some Protestants are feeling insecure and that some believe that they are facing increasing discrimination in employment, coupled with the evidence of underrepresentation in key areas of the public sector, might also lead to proactive measures to show that equality policy is of benefit to both ethno-religious communities. At the same time, non-religious dimensions, such as disability and social class, are becoming increasingly important in debates about social inequality in Northern Ireland. This more complex environment could possibly be harder to navigate than in the past, when the issue was more clearly defined as the search for equality for a disadvantaged Catholic community. Nevertheless, there are clear benefits in showing that equality policy and the ECNI can adapt to these changed circumstances.

The presence of new (and not so new) forms of inequality also means that there should be more effort to learn about the causes and origins of social and labour market differentials. Surprisingly little is known about the dynamics of inequality – how people become disadvantaged or advantaged, and the paths that they follow into and out of education, employment and joblessness. New research could very usefully be tied into the attempts in Northern Ireland to develop longitudinal studies, in which people (or households) are followed through several years to understand more about the factors that shape their experience. It is probable that the construction and analysis of these kinds of dataset will move increasingly into the mainstream of equality research. The Northern Ireland Household Panel Survey offers just such an opportunity.

Beyond these rather 'applied' and practical issues, social and economic change in Northern Ireland could present a number of broader challenges (and opportunities) for equality policy. The issue of migration, where for the first time Northern Ireland is becoming an area of immigration, raises broader questions about workers' rights, which go well beyond the usual 'two communities' discourse. The ECNI, however, is well placed to answer these questions, given the range of activities and remits it encompasses. At the same time, emigration suggests other challenges for policy and particularly the extent to which equality can be measured and encouraged in a rather small region that is open to cross-border flows, cross-channel flows to the rest of the UK, and increasingly to international migrants. Just looking at what happens in Northern Ireland could lead to a distorted picture of what happens to *people* from Northern Ireland, especially given the consequences of the longstanding exodus of Protestant students.

Social polarisation and access to new economic opportunities are also issues that require further attention. Whilst some people (and areas) have engaged successfully with the new service economy, there is evidence of social and geographical polarisation in economic well-being. Falls in unemployment rates have neither erased long-term unemployment nor geographically concentrated pockets of unemployment (as measured in terms of registered unemployment). General decreases in unemployment have also not always been matched by an expansion in economic activity and employment rates, and so *joblessness* (as measured by low economic activity and employment levels, and benefit dependency) remains a significant problem in many parts of Northern Ireland. This polarisation is mainly a social class issue. The reduction of these socio-economic inequalities is important in its own right. However, social inequality and the concentrated nature of poverty underpin some aspects of community differentials, such as lower Catholic employment rates and Protestant working-class disadvantage. Tackling poverty and helping access to employment might therefore be another way to reduce communal differentials, using different avenues to the ones discussed in this book, as well as moving towards a more equal society in general.

As Northern Ireland's society changes and the structure of the labour market alters, it is important that opportunities are taken to learn from elsewhere and, where appropriate, other jurisdictions can learn from the particular experiences of fair employment in Northern Ireland. Particularly important are the opportunities presented through developing contacts and communications with all the equality bodies in Ireland and the rest of the UK, as symbolised by recent common research projects. We take this type of dialogue and co-operation as representing the new relationships encouraged by the Belfast Agreement.

Taken together, these thoughts suggest that, despite the easing of Catholic/Protestant inequalities, employment equality policy has not become irrelevant in the twenty-first century. Rather, there is a case for a new and transformed equality policy to meet the needs of new times. The Northern Ireland Executive's commitment to a Single Equality Act will enable a more sophisticated approach to equality that incorporates the multiple identities which people have. The effectiveness of the strong fair employment intervention leads to the clear need to incorporate these powers wherever possible for the other equality dimensions covered by the unified legislation. Finally, government has still to demonstrate that it can drive forward the other complementary equality policy of New TSN and can also effectively incorporate the mainstreaming equality provisions of Section 75 of the Northern Ireland Act 1998. There is much still to do.

Notes

Chapter 1

1 The equality legislation now covers sex and equal pay, disability, race, as well as fair employment. This book is concerned with fair employment but does not seek to diminish the importance of the other equality areas.

2 It is notable that employers have taken a completely different response to sex inequality by resisting the investigations initiated by the Equal Opportunities Commission (EOC).

3 It is legitimate to ask how effective the ECNI has been in progressing its responsibilities, especially for Section 75. As one of the editors (Osborne), at the time of writing, is a member of the Commission, this task must be for others to examine.

Chapter 2

1 This chapter was written on behalf of the ECNI.

2 The 1989 Act required certain employers to register with the FEC, and submit annual monitoring returns detailing the community composition of their workforces, applicants and appointees. All public sector employers identified in the Fair Employment (Specification of Public Authorities) Order (Northern Ireland) are deemed to be automatically registered. In January 1990 all private sector employers with 26 or more employees were required to register. From January 1992, this requirement was extended to all concerns with 11 or more employees. The regulations do not require the monitoring of certain groups within the workforce, i.e. the self-employed, unemployed, schoolteachers, those on government training schemes, and those working in concerns with 10 or less employees. Full details of the monitoring regulations are provided in the annual Monitoring Reports.

Employer compliance with the monitoring regulations has generally been excellent, and far exceeded expectations at the time. In 1990, only seventeen employers (0.90%) were convicted for failing to submit a monitoring form, out of a total of 1,857 scheduled returns. In 2001, twenty-six employers (0.67%) were in default out of a total of 3,835.

3 The 'economically active' includes all those aged 16 or over who are in paid employment (both employees and the self-employed), those on government training or work schemes, those doing unpaid family work (for a business they own or that is owned by a relative), and also those classed as unemployed and seeking work (NISRA, 2001).

When making any comparison between the composition of the monitored workforce and the composition of the economically active, it should be borne in mind that the monitored workforce is only one component of the economically active. Further, adopting the economically active as a benchmark does not take into consideration those persons among the economically inactive who may like to work if suitable employment were available.

4 The proportion of people working in public administration, education and health in Northern Ireland in June 2000 was 10 percentage points higher than that for the UK as a whole (DETI, 2001).

5 An individual is counted as an applicant only once by an employer in any given year, even if that individual has made more than one application for employment. Employees who apply internally for vacancies are not included. Although all appointees are monitored, including part-time posts, the monitoring return form only includes data on those appointees who were appointed during the monitoring year and are still employed at the anniversary date of registration.

Care should be taken in making detailed comparisons between Tables 2.12 and 2.13. First, a proportion of applicant and appointee data in an individual year may not necessarily refer to the same recruitment exercises. Second, employer returns may not cover all applicants and appointees. Temporary staff, for example, who were recruited during the monitoring year but left employment before the anniversary date of registration, would not be included in the employer's return. These anomalies are a product of the Monitoring Regulations.

Chapter 3

1   ESRC Grant R0002353967, principal investigator Richard Breen.
2   Social Science Research Council (SSRC) Grant HR1430, principal investigators Sugiyama Iutaka and John Jackson.
3   The most comprehensive report of the design and fieldwork of the original Irish mobility study can be found in Jackson (1979).
4   However, the ordering of their relative strengths is reversed in the two datasets.
5   Though one should note that the size of the coefficient is small (0.085) and the level of statistical significance ($p < 0.05$) is not that high for a large sample.
6   One might expect either that people who had attained some success would be more likely to have married or that married respondents might be more stable in their careers and that, either way, being married could translate into enhanced chances of upward mobility.
7   Having a partner with a higher job status might either enhance one's own chances of high status or, perhaps, the converse if couples decided on a strategic 'trade-off', where one concentrates upon earnings while the other provides support through assuming more domestic responsibilities.
8   Testing for the effect of 'number of siblings' can be considered as evaluating whether increased demands upon family resources (competition for either material resources or the time available for individual support and socialisation from the parents) has an adverse effect on upward mobility (this being confirmed as far as education is concerned). In contrast, 'number of older siblings' can be considered as in effect evaluating whether birth order affects mobility chances (a respondent with '0' older siblings is first in birth order, a respondent with '3' older siblings falls fourth in birth order and so on). Children born early in birth order may have better chances of access to scarce family resources and receive more attention from their parents. Conversely, children born later in large families may receive material support from older brothers and sisters who are earning and hence,

paradoxically, may have *more* rather than *fewer* family resources to draw on.
9   One may hypothesise that there could be advantages to having *both* parents with higher educational attainment or job position – more than the simple additive effect of each parent's attainment considered separately.
10 Full details are available from the author.

Chapter 4

1   In Craigavon, the transfer is deferred with all pupils leaving primary schools to go to Junior High Schools. At age 14, academic selection takes place. For an evaluation, see Alexander et al, 1998.
2   In part these differences may stem from different transfer rates from secondary to grammar schools, post age 16. Preliminary evidence, however, suggests that post-16 provision in secondary schools is broadly similar (personal communication from DENI, 29 July 2003).
3   The 2001 Census differed from previous censuses in an important respect. For the first time a religion variable was created by asking those who did not indicate a current religion which religion they had been brought up in and adding these to those who did indicate an affiliation to form a community background variable. Also, those who did not answer either question had an imputed religion under the 'one number' methodology. These too were added to the community background numbers.

Chapter 5

1   Just-in-time production means the flexible sourcing of supplies and raw materials at the last minute to maintain flexibility of production and to keep the costs of maintaining huge stocks of supplies and components to a minimum.
2   Unemployment numbers passing the million mark in the 1970s were thought to presage social crisis, a fear that later seemed naïve, given the labour market experience of the 1980s with soaring unemployment levels.

Chapter 6

1   Defined as individuals actively seeking work and registered as unemployed.
2   Calculated by dividing the unemployment rate of Catholics by that of Protestants.

Chapter 7

1   The focus for this chapter is mainly on the Fair Employment Commission, as it was the regulatory body for fair employment from 1990 to 1999. However, some of the period covered in this chapter includes the Equality Commission for Northern Ireland since it took over the powers of the FEC, amongst others, from 1999 onwards. References to the Commission refer to the FEC unless otherwise indicated.
2   We have performed linear regressions to test the significance of agreements as a factor in change. The results of these suggest that agreements are a statistically significant factor in both employment growth for the underrepresented group and shifts in the community balance of employment. We are not, however, satisfied that all relevant variables have been accounted for in these regressions – in particular, we have no measure of geographic variations, and as such we have not included them in this analysis. Nevertheless, the fact that agreements seem consistently to influence the pattern of change in the expected direction is encouraging.
3   Information in this section concerning the strategies employed by the FEC is based on communications to us from staff at the ECNI.
4   We have also included the important agreement reached with the Civil Service in 1988.
5   For further discussion of segregation in occupation categories, see Chapter 2.
6   It is included here under 1990 monitoring return figures, as we do not possess figures for 1988.
7   We are again here considering only those agreement firms for which we possess a full eleven-year set of monitoring returns. Otherwise, new registrations or deregistrations could cause large, and spurious, shifts in employment growth and workforce integration amongst a relatively small group of firms. Using this method, we are examining the same group of firms for the entire decade. Thus all employment growth or decline and proportion changes in these figures are the result of employment changes at concerns that remained active throughout the 1990s.
8   This restriction is applied only because the Catholic underrepresentation agreement group is larger; the number of Protestant underrepresentation agreements is too small to split into two categories, as, when considering employment growth amongst such small groups of firms, large changes in the employment figures at one or two firms could have a disproportionate impact on the overall figures, and create a misleading picture of overall change.
9   A memorandum from the Commission indicates that the non-determined proportion of the public sector workforce was much higher in 1990, at 8 per cent of the total workforce, than the 3.6 per cent non-determined in the private sector, perhaps due to the presence of non-UK staff in the health sector. By 2001, the non-determined proportion in the public sector had fallen to 5.7 per cent and risen to 4.1 per cent in the private sector. There have thus been large changes in the size of the non-determined workforce over the decade. As we have indicated, these shifts may affect the overall pattern of change and need to be considered more carefully.

Chapter 8

1   I am particularly grateful to Eileen Lavery, Director of Research, and Mary Kitson, Senior Legal Officer, ECNI, for comment and advice on an earlier draft of this paper. This chapter was written on behalf of the ECNI.
2   The Fair Employment (Northern Ireland) Act 1989 established the Fair Employment Commission to replace the Fair Employment Agency.
3   See Article 11 of the Fair Employment and Treatment (Northern Ireland) Order 1998 (FETO).
4   An extensive review of all significant FET and higher court decisions on religious and political discrimination is contained in Fair Employment Commission, 1999.
5   It should also be noted that the vast bulk of cases assisted by the FEC

resulted in favourable settlements, from the FEC's perspective. See the Annual Reports of the FEC and the ECNI. Unfortunately, a review of these settlements is outside the scope of this paper.

6   A potentially significant reform in the FETO, also outside the scope of this paper, was the extension of 'fair employment' legislation into the fields of goods, facilities and services, a development which in any event has to date been significantly underutilised.

7   It is not proposed to examine case law on the scope of the legislation. However, a significant decision for equality law generally was *Loughran and Kelly* v. *Northern Ireland Housing Executive* ([1998] IRLR 593 (HL)), in which the House of Lords permitted designated solicitors, applying to provide services to the NIHE, to be treated as having been 'seeking employment' for the purposes of their claim under the 1989 Act.

8   See also Article 7 of the 1976 Order.

9   Nonetheless, the 'comparative' approach can frustrate a genuine examination of whether 'discrimination' has occurred. For example, in *Denvir* v. *J E Coulter Ltd* (20 November 1992 FET), the FET refused to compare a Catholic dismissed for failing to report three absences and a Protestant who received a written warning for one such absence. The ECNI proposes a test of direct discrimination based on the notion of 'disadvantage of grounds of' the prohibited factor, allowing a much wider examination of patterns of behaviour which might reveal a discriminatory approach to the issues.

10   See also the significant decision in *Willis* v. *Police Authority for Northern Ireland and others*, 29 May 2002 FET.

11   *Sudhir Kumar Tundon* v. *James P Corry (Holdings) Ltd*, a case settled after a three-day hearing during which the applicability of 'religious belief' to the applicant's religion appeared beyond dispute. See Bell (1996) at 74 and fn. 23.

12   See also *Kennedy* v. *Gallaher Ltd*, 17 December 1991 FET, 21 October 1993 NICA, and *Verner* v. *Templepatrick Properties Ltd*, 4 March 1996 FET.

13   The Court of Appeal had however already decided that non–reliance on service conditions was not a 'requirement or condition', as being 'an absolute bar', within the definition of indirect discrimination based on the much criticised English Court of Appeal decision in *Perrera* v. *Civil Service Commission* ([1988] IRLR 166 (CA)).

14   The case of *McClean* v. *Shorts Brothers*, heard in 1995, involved prolonged examination of statistical evidence but was settled before a tribunal decision was issued.

15   Implementing the FEED 2003, in particular Article 2(3).

16   As *Devlin* was being lodged in Strasbourg, the FETO (Article 80) was amending the process so that a Security Tribunal, established under Section 91 of the Northern Ireland Act 1998, could determine '(a) [whether] the act specified in the certificate was done for the certified purpose; and (b) [whether] the doing of the act was justified by that purpose'.

17   Many Section 42 cases, long delayed in the tribunal system while these judgments were awaited, have recently been settled without hearing on favourable terms to the ECNI.

18   See the sex discrimination case, *Wallace* v. *South Eastern Education and Library Board* [1980] IRLR 193 (NICA), and religious and political discrimination cases of *Department of the Environment for Northern Ireland* v. *Fair Employment Agency* [1989] NI 149 (NICA) and *Belfast Port Employers' Association* v. *Fair Employment Commission for Northern Ireland*, 29 June 1994 NICA.

19   *O'Gara* v. *Limavady Borough Council*, 31 July 1992 FET; *Elder* v. *British Shoe Corporation Ltd*, 3 August 1993 FET; *Grimes* v. *Unipork*, 17 February 1992 FET.

20   *Re Limavady Borough Council's Application*, 18 June 1993 QBD; *Re Ballymena Borough Council's Application*, 18 June 1993 QBD.

21   See also *McVeigh* v. *United Kingdom Passport Agency*, 11 January 2000. On the other hand, the Court of Appeal in *Sergeant A* considered the proposition of a police officer discriminating against a co–religionist as a 'remarkably unlikely conclusion'.

22   See, for example, *McEwan* v. *British Broadcasting Corporation*, 21 November 1995 FET and, more recently, *O'Donnell* v. *Chief Constable of the Royal Ulster Constabulary and others*, 5 March 2002 FET, and *Fraser* v. *The Queen's University of Belfast*, 20 May 2003 FET.

23   See also *Johnson* v. *Belfast City Council*, 4 August 2002 FET.

24   In comparison, *Ryan* v. *Ulsterbus* (30 July 2001 FET) is an example of a case in which 'a reasonably thorough investigation' had been undertaken.

25   The liability of employers for harassment perpetrated by third parties has now been called into some doubt by the recent House of Lords decision in *Macdonald* v. *Ministry of Defence* ([2003] IRLR 512 (HL)), in which a previous pivotal judgment on such harassment, *Burton* v. *De Vere Hotels* ([1996] IRLR 596 (EAT)), was overruled.

26   Any lack of clarity on this point has been removed by the enactment of the proposed FETO Amendment Regulations, proposed Article 3A.

27   For an early analysis of FET compensation orders in comparison with those in sex discrimination cases, see Hegarty and McKeown, 1994.

28   SACHR (1987, 151) proposed that the maximum should not be 'as low as' the maximum in the SDO 1976.

29   Compensation awards in equality law differ from those in unfair dismissal and most other employment law cases in that 'non-pecuniary loss' can be compensated on the basis of the award which would be open to the County Court as if the case was one in tort.

30   The extraordinary effect of *Duffy* can be judged by average awards for injury to feelings in employment tribunals in Great Britain in the year 2000, namely £7,216 in race cases, £3,737 in sex cases and £5,802 in disability cases (*Equal Opportunities Review* 100 (2001) 12).

31   It is now well established that damages on the basis of tort compensation can include damages for personal injury, including psychiatric damage.

32   The EAT had substituted figures of £25,000 for injury to feelings and £5,000 for aggravated damages.

33   The ECNI's position papers on the Single Equality Act can be found on its website, www.equalityni.org.

34   The ECNI also proposes a range of more proactive remedies for equality cases, such as orders to change practices and procedures and the carrying out of equality audits.

Chapter 9

1   The author would like to thank Dr Katrina Lloyd for her assistance with statistical analysis.

2   Some employment questions first used in 1994 were reintroduced to the 2001 survey. For the purposes of comparison, data from both years are referenced in this chapter.

3   Devolution first went live in November 1999 but has since been suspended three times. At the time of writing it remains suspended.

4   Aughey lists the concessions the British government made to republicans in an effort to secure that the latter would engage in 'exclusively democratic' processes. These included: the continued early release of prisoners; the reduction of troop levels (despite continued paramilitary involvement in punishment beatings and intimidation); an agreement to meet a long-standing republican demand for an inquiry into the events of Bloody Sunday; the acceptance of the central recommendations of the Patten Report on police reforms (which were lambasted by unionists); permission, against the advice of the Speaker, that Sinn Féin MPs should be allowed access to the facilities of the House of Commons, without having taken an oath of allegiance; and, crucially, the persuasion of David Trimble that he should advise his party to share power with Sinn Féin. This was based on an understanding that the IRA would co-operate with an International Decommissioning Body and there would be some gesture on arms to satisfy unionist sceptics. Neither happened, but devolved government went 'live' in November 1999 (Aughey, 2001: 217).

5   Most of the analysis presented here is based on post-1998 surveys. The exception is in the area of employment, where some questions included for the first time in 1994 were included again in 2001.

6   Statistical note: Any p value less than 0.05 is statistically significant and indicates that there is a 5 per cent probability that the result is due to chance; a p value less than 0.01 indicates that there is a 1 per cent probability that the result is due to chance; while a p value greater than

0.05 indicates that the result is not statistically significant.

7   Although the term 'preferential treatment' is not defined in the question, it is not unreasonable to assume that respondents interpret it in terms of positive discrimination.

8   Of thirteen schools that have accepted the option to transform to integrated status, none is from the Catholic-maintained sector (Hughes and Donnelly, 2002).

References

ABELLA, R. (1984) *Equality in Employment: A Royal Commission Report, Volume 1*, Ministry of Supply and Services, Ottawa

ALEXANDER, J., DALY, P., GALLAGHER, A., GRAY, C. and SUTHERLAND, A. (1998) *An Evaluation of the Craigavon Two-Tier System*, Research Report No. 12, DENI, Bangor

ANDERSON, J. and SHUTTLEWORTH, I. (1998) 'Sectarian demography, territoriality, and political development in Northern Ireland', *Political Geography*, 17, 187–208

ANYADIKE-DANES, M. (2003) *Is this as Good as it Gets? Regional Gradients in UK Male Non-Employment*, Northern Ireland Economic Research Centre, Belfast

APPLEBY, G. and ELLIS, E. (1991) 'Law and employment discrimination: the working of the Northern Ireland Fair Employment Agency', in R. Cormack and R. Osborne (eds), *Discrimination and Public Policy in Northern Ireland*, Clarendon Press, Oxford

ARMSTRONG, D. (1999) 'Hidden male unemployment in Northern Ireland', *Regional Studies*, 33, 499–511

AUGHEY, A. (2001) 'British policy in Northern Ireland', in S. Savage and R. Atkinson (eds), *Public Policy under Blair*, Palgrave, Basingstoke

AUNGER, E. (1975) 'Religion and social class in Northern Ireland', *Economic and Social Review*, 7, 1–18

BARRITT, D. and CARTER, C. (1962) *The Northern Ireland Problem*, Oxford University Press, Oxford

BEATTY, C. and FOTHERGILL, S. (1996) 'Labour market adjustment in areas of chronic labour market decline: the case of the UK coalfields', *Regional Studies*, 30, 627–40

BEATTY, C., FOTHERGILL, S. and MacMILLAN, R. (2000) 'A theory of employment, unemployment and sickness', *Regional Studies*, 34, 617–30

Belfast Agreement, The: An Agreement Reached at the Multi-Party Talks on Northern Ireland (1998), Cm 3883, The Stationery Office, London

BELL, C. (1996) 'The case law of the Fair Employment Tribunals', in D. Magill and S. Rose (eds), *Fair Employment Law in Northern Ireland: Debates and Issues*, Standing Advisory Committee on Human Rights, Belfast

BELL, D. (1974) *The Coming of Post-Industrial Society: A Venture in Social Forecasting*, Heinemann Educational, London

BEW, P., PATTERSON, H. and TEAGUE, P. (1997) *Between War and Peace: The Political Future of Northern Ireland*, Lawrence and Wishart, London

BLAU, P. and DUNCAN, O. (1967) *The American Occupational Structure*, John Wiley & Sons, New York

BLOCK, W. and WALKER, M. (1985) *On Employment Equity: A Critique of the Abella Royal Commission Report*, Fraser Institute, Vancouver

BOOTH, H. and BERTSCH, K. (1989) *The MacBride Principles and US Companies in Northern Ireland*, Investor Responsibility Research Center, Washington

BOROOAH, V. (1999) 'Is there a penalty to being a Catholic in Northern Ireland?: an econometric analysis of the relationship between religious belief and occupational success', *European Journal of Political Economy*, 15, 163–92

BOROOAH, V. (2000) 'Targeting social need: why are deprivation levels in Northern Ireland higher for Catholics than for Protestants?, *Journal of Social Policy*, 29, 281–301

BOUND, H. and FREEMAN, R. (1989) 'Black economic progress: erosion of post-1965 gains in the 1980s?, in S. Shulman and W. Darity (eds), *The Question of Discrimination: Racial Inequality in the US Labor Market*, Wesleyan University Press, Middletown, Connecticut

BOWEN, W. and BOK, D. (1997) *The Shape of the River: Long-Term Consequences of Considering Race in University Admissions*, Princeton University Press, Princeton

BREEN, R. (2000) 'Class inequality and social mobility', *American Sociological Review*, 65, 392–406

BREEN, R. and GOLDTHORPE, J. (2001) 'Class, mobility and merit: the experiences of two British birth cohorts', *European Sociological Review*, 17, 81–101

BRYNIN, M. (2002a) 'Overqualification in employment', *Work, Employment and Society*, 16, 637–54

BRYNIN, M. (2002b) 'Graduate density, gender and employment', *British Journal of Sociology*, 53, 363–81

BRYSON, A. and McKAY, S. (1994) *Is it Worth Working?*, Policy Studies Institute, London

BURNS REPORT (2001) *Education for the 21st Century: Report of the Post-Primary Review Body*, Department of Education for Northern Ireland, Bangor

BYNNER, J., ELIAS, P., McKNIGHT, A., PAN, H. and PIERRE, G. (2002) *Young People's Changing Routes to Independence*, Joseph Rowntree Trust, York

CARMICHAEL, P. and KNOX, C. (1999) 'Towards a new era? Some developments in the governance of Northern Ireland', *International Review of Administrative Sciences*, 65, 103–16

COMPTON, P. (1981) *The Contemporary Population of Northern Ireland and Populated Related Issues*, Institute of Irish Studies, Queen's University of Belfast, Belfast

COMPTON, P. (1991) 'Employment differentials in Northern Ireland and job discrimination: a critique', in P. Roche and B. Barton (eds), *The Northern Ireland Question: Myth and Reality*, Avebury, Aldershot

CORMACK, R. and OSBORNE, R. (eds) (1983) *Religion, Education and Employment: Aspects of Equality of Opportunity in Northern Ireland*, Appletree Press, Belfast

CORMACK, R.J. and OSBORNE, R. (eds) (1991) *Discrimination and Public Policy in Northern Ireland*, Clarendon Press, Oxford

CORMACK, R. and OSBORNE, R. (1993) 'Higher Education in Northern Ireland', in R. Osborne, R. Cormack and A. Gallagher (eds), *After the Reforms: Education and Policy in Northern Ireland*, Avebury, Aldershot

CORMACK, R. and OSBORNE, R. (1994) 'The evolution of the Catholic middle class', in A. Guelke (ed.), *New Perspectives on Northern Ireland*, Avebury, Aldershot

CORMACK, R., OSBORNE, R. and THOMPSON, W. (1980) *Into Work? Young School Leavers and the Structure of Opportunity in Belfast*, Fair Employment Agency, Belfast

CORMACK, R. and ROONEY, E. (n.d.) *Religion and Employment in Northern Ireland, 1921–1971*, Department of Sociology, Queen's University of Belfast, Belfast

DARBY, J. and MURRAY, D. (1980) *The Vocational Aspirations and Expectations of School Leavers in Londonderry and Strabane*, Fair Employment Agency, Belfast

DEAKIN, S. and REED, H. (2000) 'River crossing or cold bath? Deregulation and employment in Britain in the 1980s and 1990s', in G. Esping-Anderson and M. Regini (eds), *Why Deregulate Labour Markets?*, Oxford University Press, Oxford

DED (1989) *Fair Employment in Northern Ireland Code of Practice*, Department of Economic Development, Belfast

DEL (2001) *New Deal for 18–24 Year Olds: Survey of Participants*, Department for Employment and Learning, Belfast

DEL (2003) *New Deal for 18–24 Year Olds: Survey of Participants, Stage 2 Report*, Department for Employment and Learning, Belfast

DELOITTE AND TOUCHE (2001) *Employability Scoping Study: Final Report for the Taskforce on Employability and Long-Term Unemployment*, Deloitte and Touche, Belfast

DENI (1998) *Adult Literacy in Northern Ireland: Summary of Key Findings*, Department of Education for Northern Ireland, Bangor

DENI (2002) *Transfer Procedure Test Results 2001/02*, Department of Education for Northern Ireland, Bangor

DENI (2003) *Enrolments at Schools and Funded Pre-School Education in Northern Ireland 2002/03*, Department of Education for Northern Ireland, Bangor

DETI (2001) 'Northern Ireland labour market data', *Labour Market Trends*, 109, 13–28

DIGNAN, T. (2003a) *New TSN Household Profile*, report prepared for the Office of the First Minister and Deputy First Minister, Belfast

DIGNAN, T. (2003b) *Community Differentials and New TSN*, Office of the First Minister and Deputy First Minister, Belfast

DONNELLY, C. (2000) 'In pursuit of school ethos', *British Journal of Educational Studies*, 48, 24–154

ECNI (2002) *A Profile of the Northern Ireland Workforce*, Monitoring Report No. 12, Equality Commission for Northern Ireland, Belfast

EDWARDS, J. (1995) *Affirmative Action in a Sectarian Society*, Avebury, Aldershot

ELLIOTT, J., DALE, A. and EGERTON, M. (2001) 'The influence of qualifications on women's work histories, employment status and earnings at age 33', *European Sociological Review*, 17, 145–68

ESRC (2003) *The Assembly Elections in Northern Ireland, 2003: What Can We Expect?*, Devolution Briefings No. 2, May 2003, Economic and Social Research Council, Belfast

EVERSLEY, D. (1989) *Religion and Employment in Northern Ireland*, Sage, London

EVERSLEY, D. (1991) 'Demography and unemployment in Northern Ireland', in R. Cormack and R. Osborne (eds), *Discrimination and Public Policy in Northern Ireland*, Clarendon Press, Oxford

FEA (1978) *An Industrial and Occupational Profile of the Two Sections of the Population in Northern Ireland: An Analysis of the 1971 Census*, Fair Employment Agency, Belfast

FEA (1983) *Report of an Investigation by the Fair Employment Agency for Northern Ireland into the Non-Industrial Northern Ireland Civil Service*, Fair Employment Agency, Belfast

FEC (1991) *A Profile of the Northern Ireland Workforce: A Summary of the 1990 Monitoring Returns*, Research Report 1, Fair Employment Commission, Belfast

FEC (1999) *Fair Employment Case Law: Religious and Political Discrimination in Northern Ireland* (4th ed.), Fair Employment Commission, Belfast

Fair Employment (Northern Ireland) Act 1989, Chapter 32, HMSO, London

Fair Employment (Specification of Public Authorities) Regulations (Northern Ireland) (1989), Statutory Rule 1989 No. 475, HMSO, London

FITZPATRICK, B. (1999) 'The new Northern Irish equality regime', *Industrial Law Journal*, 28, 336–47

FITZPATRICK, B., HEGARTY, A. and MAXWELL, P. (1996) 'A comparative review of fair employment and equality of opportunity law', in D. Magill and S. Rose (eds), *Fair Employment Law in Northern Ireland: Debates and Issues*, Standing Advisory Committe on Human Rights, Belfast

FOTHERGILL, S. and GUDGIN, G. (1982) *Unequal Growth: Urban and Regional Employment Change in the UK*, Heinemann Educational, London

GALLAGHER, A. (1995) 'The approach of government: community relations and equity', in S. Dunn (ed.), *Facets of the Conflict in Northern Ireland*, St Martin's Press, London and New York

GALLAGHER, A., OSBORNE, R. and CORMACK, R. (1994a) *Fair Shares? Employment, Unemployment & Economic Status*, Fair Employment Commission, Belfast

GALLAGHER, A., OSBORNE, R. and CORMACK, R. (1994b) 'Religion, equity and education in Northern Ireland', *British Educational Research Journal*, 29, 507–18

GALLAGHER, A. and SMITH, A. (2000) *The Effects of the Selective System of Secondary Education in Northern Ireland, Volumes 1 and 2*, Department of Education for Northern Ireland, Bangor

GLAZER, N. (1988) 'The affirmative action stalemate', *Public Interest*, 90

GORDON, I. (1999) 'Move on up the car: dealing with structural unemployment in London', *Local Economy*, 14, 87–95

GRANOVETTER, M. (1995) *Getting a Job: A Study of Contacts and Careers* (2nd ed.), Chicago University Press, Chicago

GRAY, J., McPHERSON, A. and RAFFE, D. (1983) *Reconstructions of Secondary Education: Theory, Myth and Practice since the War*, Routledge, London

GREEN, A. (1997) 'Exclusion, unemployment and non-unemployment', *Regional Studies*, 31, 505–20

GREEN, A. (2001) 'Unemployment, non-unemployment and labour market disadvantage', *Environment and Planning A*, 33, 1361–4

GREEN, A. and OWEN, D. (1998) *Where are the Jobless? Changing Unemployment and Non-Employment in Cities and Regions*, Policy Press, Bristol

GREEN, A., SHUTTLEWORTH, I. and LAVERY, S. (2003) *Young People, Job Search and Local Labour Markets: The Example of Belfast*, Employability Seminar, University of Warwick

GREGG, P. and WADSWORTH, J. (1998) 'Unemployment and non-employment: unpacking economic activity, London', *Employment Policy Institute Economic Report*, 12, London

GUDGIN, G. and BREEN, R. (1996) *Evaluation of the Ratio of Unemployment Rates as an Indicator of Fair Employment*, Central Community Relations Unit, Belfast

HAKIM, C. (2000) *Work-Lifestyle Choices in the 21st Century*, Oxford University Press, Oxford

HARBISON, J. and HODGES, W. (1991) 'Equal opportunities in the Northern Civil Service', in R. Cormack and R. Osborne (eds), *Discrimination and Public Policy in Northern Ireland*, Clarendon Press, Oxford

HAYES, B. (1987) 'Female intergenerational occupational mobility within Northern Ireland and the Republic of Ireland: the importance of maternal occupational status', *British Journal of Sociology*, 38, 66–76

HAYES, B. (1990) 'Female intergenerational occupational mobility within Northern Ireland: do parental background characteristics matter?', in M. Maguire (ed.), *Unequal Labour: Women and Work in Northern Ireland*, Policy Research Institute, Belfast

HAYES, B. and MILLER, R. (1993) 'The silenced voice: female social mobility patterns with particular reference to the British Isles', *British Journal of Sociology*, 4, 653–72

HEGARTY, A. and McKEOWN, C. (1994) 'Figuring out equality: an analysis of tribunal remedies in individual complaints of discrimination, *Review of Employment Topics*, 2, 80–103

HEPBURN, A. (1983) 'Employment and religion in Belfast, 1901–1951', in R. Cormack and R. Osborne (eds), *Religion, Education and Employment: Aspects of Equal Opportunity in Northern Ireland*, Appletree Press, Belfast

HEPPLE, B. (1990) 'Discrimination and equal opportunity in Northern Ireland', *Oxford Journal of Legal Studies*, 10, 408–21

HILLS, J., LE GRAND, J. and PIACHAUD, D. (eds) (2002) *Understanding Social Exclusion*, Oxford University Press, Oxford

HOUT, M. (1989) *Following in Father's Footsteps*, Harvard University Press, London

HUGHES, J. (2001) 'Constitutional reform in Northern Ireland:

implications for community relations policy and practice', *International Journal of Conflict Management*, 12, 154–73

HUGHES, J. and DONNELLY, C. (2002) 'Ten years of social attitudes to community relations in Northern Ireland', in G. Robinson, A. Gray and D. Heenan (eds), *Social Attitudes in Northern Ireland: The Eighth Report*, Pluto Press, London

IER (2001) *Projections of Occupations and Qualifications: 2000/2001*, Research in Support of the National Skills Task Force, Institute for Employment Research, University of Warwick, Coventry

JACKSON, J. (1979) *Determinants of Occupational Status and Mobility in Northern Ireland and the Irish Republic*, final report to the Social Science Research Council

JESSOP, B. (2003) *From Thatcherism to New Labour: Neo-Liberalism, Workfarism, and Labour Market Regulation*, Department of Sociology, University of Lancaster, Lancaster

KENNEDY, G. (2000) *The 2000 NI Social Omnibus Survey*, Labour Market Bulletin 14, 39–44, Department of Higher and Further Education, Training and Employment, Belfast

LEITH, H., OSBORNE, R. and GALLAGHER, A. (2000) *Skill Development and Enhancement: A Study of Northern Ireland Graduates*, University of Ulster, Jordanstown

LEVITAS, R. (1998) *The Inclusive Society? Social Exclusion and New Labour*, Macmillan, Basingstoke

MACKAY, F. and BILTON, K. (2000) *Learning from Experience: Lessons in Mainstreaming Equality*, Governance of Scotland Forum, University of Edinburgh, Edinburgh

MacKAY, R. (1999) 'Work and non-work: a more difficult labour market', *Environment and Planning A*, 31, 1919–34

McCRUDDEN, C. (1991) 'The evolution of the Fair Employment (Northern Ireland) Act 1989 in parliament', in R. Cormack and R. Osborne (eds), *Discrimination and Public Policy in Northern Ireland*, Clarendon Press, Oxford

McCRUDDEN, C. (1992) 'Affirmative action and fair participation: interpreting the Fair Employment Act 1989, *Industrial Law Journal*, 1, 184–214

McCRUDDEN, C. (2001) 'Equality', in C. Harvey (ed.), *Human Rights, Equality and Democratic Renewal in Northern Ireland*, Hart, Oxford

McGARRY, J. and O'LEARY, B. (1995) *Explaining Northern Ireland*, Blackwell, Oxford

MacGILL, P. (1996) *Missing the Target: A Critique of Government Policy on Targeting Social Need in Northern Ireland*, Northern Ireland Council for Voluntary Action, Belfast

MacGINTY, R. and WILFORD, C. (2002) 'More knowing than

knowledgeable: attitudes towards devolution', in G. Robinson, A. Gray and D. Henan (eds), *Social Attitudes in Northern Ireland: The Eighth Report*, Pluto Press, London

McLAUGHLIN, E. and QUIRK, P. (1996a) 'Targeting social need', in E. McLaughlin and P. Quirk (eds), *Policy Aspects of Employment Equality in Northern Ireland*, Standing Advisory Committe on Human Rights, Belfast

McLAUGHLIN, E. and QUIRK, P. (eds) (1996b) *Policy Aspects of Employment Equality in Northern Ireland*, Standing Advisory Committee on Human Rights, Belfast

MCQUAID, R. and LINDSAY, C. (2002) 'The employability gap: long-term unemployment and barriers to work in buoyant labour markets', *Environment and Planning C*, 20, 613–28

McRAE, S. (1997) *Changing Britain: Families and Households in the 1990s*, Oxford University Press, Oxford

McVEY, J. and HUTSON, N. (eds) (1996) *Public Views and Experiences of Fair Employment and Equality Issues in Northern Ireland*, Standing Advisory Committee on Human Rights, Belfast

McVICAR, D. (ed.) (2000) *Young People and Social Exclusion in Northern Ireland: Status 0 Four Years On*, Department of Higher and Further Education, Training and Employment

McWHIRTER, L., DUFFY, U., BARRY, R. and McGUINESS, G. (1987) 'Transition from school to work: cohort evidence', in R. Osborne, R. Cormack and R. Miller (eds), *Education and Policy in Northern Ireland*, Policy Research Institute, Belfast

MAGILL, D. and ROSE, S. (eds), (1996) *Fair Employment Law in Northern Ireland: Debates and Issues*, Standing Advisory Committee on Human Rights

MILLER, R. (1978a) 'Opinions on school de-segregation in Northern Ireland', in *Proceedings of the 4th Annual Conference of the Sociological Association of Ireland, Ballymascanlon*, Department of Social Studies, Queen's University of Belfast, Belfast

MILLER, R. (1978b) *Attitudes to Work in Northern Ireland*, Fair Employment Agency, Belfast

MILLER, R. (1979) *The Occupational Mobility of Protestants and Catholics in Northern Ireland*, Fair Employment Agency, Belfast

MILLER, R. (1981) 'A model of social mobility in Northern Ireland', in P. Compton (ed.), *The Contemporary Population of Northern Ireland and Population-Related Issues*, Institute of Irish Studies, Queen's University of Belfast, Belfast

MILLER, R. (1983) 'Religion and occupational mobility', in R. Cormack and R. Osborne (eds), *Religion, Education and Employment: Aspects of Equal Opportunity in Northern Ireland*, Appletree Press, Belfast

MILLER, R. (1996) 'Public opinion on fair employment issues: evidence from the Northern Ireland social attitudes surveys', in J. McVey and N. Hutson (eds), *Employment Equality in Northern Ireland, Volume 3: Public Views and Experiences of Fair Employment and Equality Issues in Northern Ireland*, Standing Advisory Committee on Human Rights, Belfast

MILLER, R., CURRY, C., CORMACK, R. and OSBORNE, R. (1991) *The Labour Market Experiences of an Educational Elite: A Continuous Time Analysis of Recent Higher Education Graduates*, University of Ulster, Coleraine

MILLER, R. and HAYES, B. (1990) 'Gender and intergenerational mobility', in G. Payne and P. Abbot (eds), *The Social Mobility of Women: Beyond Male Mobility Models*, Falmer, London

MILLER, R., WILFORD, R. and DONOGHUE, F. (1996) 'Attitudinal support and low participation in integrated education: a Northern Ireland conundrum', *Administration*, 44, 61–9

MORAHAN, T. (2000) 'The fastest improving regional economy in the UK', *Labour Market Bulletin*, 14, Department of Higher and Further Education, Training and Employment, Belfast

MORRIS, A. (1997) 'Same mission, same methods, same results? Academic and religious outcomes from different models of Catholic schooling', *British Journal of Educational Studies*, 45, 378–91

MORRISSEY, M. and GAFFIKIN, F. (2001) 'Northern Ireland: democratizing for development', *Local Economy*, 16, 2–13

MURPHY, A. and ARMSTRONG, D. (1994) *A Picture of the Catholic and Protestant Male Unemployed*, Central Community Relations Unit, Belfast

MURRAY, R. and OSBORNE, R. (1983) 'Educational qualifications and religious affiliation', in R. Cormack and R. Osborne (eds), *Religion, Education and Employment: Aspects of Equal Opportunity in Northern Ireland*, Appletree Press, Belfast

National Statistics (2001), *International Student Assessment: Results for Northern Ireland 2000*, National Statistics, London

NICAISE, I., BOLLENS, J., DAWES, L., LAGHAEI, S., THAULOW, I., VERIDE, M. and WAGNER, A. (1995) *Pitfalls and Dilemmas in Labour Market Programmes for Disadvantaged Groups and How to Avoid Them*, Avebury, Aldershot

NICRA (1964) *The Plain Truth*, Northern Ireland Civil Rights Association, Belfast

NICVA (2001) 'Response to the Northern Ireland Executive's Draft Programme for Government and Budget, 2002–2003', Northern Ireland Council for Voluntary Action, Belfast

NIEC (1998) *Growth with Development: A Response to New TSN*, Northern Ireland Economic Council, Belfast

NISRA (2001) *A Profile of Protestants and Roman Catholics in the Northern Ireland Labour Force*, Northern Ireland Statistics and Research Agency Monitor 2/01, Belfast

NISRA (2003a) 'Census of population, economically active persons of working age in Northern Ireland by age and sex and community background (religion or religion brought up in)', unpublished table, Northern Ireland Statistics and Research Agency, Belfast

NISRA (2003b) *Northern Ireland Census 2001, Standard Table S325: Age and Highest Level of Qualification by Sex and Community Background (Religion Or Religion Brought Up In)*, Northern Ireland Statistics and Research Agency, Belfast

Northern Ireland Affairs Select Committee (1997) *Underachievement in Northern Ireland Secondary Schools*, HC79, HMSO, London

Northern Ireland Affairs Select Committee (1999) *The Operation of the Fair Employment (Northern Ireland) Act, Fourth Report*, HMSO, London

O'DOWD, L., ROLSTON, B. and TOMLINSON, M. (1980) *Northern Ireland: Between Civil War and Civil Rights*, CSE Books, London

Office of the First Minister and Deputy First Minister (2001) *Programme for Government: Making a Difference 2001–04*, Economic Policy Unit, Belfast

O'LEARY, B. and McGARRY, J. (1993) *The Politics of Antagonism, Understanding Northern Ireland*, Athlone Press, London

O'NEILL, S. (2000) 'Liberty, equality and the rights of cultures: the marching controversy at Drumcree', *British Journal of Politics and International Relations*, 2, 26–45

ONS (1998) *Social Focus on the Unemployed*, Office for National Statistics, HMSO, London

OSBORNE, R. (1991) 'Discrimination', in P. Stringer and G. Robinson (eds), *Social Attitudes in Northern Ireland, 1990–1991*, Blackstaff Press, Belfast

OSBORNE, R. (1992) 'Fair employment and employment equity: policy learning in a comparative context, *Public Money and Management*, 12, 11–18

OSBORNE, R. (1993) 'Research and policy: a Northern Ireland perspective', *Government and Policy*, 11, 465–77

OSBORNE, R. (1996a) *Higher Education in Ireland: North and South*, Jessica Kingsley, London

OSBORNE, R. (1996b) 'Policy dilemmas in Belfast', *Journal of Social Policy*, 25, 181–96

OSBORNE, R. (1999) 'Higher education participation in Northern Ireland', *Journal of the Statistical and Social Inquiry Society of Ireland*, 28, 265–98

OSBORNE, R. (2001) 'Higher education, participation and devolution: the case of Northern Ireland', *Higher Education Policy*, 14, 45–60

OSBORNE, R. (2003a) 'Widening access in the UK and Ireland', paper given at the Society for Research on Higher Education/Northern Ireland Higher Education Council seminar 'The Widening Access Policy Agenda in Northern Ireland', Belfast

OSBORNE, R. (2003b) 'Progressing the equality agenda in Northern Ireland', *Journal of Social Policy*, 32, 339–60

OSBORNE, R. and CORMACK, R. (1989) 'Fair employment: towards reform in Northern Ireland', *Policy and Politics*, 17, 287–94

OSBORNE, R., CORMACK, R., REID, N. and WILLIAMSON, A. (1983) 'Political arithmetic, higher education and religion in Northern Ireland', in R. Cormack and R. Osborne (eds), *Religion, Education and Employment: Aspects of Equal Opportunity in Northern Ireland*, Appletree Press, Belfast

OSBORNE, R., GALLAGHER, A., CORMACK, R. with SHORTALL, S. (1996) 'The implementation of the policy appraisal and fair treatment guidelines', in E. McLaughlin and P. Quirk (eds), *Policy Aspects of Employment Equality in Northern Ireland*, Standing Advisory Commission on Human Rights, Belfast

OSBORNE, R., MILLER, R., CORMACK, R. and WILLIAMSON, A. (1987) 'Graduates: geographical mobility and incomes', in R. Osborne, R. Cormack and R. Miller (eds), *Education and Policy in Northern Ireland*, Policy Research Institute, Belfast

OSBORNE, R., MILLER, R., CORMACK, R. and WILLIAMSON, A. (1988) 'Trends in higher education participation in Northern Ireland', *Economic and Social Review*, 19, 283–301

OSBORNE, R. and MURRAY, R. (1978) *Educational Qualifications and Religious Affiliation in Northern Ireland*, Fair Employment Agency, Belfast

OSBORNE, R. and SHUTTLEWORTH, I. (2003) *Potential Skills Shortages in the Northern Ireland IT and Electronic Engineering Sectors – and Inequalities in Educational Uptake*, Department for Employment and Learning, Belfast

PATERSON, L. (2000) 'Salvation through education? The changing social status of Scottish Catholics', in T. Devine (ed.), *Scotland's Shame? Bigotry and Sectarianism in Modern Scotland*, Mainstream Publishing, Edinburgh

Patten Report (1999) *A New Beginning: Policing in Northern Ireland*, Report of the Independent Commission on Policing for Northern Ireland, HMSO, London

PECK, J. (2001) *Workfare States*, Guildford Press, London

Police (Northern Ireland) Act 2000 (2000), Chapter 32, The Stationery Office, Belfast

REES, T. (1998) *Mainstreaming Equality in the European Union*, Routledge, London

ROWTHORNE, B. and WAYNE, N. (1988) *Northern Ireland: The Political Economy of Conflict*, Polity Press, London

Royal Statistical Society (1995) *Report of the Working Party on the Measurement of Unemployment in the UK*, Royal Statistical Society, London

RUANE, J. and TODD, J. (1996) *The Dynamics of Conflict in Northern Ireland: Power, Conflict, and Emancipation*, Cambridge University Press, Cambridge

SACHR (1987) *Religious and Political Discrimination and Equality of Opportunity in Northern Ireland: Report on Fair Employment*, HMSO, Belfast

SACHR (1990) *Religious and Political Discrimination and Equality of Opportunity in Northern Ireland, Second Report*, HMSO, London

SACHR (1991) *Sixteenth Report (1990–1991)*, HMSO, London

SACHR (1997) *Employment Equality: Building for the Future*, HMSO, Belfast

SHAVIT, Y. and MULLER, W. (eds) (1998) *From School to Work: A Comparative Study of Educational Qualifications and Occupational Destinations*, Clarendon Press, Oxford

SHUTTLEWORTH, I. (1995) 'The relationship between social deprivation, as measured by free school meals eligibility, and educational attainment at GCSE in Northern Ireland: a preliminary investigation', *British Educational Research Journal*, 21, 487–504

SHUTTLEWORTH, I. (1999) 'Religion, education, "first destinations" and later careers: evidence on the persistence of inequalities in the transition from school in Northern Ireland', in T. Lange (ed.) *Understanding the School-to-Work Transition*, Nova Science Publishers, New York

SHUTTLEWORTH, I. and TYLER, P. (2002) 'What happened to the former Harland & Wolff workers – a further follow-up', *Labour Market Bulletin*, Department for Employment and Learning, 16, 117–22, Belfast

SMITH, D. (1987) *Equality and Inequality in Northern Ireland Part I: Employment and Unemployment*, Policy Studies Institute, London

SMITH, D. and CHAMBERS, G. (1991) *Inequality in Northern Ireland*, Clarendon Press, Oxford

Social Disadvantage Research Centre (2001) *Measures of Deprivation in Northern Ireland*, Social Disadvantage Research Centre, Department of Social Policy and Social Work, University of Oxford

SUNLEY, P., MARTIN, R. and NATIVEL, C. (2001) 'Mapping the New Deal: local disparities in the performance of Welfare-to-Work', *Transactions Institute of British Geographers*, 26, 484–512

Taskforce on Employability and Long-Term Unemployment (2002), *Report of the Taskforce on Employability and Long-Term Unemployment*, Department for Employment and Learning, Belfast

TAYLOR, R. (1988) 'Social scientific research on the troubles in Northern Ireland: the problem of objectivity', *Economic and Social Review*, 19, 123–45

'UUP peer hits out at "secrecy" of PSNI test scores', *Belfast Telegraph*, 2, November 2001

'We have the facts now let's do the debate' (Morning View), *News Letter*, 16 May 2003

White Paper (1988) *Fair Employment in Northern Ireland*, HMSO, Belfast

White Paper (1998) *Partnership for Equality*, HMSO, Belfast

WHYTE, J. (1983) 'How much discrimination was there under the Unionist regime, 1921–1968?', in T. Gallagher and J. O'Connell (eds), *Contemporary Irish Studies*, Manchester University Press, Manchester

WHYTE, J. (1990) *Interpreting Northern Ireland*, Clarendon Press, Oxford

Index